Philo of Alexandria

Philo of Alexandria

A Sourcebook

Nélida Naveros Córdova, CDP

LEXINGTON BOOKS/FORTRESS ACADEMIC
Lanham • Boulder • New York • London

Published by Lexington Books/Fortress Academic
Lexington Books is an imprint of The Rowman & Littlefield Publishing Group, Inc.
4501 Forbes Boulevard, Suite 200, Lanham, Maryland 20706
www.rowman.com

86-90 Paul Street, London EC2A 4NE, United Kingdom

Copyright © 2023 by The Rowman & Littlefield Publishing Group, Inc.

All rights reserved. No part of this book may be reproduced in any form or by any electronic or mechanical means, including information storage and retrieval systems, without written permission from the publisher, except by a reviewer who may quote passages in a review.

British Library Cataloguing in Publication Information Available

Library of Congress Cataloging-in-Publication Data Available

ISBN 9781978708617 (cloth : alk. paper) | ISBN 9781978708624 (ebook)

♾️™ The paper used in this publication meets the minimum requirements of American National Standard for Information Sciences—Permanence of Paper for Printed Library Materials, ANSI/NISO Z39.48-1992.

In memory of my Doktorvater, Thomas H. Tobin. His love for Philo and method of interpretation greatly influenced my scholarship.

Contents

Introduction	ix
Chapter 1: Philo's Theology	1
Chapter 2: Philo's Doctrine of Creation	25
Chapter 3: Philo's Anthropology	47
Chapter 4: Philo's Doctrine of Ethics	81
Chapter 5: Biblical Characters	123
Chapter 6: Jewish Law and the *Decalogue*	141
Chapter 7: Jewish Worship and Major Observances	155
Index	187
About the Author	197

Introduction

In recent decades, Philo of Alexandria has become an influential first century CE author in the study of the New Testament. Particularly graduate students, who are not "experts" on Philo, often encounter the Jewish exegete and his writings in their academic studies and research. This sourcebook is, therefore, suited to the beginner, and for anyone who has an interest in knowing and learning about Philo. Although the presence of Philo in both biblical and classical studies has been marginal, in the last two decades Philonic research has grown rapidly. Outstanding studies have been published by seasoned and respected scholars in *The Studia Philonica Annual*, *The Studia Philonica Monograph Series,* the Philo of Alexandria Commentary Series, as well as in other noted journals and publishers. We have also a considerable number of works published by emerging young scholars. The recognition of the relevance and value of Philo in early Christianity has led Philonic experts to have a meritorious and well-deserved spot in national and international conferences, for example, the Society of Biblical Literature and the Society of New Testament Studies. These avenues have offered new approaches, methods, and interpretations; without a doubt they have enriched our understanding of Philo's writings and have facilitated the availability of secondary sources and, why not to say, the exposure to Philo of Alexandria and his writings in a larger scope.

In my knowledge, surprisingly, there are only two works that are devoted to some extent to Philo's major topics and themes. In 1960, Hans Lewy produced a short and meager anthology in *3 Jewish Philosophers*.[1] In it, Lewy put together selections of the writings of Philo. Twenty years later (1981), David Winston assembled an anthology from Philo's works in his book *Philo of Alexandria: The Contemplative Life, the Giants, and Selections*.[2] In his work, Winston offered a full translation of Philo's treatise, *The Contemplative Life and the Giants*. He carefully selected sections from other Philonic treatises presented under random but important themes of Philo's thought. What is highly valued about his contribution is that Winston introduced the reader to Philo's broader range of his thought in a more balanced appreciation than was available in Lewy. Today, scholars unanimously recognize Winston's brilliant anthology, for it offered a doorway into Philo's complex thinking, an influential yet enigmatic ancient Jewish philosopher who was deeply immersed in two highly influential cultures, the Jewish and the Greek, in first century CE Alexandria.

WHO IS PHILO?

Philo the Jew or *Philo Judaeus* was most likely born circa 20 BCE in Alexandria, a great *polis* in the East founded by Alexander the Great. He died some time at the beginning of Claudius's reign circa 50 CE. Significantly, he was a contemporary of Jesus, the Apostle Paul, as well as the Rabbi Gamaliel (Acts 5:34; 22:3). While Philo played an important role in the history of Judaism, paradoxically he was an unknown figure among the Jews themselves. From his own writings, we have important biographical facts; in 38 CE Philo might have abandoned his work as a philosopher (*Spec.* 3.1); later in his career, as he writes when he "was old in age" (*Legat.* 182), he presided over the delegation of the Alexandrian Jews, who attempted to speak on behalf of the Jews in Alexandria before the Emperor Gaius Caligula in 39–40 CE (Josephus, *J. A.* 18.259); and he made a trip to the Temple in Jerusalem at least once in his lifetime (*Prov.* 2.64). He had a privileged life; he belonged to a wealthy and influential Jewish family in Alexandria and probably held a triple citizenship: Jewish citizenship of Alexandria, Alexandrian citizenship, and Roman citizenship. The opulent economic position and the connections of his family with the Herodian dynasty placed Philo and his family on a favorable position among the elite few. An interesting fact is that his brother Alexander Lysimachus was the Alabarch of the Jewish community in Alexandria (Josephus, *J. A.* 18.159, 259; 20.100; *B. J.* 5.201–205); the actual nature of his political functions, however, is unknown. Alexander's immense wealth is recorded in Josephus's *Jewish War*; the Jewish historian described that Philo's brother donated the sum of 200,000 drachmae (about $54,000) to Agrippa, grandson of Herod the Great, and sufficient gold and silver to cover the nine gates of the Temple in Jerusalem (Josephus, *B. J.* 5.205). Certainly, Alexander's political stand presumes the idea that there was a solid relation between Philo's family and the imperial house of Rome. Another interesting fact is that Philo's nephew, Tiberius Julius Alexander, apostatized from Judaism and embraced the pagan beliefs, converting himself into an enthusiastic practicer of the philosophical doctrines, which were contrary to the beliefs of his forefathers (Josephus, *A. J.* 20.101). However, it is important to note that the extent of his renouncement of Judaism is unknown and is still a matter of speculation.

Philo's privileged position allowed him to receive a good Greek and Jewish education, as well as the leisure to write treatises. His writings reflect an advanced intellectual formation, even though there is little information about his personal life and professional career. We deduce that he received an education according to the Greek *paideia*. The high quality of his language, the profound and complex level of his thinking, and his versatility as well as his sophistication in using Greek philosophy in his biblical exegesis demonstrate that he went beyond the preliminary exercises of the *progymnasmata* to receive an advanced level of Greek general education called encyclical training at school. Philo's rich philosophical formation is strongly reflected in his use of the various philosophical doctrines of Plato, Aristotle, Pythagoras, the Stoa, and Middle Platonism. Philo also studied Greek literature, including Homer, the tragedians, the poets, and the historians. At the same time, his writings attest to his excellent Jewish education in Greek. As it was true for Hellenistic Jews living in the Greek Diaspora, he studied the Septuagint (LXX). His writings evince his appreciation for the Jewish Scripture, the Jewish way of life, the beliefs of Judaism (e.g., monotheism, circumcision, Temple, food laws), and his strong commitment to the value of the ethical character of the Mosaic Law. Without a doubt, these practices helped him to form his character. Some scholars argued that Philo might have practiced an austere, perhaps conventual way of life. What is clear, however, is that Philo deeply admired the Essenes and another, similar Jewish group in Egypt called the Therapeutae, discussed in *On the Contemplative Life*. Significantly, Philo's testimony about this group is the only one we know from the ancient literature that explicitly refers to this Jewish group with similar characteristics to the Essenes in Israel.

Certainly, Philo was a Hellenistic Jewish intellectual; while he was a profound admirer of Greek wisdom, he also was a pious Jew, zealous for the traditions of his ancestors and practice of the ethical commandments of the Mosaic Law. Winston explained it this way: Philo was "a convinced and ardent Platonist, passionately goaded by the charms of philosophy to attempt to lead others into her delightful embrace," but at the same time, "he cherished a deep and devoted loyalty to his ancestral tradition, and believed he could bridge the chasm" between the Greek and Jewish worlds.[3] Philo spent much of his time writing exegetical and apologetical works of the Pentateuch, especially Genesis. His writings show that Philo did not see opposition between both intellectual worlds, the Hellenistic and the Jewish; for him, both worlds complemented each other. He tried to reconcile both traditions through philosophy, amply observed in his application of philosophical categories and vocabulary into his biblical interpretations and allegories. I believe that he was a representative of the history and development of the traditions of interpretations.

Another important aspect of Philo's reconciliatory character is that he accepted and employed the literal and allegorical interpretations of the biblical passages; in other words, he embraced the allegorical method of interpretation without rejecting the literal meaning of Genesis (e.g., Temples, circumcision, food laws). He was familiar with the Hellenistic Jewish authors who preceded him, such as Aristeas, Aristobulus, and Artapanus (ca. second century BCE), but his own allegorical and philosophical interpretations moved beyond these. It is important to note that Philo was not a (professional) philosopher in all the extent of the word; he was not affiliated with a particular philosophical school or *airesis*. Indeed, he did not write philosophical expositions or systems like Plato, Aristotle, the Stoics, or the Middle Platonists. I suggest that Philo was a de facto Middle Platonist—that is, a representative of Middle Platonism.[4] His fondness for Middle Platonism is strongly perceived in the way he drew on what he believed to be the best from each philosophical tradition and incorporated it into his own thought. His combination of Greek philosophical ideas and his consistent use of Platonic categories placed Philo at the beginning of emerging Middle Platonism. His writings show the trends of Middle Platonism of the first century CE, a time of coalescing philosophies. He masterfully combined and interconnected the various philosophical strands, a fact that became a major characteristic during the Middle Platonic period (ca. 25 BCE–40 CE).[5]

The Philonic Corpus

While it is true that Philo was not the first Hellenistic Jewish writer of antiquity, he certainly achieved the highest fame in the ancient world. Particularly, he held a prominent place in the Alexandrian Jewish exegetical tradition. Impressively, today we have about 2,500 pages of his writings, and there were a significant number of manuscripts that did not survive. Scholars suggest that the Philonic corpus was probably composed of more than seventy treatises, some thirty-seven of which have survived to us. Most of his writings came to us in their original language, Greek, but in some cases, some of his writings survived in Armenian, including in Latin. It is quite surprising to know that Philo was not known by early Jews; in fact, all his writings were preserved in Christian manuscripts only, especially by the early Church Fathers (e.g., Origen, Eusebius, Ambrose of Milan, and Clement of Alexandria), who not only preserved Philo's treatises (probably in their library), but also appreciated his method of interpretation of Scripture and his biblical exegesis. These early Christian authors, especially Origen, Ambrose, and Clement, found in Philonic exegesis an inexhaustible fountain of theories and concepts adaptable to basic doctrines in early Christianity. Philo's popularity among Christians was so immense that some Church Fathers called him "Philo the Bishop," and Eusebius of Caesarea believed that Philo was a Christian. Harry Wolfson once wrote, Philo was the "first Christian philosopher," and David T. Runia made an astounding statement: "Between Josephus in the first century and the Renaissance there is not a single explicit reference to Philo in a Jewish or a non-Christian Greek or Latin source."[6]

The division of Philo's works is debated; there is not a unanimous agreement concerning the classification and order of Philo's treatises known to us. Most scholars divide the Philonic corpus into five series: the Exposition of the Laws, the Allegorical Commentary, the Philosophical Works, the Apologetical Works, and the Questions and Answers. What is characteristic about the Philonic thought is that Philo treated philosophical topics and themes apropos of his time fundamentally following the Platonic tradition.[7] For example, the philosophical treatises, which discuss God and the cosmos, do not have anything particularly Jewish *per se*, and the historical-apologetic treatises have in nature a historical character. For instance, we know that Philo led an embassy to Rome to discuss with Gaius Caligula the anti-Semitic sentiments in Alexandria stirred as a consequence of the visit of Agrippa I to Alexandria. The Series of the Questions and Answers have as their main purpose the understanding of the Scriptures. These are commentaries of the Books of Genesis and Exodus, in the Armenian translation, where Philo commented verse by verse each of these books, as part of the study of the biblical texts. The context in which these commentaries took place might have been in synagogues or what was called *proseuchē*, or a house of prayer.

We have other groups of voluminous texts where Philo explained themes from the Ten Commandments (the *Decalogue*), such as the meaning of the Jewish Law, the figures of Moses and Abraham. What is characteristic about Philo's interpretation is his technique of allegorism. On the one hand, Philo affirmed that the biblical texts have a literal significance, presuming that these texts were divine texts. On the other hand, they also have a hidden message where, according to Philo, the reader finds the true message behind these texts. There are treatises where the allegory profoundly reaches high levels, as it is found in his rereading of the stories of Abraham and the allegory of the soul in *Legum Allegoriae*. For Philo, what the biblical text describes is not only about a historical figure, at least from the perspective of the ancient Jews, but it truly describes the soul's journey and the way the soul is able to come near to God.

Philo was committed to his Judaism in the Diaspora of Alexandria, manifested in his interest on the Jewish practice and the themes of Scriptures. He read the texts as another Jew, but his interpretation reached a profound and hidden meaning of the biblical texts. He intended to interpret the Jewish culture and the Jewish texts in function of the Greek culture, precisely by trying to find in Judaism those messages that he and his audience knew of the Greek world. In this way, in his writings he was able to revalue Judaism before the eyes not only of his fellow Jews but also of non-Jews, so that they could discover great wisdom in the Jewish texts.

ABOUT THIS SOURCEBOOK

This sourcebook is primarily for students who are studying Philo, are writing a master's or doctoral thesis, and need an introductory source for the central topics and themes of Philo of Alexandria. I intend to offer the reader a friendly introduction to Philo and his thought. It has already been recognized that the Philonic corpus is immense and his style verbose. Considering the complexity of his biblical interpretation and allegories, I selected, based on my personal judgment, the most relevant topics and themes in the study of Philo. My experience in studying and researching Philo has helped me to choose key texts that I would have appreciated to have in a sourcebook when I was a doctoral student. My hope is that the reader finds a practical and friendly avenue to Philo's major topics and themes, and that the reader would get a good sense of who Philo was and what his most important themes are within the contexts of Hellenistic Jewish and Greek philosophical traditions.

I confidently say that this is the first sourcebook that puts together the major Philonic topics and themes from the entire corpus. I have not included translations of the texts of Questions and Answers of Genesis (*QG*) and of Exodus (*QE*). These two treatises survived in Armenian. So, the reader can wisely use the translations of the Loeb Classical Library (LCL). However, I have included in the translations some relevant texts from *QG* and *QE* as references that may be helpful for the reader. The uniqueness of this sourcebook is both the nature of the translations and its ethical focus, which I shall explain next. My goal is not to offer an embellished English translation. I intend to provide an organic translation that highlights Philo's Greek thought. It is necessary to note that all translations are interpretations of the translator. It is also important to clarify that Philo's Greek is, in many cases, difficult to translate, and sometimes simply untranslatable. Consequently, some translations cannot represent Philo's thought adequately. Thus, to offer an effective translation of Philo's difficult Greek, in the best possible way, I have consulted other translations and opted for the most acceptable translations of Philo's Greek.

In my opinion, other modern translations of Philo's writings have sought a high degree of interpretation and (philosophical) sophistication. Regarding the former, a good example is the translation of C. D. Yonge and David M. Scholer, *The Works of Philo Complete and Unabridged*.[8] In my opinion, the translators have stretched Philo's Greek by incorporating too much interpretation into their renderings. The translation that incorporates both interpretation and (philosophical) sophistication is that of F. H. Colson and G. H. Whitaker in the Loeb Classical Library translations (Philo, volumes I–XII). This is the translation that I have consulted for the most part, and that modern scholars and graduate students use for their scholarly works on Philo; indeed, it is highly recommended, since it is believed that the translation has achieved a high degree of "accuracy" of Philo's thought and Greek philosophical influence on his thinking. Remarkably, the Loeb translations are polished and employ an advanced philosophical technical character as well as terms. For these reasons, the reader receives the most reliable and/or acceptable interpretations of Philo's thought in the academic world.

This sourcebook offers careful and readable translations. An important feature about my translation is that the reader receives fresh translations of Philo's thought. Perhaps in the passages the reader may encounter sections where sentences do not flow as smoothly as expected in the English language. The reader should know that Philo is not consistent in clearly describing his ideas for modern readers. Let's remember, we are dealing with treatises written two thousand years ago! My intention in this sourcebook, therefore, is not to offer a perfect translation and/or interpretation, but to provide translations, more than interpretations, that would serve the introductory reader to have a good understanding of Philo's major topics and themes and the basic structure of his thought.

Another important peculiarity of this sourcebook is its ethical character. From start to finish I have intended to focus on the ethical character of Philo, the basic spectrum of his biblical exegesis. The rationale of this approach is that in Philo's interpretation of the Pentateuch (LXX) there is a unity; his theology, cosmology, anthropology, ethics, his metaphorical description of biblical characters, the *Decalogue*, and Jewish observances, all these point toward the ethical character of his thought. Within Philo's ethics, then, I have developed seven chapters that put in perspective the importance of Philo's large *oeuvre*: theology, cosmology, anthropology, ethics, biblical characters, the Jewish Law/*Decalogue*, and Jewish worship and observances. Each chapter is divided into topics, and under each topic I have provided themes commonly studied in Philo. It is important that the reader knows that the Jewish exegete neither developed a list of topics or themes nor offered explicit definitions or descriptions of each topic and theme. Thus, both the topics and themes of this sourcebook derive from his biblical exegesis or biblical interpretation. They were carefully chosen based on Philo's emphasis throughout his corpus and their ethical significance. To help the reader in their "getting acquainted with

Philo," each chapter is introduced by a summary of Philo's teachings on the topic to which the chapter is devoted. I highlight the nature of Philo's philosophical thought and explain the significance of specific terms and features related to the various topics and themes. To enrich the reader's knowledge of Philo's Jewish and philosophical thought and interpretation, I provide extra summaries (or notes) related to some of the most relevant themes presented under the topics/themes. Lastly, under each chapter I have included a brief bibliography as a supplement for further reading in order to facilitate the reader on their study or research. At the end of each theme, I also add in the notes other texts in case the reader needs other useful texts to explore.

LIST OF PHILO'S TREATISES

Abr. = *On Abraham* (*De Abrahamo*)
Aet. = *On the Eternity of the World* (*De Aeternitate Mundi*)
Agr. = *On Agriculture* (*De Agricultura*)
Cher. = *On the Cherubim* (*De Cherubim*)
Conf. = *On the Confusion of Tongues* (*De Confusione Linguarum*)
Congr. = *On Mating with the Preliminary Studies* (*De Congressu Quaerendae Eruditionis Gratia*)
Contempl. = *On the Contemplative Life* (*De Vita Contemplativa*)
Decal. = *On the Decalogue* (*De Decalogo*)
Det. = *That the Worse Attacks the Better* (*Quod Deterius Potiori Insidiari Soleat*)
Deus = *On the Unchangeableness of God* (*Quod Deus Sit Immutabilis*)
Ebr. = *On Drunkenness* (*De Ebrietate*)
Flacc. = *Against Flaccus* (*In Flaccum*)
Fug. = *On Flight and Finding* (*De Fuga et Inventione*)
Gig. = *On the Giants* (*De Gigantibus*)
Her. = *Who Is the Heir of Divine Things?* (*Quis Rerum Divinarum Heres Sib*)
Hypoth. = *Hypothetica* (*Apologia pro Iudaeis*)
Ios. = *On Joseph* (*De Iosepho*)
Leg. = *The Allegorical Laws, 1–3* (*Legum Allegoriae*)
Legat. = *On the Embassy to Gaius* (*De Legatione ad Gaium*)
Migr. = *On the Migration of Abraham* (*De Migratione Abrahami*)
Mos. = *On the Life of Moses, 1–2* (*De Vita Mosis*)
Mut. = *On the Change of Names* (*De Mutatione Nominum*)
Opif. = *On the Creation* (*De Opificio Mundi*)
Plant. = *On Noah's Work as a Planter* (*De Plantatione*)
Post. = *On the Posterity and Exile of Cain* (*De Posteritate Caini*)

Praem. = *On Rewards and Punishments* (*De Praemiis et Poenis*)
Prob. = *Every Good Person Is Free* (*Quod Omnis Probus Liber Sit*)
Prov. = *On Providence, 1–2* (*De Providentia*)
QE = *Questions and Answers on Exodus* (*Quaestiones et Solutiones in Exodum*)
QG = *Questions and Answers on Genesis* (*Quaestiones et Solutiones in Genesin*)
Sacr. = *On the Sacrifices of Abel and Cain* (*De Sacrificiis Alebis et Caini*)
Sobr. = *On Sobriety* (*De Sobrietate*)
Somn. = *On Dreams, 1–2* (*De Somniis*)
Spec. = *On the Special Laws, 1–4* (*De Specialibus Legibus*)
Virt. = *On the Virtues* (*De Virtutibus*)

WORKS BY OTHER AUTHORS

B. J. = *Jewish War* (*Bellum Judaicum*)
J. A. = *The Antiquities of the Jews* (*Antiquitates Judaicae*)
SVF = *Stoicorum Veterum Fragmenta*
Tim. = *Timaeus*
Wis. = *Wisdom of Solomon*

NOTES

1. Hans Lewy, Isaak Heinemann, and Alexander Altmann, eds., *3 Jewish Philosophers: Philo: Selections, Saadya Gaon: Book of Doctrines and Beliefs, Yehuda Halevi: Kuzari* (Cleveland: Jewish Publication Society, 1960).

2. David Winston, *Philo of Alexandria: The Contemplative Life, the Giants, and Selections* (Mahwah, NJ: Paulist Press, 1981).

3. Winston, *Philo of Alexandria*, 1.

4. David T. Runia, "Was Philo a Middle Platonist? A Difficult Question Revisited," *Studia Philonica* 5 (1993): 112–40 at 130.

5. Cf. John Dillon, *Alcinous: The Handbook of Platonism* (Oxford: Clarendon Press, 2001), xl.

6. Runia, "Philo and the Patristic Tradition: A List of Direct References," in Seland Torrey, ed., *Philo: A Handbook to Philo of Alexandria* (Grand Rapids, MI: Eerdmans, 2014), 268–86, at 270.

7. For a basic and informative survey on Philo and his writings, see Kenneth Schenck, *A Brief Guide to Philo* (Louisville: WJK, 2005).

8. C. D. Yonge and David M. Scholer, *The Works of Philo Complete and Unabridged* (Peabody: Hedrickson Publishers, 1993). This translation is also available online,

"Early Jewish Writings": http://www.earlyjewishwritings.com/philo.html. For other Philonic sources see Seland Torrey website: https://torreys.org/bible/.

BIBLIOGRAPHY

Mendelson, Alan. *Philo's Jewish Identity.* Brown Judaic Series 161. Atlanta: Brown Judaic Studies, 1988.

Morris, Jenny. "The Jewish Philosopher Philo." Pages 809–89 in vol. 3 of Emil Schürer, *The History of the Jewish People in the Age of Jesus Christ (175 B.C.– A.D. 135).* Edited by Geza Vermes et al. Edinburgh: T & T Clark, 1973–1987.

Niehoff, Maren. *Philo of Alexandria: An Intellectual Biography.* New Haven, London: Yale University Press, 2018.

Royse, James R. "Philo's Division of his Works into Books." *The Studia Philonica Annnual* 12 (2001): 59–85.

Runia, David T. *Philo in Early Christian Literature: A Survey.* Compendia Rerum Iudaicarum ad Novum Testamentum III. Minneapolis: Fortress Press, 1993.

Seland, Torrey, ed. *Reading Philo: A Handbook to Philo of Alexandria.* Grand Rapids, MI: Eerdmans, 2014.

Sterling, Gregory E. "Philo." Pages 1063–70 in *The Eerdmans Dictionary of Early Judaism.* Edited by John J. Collins and Daniel C. Harlow. Grand Rapids, MI: William B. Eerdmans Publishing Company, 2010.

Sterling, Gregory E. "'Philo Has Not Been Used Half Enough': The Significance of Philo of Alexandria for the Study of the New Testament." *Perspectives in Religious Studies* 30, no. 3 (2003): 251–69.

Chapter 1

Philo's Theology

In this chapter, Philo's theology covers the most important and relevant passages in connection with his ethics. From his scriptural exegesis, the first observation that I want to point out is Philo's description of God within the Jewish and Platonic traditions. Philo identifies God as the Existent One (*ho ōn; to on*), the identification of Yahweh in Exod. 3:14, in Platonic terms (*to on*).[1] With the expression the "All" or the "whole" (*holos*) Philo generally refers either to the world or the universe. The Greek word *anthrōpos* or its plural (*anthrōpoi*) is usually translated as human(s) or human beings, sometimes as person, man, or men, depending on the context.

While Philo's identification of God as Creator, Father, and Maker of the world follows his Jewish tradition, the reader encounters explicit philosophical features, besides Philo's identification of God as the Existent One or He Who Is. God's superior qualities in His nature are Platonic in character; but his understanding of the Logos (sometimes translated as Reason or Word), defined or described in many forms, and the Spirit (*pneuma*) are Stoic in orientation. Philo speaks of the Spirit as the human Spirit and as the Spirit of God, and in a few instances, he connects it with virtue. Philo's conception of God's preexistence and transcendence are expressed in (Middle) Platonic categories, as well as His self-sufficiency. Within this philosophical context, God's transcendent nature and His disassociation from evil or passions are consistently present. Philo strongly argues that God is not anthropomorphic; he links God only with the mind (*nous*) and the good. Philo recognizes other deities (gods); however, he makes clear emphasis on the superiority of the Jewish God, the Existent One, Who is the true God. When speaking of the Jewish God the reader will find Philo's repetition in the way he describes God as the One Who fills and contains everything and needs nothing for Himself. A key feature regarding God's transcendent nature is that Philo consistently emphasizes the notion that human beings can know God's existence but claims and defends that human beings cannot apprehend His nature; in other words, human beings cannot grasp God's nature or essence, not even know

His name. Moses, the Lawgiver, cannot find the essence of He Who Is. One detail that the reader cannot miss is the beautiful, sublime, poetic language that Philo uses to explain his understanding of God and Who God Is. Indeed, Philo spends a good deal expounding profoundly his interpretation of the Jewish expression "I AM the Lord/God."

Following philosophical traditions (Platonic, Stoic, and Middle Platonism), Philo introduces God's powers or potencies as inferior to the Existent One, and the relationship between God and both the Monad (God/active principle) and Dyad (matter/passive principle), two philosophical terms peculiar to Middle Platonists, used in their interpretation of Plato's *Timaeus*, which was Philo's source for his exposition of the creation of the world and the human. Angels are, too, powers or potencies (*QG* 3.12). The reader learns that despite Philo's strong emphasis on God's transcendent reality that is unreachable to humans, interestingly, there is a way for human beings to get closer to the Existent One and develop a relationship with Him through vocal or mental prayer and petitions. God listens, is compassionate, and reaches the minds of humans. God is always associated with goodness and virtues only; He is identified as the Lover of virtues. The unity of Philo's theology comes to be expressed in the divine and transcendent qualities, which ultimately are reflected Platonically in virtues and not in vices or wickedness.

THE NATURE OF GOD

Note

In conversation with the larger Greco-Roman world, Philo uses *Greek philosophical* language to describe the Existent One as the Creator: Maker of heaven and earth, Husband and Father of the universe, Author of all things, Master and Sovereign of the universe, Architect, Artificer of the universe, Archetype, Cause of all things, Begetter of the universe, Source of all good things, Primal Cause, and most ancient Cause of all. Philo appropriates (*Middle*) *Platonic* language to describe the Existent One as Unchanged, Uncreated, Incorruptible, Transcendent, Immaterial, Invisible, Eternal, Possessor of knowledge, Fountain of Reason, Self-Existent, Self-Sufficient, Existent God, and Existing Being.[2] Philo also ascribes further *characteristics of* the Existent One: Goodness, True Good, Benefactor, Prince of Peace, Peace-Keeper, and Peace-Maker. In convergence with other Hellenistic Jewish writers, Philo emphasizes the *superiority of Judaism* by describing the Existent One as Universal Ruler, Superior to all things, Superior to virtue, King of kings and God of gods, All-sovereign, Sovereign of the universe, Great King, Prince of Peace, Commander and Ruler, Ruler of the universe, and Savior.[3] As was true for all Jews, for Philo the Supreme Jewish God is One,[4] the true and only God.[5] However, what is unique about Philo's understanding of God is that Philo never describes God as YHWH; instead, he identifies the Jewish God as "the Existent One," and he intentionally omits Jewish elements (e.g., the God of Israel, I am your God, and you are my people, etc.).

Philo uses the term of providence (*pronoia*) primarily in theological, cosmological, ethical, and anthropological statements. Philo knew and adopted for his own interpretation the traditions he inherited and incorporated these ancient ways of interpreting divine providence in his own doctrine: if God exists, then there is divine providence (*Ebr.* 19). For Philo the Existent One (*ho ōn* [Exod. 3:14; cf. Deut. 32:39], *to on*), who is transcendent, can relate directly to human beings and be a Provident Father.[6] For Philo, God provides for the world and exercises providence over everything He created. Although this idea that God is Provident is dependent on philosophical traditions, his reinterpretation is governed by his Jewish monotheism and his theocentric view. At the beginning of his treatise, *On the Creation,* he praises both piety and divine providence as "the most beneficial and indispensable" (*Opif.* 9), and at the end of the treatise, when Philo declares his credal formulation (*Opif.* 171–172), he connects again God's providential care with the virtue of piety.[7] The anthropomorphic image of human fatherhood applied to God served Philo as a congenial means of connecting the idea of providence to the concept of God as to render comprehensible to his audience the belief that God the Father takes immanent care of His creation and humanity.[8]

The Existent One

Post. 28–31: An oracle in the clearest light declared by the all-wise Moses, who is the most worthy and steadfast man of good health, is as this: "but you stand here by me" (Deut. 5:31). In this oracle two things are present: one that the Existent One (*QE* 2.122–123), Who moves and turns all else, is motionless and unchangeable (*QE* 2.61); and the other is that He makes the worthy man sharer of His own nature, which is repose. For I think that, just as a correct ruler guides straight the crooked things; so, moving things are brought to stop and made stationary by the force of Him Who stands. 29 Here, He summons another to stand by Him. Elsewhere He says, "I will go with you to Egypt, and I will bring you up to the end" (Gen. 46:4), not "you with me." Why is this so? Because both quiescence and abiding are God's own characteristics but change of place and all movement that causes change is characteristic of creation. 30 When, therefore, He speaks of His own goodness, He means "you stand with me," not "I stand with you." For God will not stand, but rather He has always stood. But when He comes to that which is fitting to creation, He will most rightly say, "I will go down with you," because for you the change of place is proper. So, with me no one will go down—for I do not turn or change—but one shall stand seeing that quiescence, which is dear to me. Though with those who go down in the sense of changing their place—for change of place is a kins-brother to them—I will go down in all-pervading Self-Presence, without changing places, for I have filled the universe with Myself. 31 To be sure I do this also in pity for the rational nature, that it may be caused to rise out of the nether world of the passions into the upper region of virtue guided step by step by Me. I AM Who leads to the road to heaven, and I have appointed a place, a highway for suppliant souls, that they might not grow weary as they tread it.

Migr. 182–183: Wherefore, even though it is said somewhere in the law book, "God in heaven above and on earth below" (Deut. 4:39), no one is supposed to speak of He that Is—because the Existent One can contain but cannot be comprehended by law—and of His power, just as He established and ordered and marshalled the whole (or universe). 183 This Lord is goodness; He has driven away from Himself envy together with its hatred of virtue and moral beauty; He is the begetter of graces through which He has shown forth what He brought into existence the things that did not exist. Because the Existent One, in my opinion, should be imagined everywhere, in reality is shown nowhere; thus, it is a totally true oracle in which the words, "Here I am," which describes Him, as if He were visible, Him that cannot be pointed out and that is invisible, are followed by the words, "before that you were made" (Exod. 17:6). For He is before all of creation, going out of that and without being present in any of the things that come after Him.

Congr. 171: Who, then, is so unholy as to suppose that God is hurtful and that He sends famine, a most pitiable death to those who are unable to live without food? He is good, the Cause of good things, a Benefactor, Savior, Nourisher, Wealth-bringer, and Munificent. He has banished the cumberers of the earth, Adam and Eve, from the garden of Eden.

Fug. 162–163: For his thoughts are busy over the untrodden dwelling place of divine natures but now being about to break into pieces in a never-ending and vain work, he is relieved from it with the compassion and providence of God, the Savior of all creatures (*QG* 2.13, 60). He from the innermost Sanctuary proclaimed, "don't draw near here" (Exod. 2:5), which is as much as to say "enter not on such an inquiry"; for the work is futility and a busy disposition, too high, that is beyond the human ability. But marvel at all the things that have come into being, but as for the reasons for which they have come into being or are decaying, cease to busy thyself with them. 163 For "the place on which you stand," it says, "is holy ground" (Exod. 3:5). What kind of nature is the place? Evidently, it is about that of causation, which He has assigned only to the divine natures, deeming no human being capable of grasping with the study of causation.

Fug. 197–198: It is time to talk about the supreme and most excellent Spring, which the Father of the whole declared through the mouths of the prophets. He said in a certain place, "Me they forsook, a Spring of life, and dug for themselves broken cisterns, which are not able to hold water" (Jer. 2:13). 198 God, therefore, is the chiefest Spring, and likewise may He be called, for this whole universe is a rain that fell from Him. But I bow in awe when I hear that this Spring is one of life. For God alone is the Cause of the soul and life, and preeminently of the rational soul and of the life that is united with prudence (*QG* 3.11). For matter is dead, but God is something more than life, an ever-flowing Spring of living as He Himself says.

Decal. 41: For if the Uncreated and the Incorruptible, and Eternal God, Who needs nothing and is the Maker of all things and the Benefactor and King of kings and God of gods, could not wait to see the most despise or humblest, God would deem worthy to banquet him of holy oracles and statutes, as though it was intended to give a feast for him alone and to make ready an effusive drinking party for the soul instructed in the holy secrets and accepted for admission to the greatest mysteries. . . . [9]

Prob. 42–43: Who can say that God's friends are not free? We recognize justly that the friends of kings possess not only freedom but also authority; they take part in their management and administration as leaders. To those who are ascribed servants of the celestial gods, who are god-lovers, and thereby god-beloved, rewarded with the same kindness, as they have shown, and in the judgment of truth are as the poets say, rulers of all and kings of kings. 43 The Legislator of the Jews in high spirits went even beyond extreme and in the practice of his naked philosophy, ventured to speak of him who was possessed by the love of the divine, and worshipped the Existent One only. It is boldly to say that he is no longer man but a god, indeed, a god to humans (Exod. 7:1), not to the different parts of nature; so that he may leave to the Father of all the place of King and God of gods.[10]

The Transcendence of God

Leg. 1.43–44: "And God planted a Paradise in Eden toward the sun-rising, and He placed there the human whom He molded" (Gen. 2:8; *QG* 1.6–8, 56). By using many words for it Moses has shown that the sublime and the heavenly wisdom has many names. For he calls it the heavenly wisdom "beginning," "Image," and "vision of God." And now he establishes through the planting of the garden that the earthly wisdom is a copy of this wisdom as of an archetype. Let not so great an impiety seize human reasoning as to suppose that God tills the soil and plants gardens. Since we should immediately be without knowing about what his real reason could be so. For it would not be to provide himself with pleasant resting-place and pleasures. Let no such fables ever enter our intellect. 44 For not even the whole world would be sufficient to make a dwelling place for God, since God is His own place and is filled by Himself and is sufficient for Himself. He fills and encompasses all other things which are in need, helpless, and empty. But He Himself is not contained by anything else, as He Himself is One and the All.

Deus 57–59: What may we say? If He is furnished with parts of the bodily organs, He has feet to move forward, but to where will He walk, if He fills everything with His presence? To whom will He go, if there is no one who is held in equal honor to Him? And on account of what will He go? For it cannot be because of his health as with us. Indeed, hands too He must have both to receive and to give; but the case is that He takes nothing from anyone, for He has no need of anything and has all the possessions as His; and when He gives, He does so using an assistant, His Logos, through which also He made the world. 58 Nor had He any need of eyes, through which no perception can take place without a sensible light. But the light is created and is perceptible by the senses, whereas God saw before creation, being Himself furnished with His own light. 59 And what need is there to speak of the organs of nourishment? If He has them, He takes nourishment and after filling up He rests, and after resting he has need again, and the rest of what follows on this I will not discuss. These are inventions of the impious, who represent the Deity in human form, but they are in fact attributing human passions to God.

Conf. 136–139: But all things have been filled by God, Who contains everything, but is not contained. To be standing both everywhere and nowhere is His property and His alone. He is nowhere, because He Himself has created a space and a place for material things, and it is repulsed by custom to say that He Who Is Creator is contained in anything that He has created (*QG* 4.114). He is everywhere, because He Himself has made His powers extend through the earth, water, air, and heaven. He has left no part of the universe desolated without His presence, and bringing everything together, He bound them fast with invisible bonds, so that they should never be loosened. . . . [11] 137 The Existent One has in His mind that He is over and above His potencies. So, it is not conceivable that He can be conceived spatially. Rather, this potency of His, by which He set and ordained all things, is called truly "God" in accordance to the derivation of that name,[12] and holds the whole and is extended through all the parts of the universe. 138 But the Divine, Invisible that cannot be reached, is present everywhere and is in reality invisible and is present nowhere. . . . [13] We have the phrase "Thus, I stand before you" (Exod. 17:6). I seem the object of demonstration and comprehension, yet I go beyond the created things, preceding all demonstration and appearances. 139 Hence, none of the names that expresses a movement from a place to place, whether up or down, to right or to left, forward or backward, fits to be in accord with

God. For no such word can conceive Him; in fact, none of the sayings about these movements is compatible with Him, nor in the translation and nor in the change of place.

Somn. 2.99–100: Coming to know for certain that such judges could never have failed to give a sound judgment, but as their training from the First has taught them Who is the King, the Lord, they hate to give homage and honor to one who appropriates the honor due to God and calls away His suppliants to do service to himself. 100 With good courage, therefore, they will say, "are not you going to be king and rule us? Or do you not perceive that we are not self-ruling but under the kingship of an Immortal, the One and only God? Are we ruled by a King? But who? Are we not under a Lord ruling us? Are we not safe under a master and have and will have the same Lord forever, bondage to whom gives us great joy like his freedom does to any other? For of all things in creation that are held in honor in this world of creation bondage to God is the best.

Somn. 1.229–232: Thus, what are we to say? He who is truly God is One, but those that are improperly called are more than one. For this reason, the holy Word has revealed in the present the One, Who is truly by means of the article saying, "I Am *the* God"; while it omits the article when affirming Him who is improperly called, saying, "Who appeared to you in a place," not "of the God," but only "of God." 230 It now gives the title "God" to His chief Logos, not because of superstitions in the arrangement of the names, but only with one goal before Him: to use words to express facts. Also, looking at other passages when inquiring if there is the same name applicable to the One Who Is, clearly, one comes to recognize that the Lord has no name, and that whatever name one may say, it will be by license of language; because the essence of the One Who Is is not proper to be spoken of, but it is simply the Existent One. 231 Moses also gives testimony to the prophetic word he learned whether there is a name for Him: "I AM He who Is" (Exod. 3:14). It was given in order that, since there are not in God things human beings can comprehend, human beings may recognize His existence. 232 Therefore, with the incorporeal souls and with His worshippers it is likely that He should reveal Himself as He Is, conversing with them as friend to friends; to those who are still in the body, He shows Himself like angels without altering His own nature, for He is immutable (*QE* 2.37). He conveys to those who receive the impression of His presence a different form of appearance, so that they may learn that the Image is not a copy but rather the same original form.

Praem. 39–40a: The Father and Savior perceiving his sincere yearning and longing gave His mercy upon him and gave power to the penetration of his eyesight and did not bear a grudge to grant him a vision of Himself just in so far as it was possible for the created and mortal nature to contain it. The vision certainly showed only that "He Is," not "what He Is." 40 For that which is better than the good, more powerful, and higher than the Monad, and purer than the Unit, cannot be discerned by anyone else; to God alone, the One, is permitted to apprehend Himself.[14]

God and the Mind

Det. 89–95: For the mind, being hastier than all things and time, is the only part of all our endowments that seems to change quickly to become itself and leaves behind the time in which it seems to find itself, and by virtue of invisible faculties, comes lightly into contact with the universe, its parts, and their causes respectively. And now, having reached not only the boundaries of the earth and of the sea, but also of the air and heaven, the mind does not stay there, because the universe is a narrow boundary for its continuous and unceasing course, and aiming to advance beyond, and apprehend, if possible, the nature of God, which except for its bare existence is inapprehensible. 90 How, then, the human mind being so tiny, like the size of the brain or a heart, should be able to contain such an immense magnitude of sky and universe, had it not been a piece of that divine and blessed soul that is not divided? For nothing is severed or detached from the divine, but only extended. Therefore, the mind having obtained a share of perfection that exists in the whole, when it conceives the universe, stretches out as widely as the bounds of the whole, for its force is susceptible of attraction. 91 Thus, these few words may be said about the essence of life, and so in the following the order, we shall give the interpretation of the phrase "the voice of blood cried loud" (Gen. 4:10) in this way. One part of our soul is dumb, and another has a voice. The nonrational part is dumb; the rational, which is the only part that has attained the conception of God, has a great voice. With the other parts we can apprehend neither God nor any other intelligible object. 92 In the vital faculty, thus, whose essence is blood, a portion has obtained, as honorable gift, the voice and the speech; not a stream that flows through the mouth and the tongue, but the fountain from which the cisterns of uttered speech are filled. The fountain is the mind through which partly voluntarily, partly involuntarily, we utter aloud our petitions and outcries to the One Who Is. 93 He, being goodness and graciousness, does not turn away from those who seek His protection, above all when they groan over the works and sufferings in Egypt without pretense and falsehood. Indeed, Moses says that their words go up to God (Exod. 2:23), and that He hears and delivers them from evils that are falling upon them. 94 All of these things happened when the king of Egypt died. Contrary to expectation, one may expect that when a tyrant ruler dies, those whom he tyrannized are glad and rejoice; yet it is then that they are said to lament, for we are told "after those many days the king of Egypt died, and the children of Israel lamented sorely" (Exod. 2:23). 95 Thus, on the one hand, the literal sentence does not comprise to reason; on the other hand, it is found in conformity with the powers that sway the soul. For the Pharaoh scatters and casts away the ideas about noble glories, when this power (the Pharaoh) shows himself quick and active to us and appears to be healthy in glory, if indeed any evil power may be said to be healthy, we drive self-control far from us, and we welcome pleasure. But when the author of our foul and licentious life becomes impotent, it may weaken and die, and we are brought all at once to a clear view of a life of temperance and turn to lamenting and bewailing for our old ways of living. Because preferring pleasure over virtue, we contaminate the immortal life with the mortal life. But He alone is gracious, taking pity on our continuous mourning, accepts our souls, and without effort dispels the Egyptian tornado of passions that had burst upon us.

Mut. 7–15: Indeed, you shall not believe that the Existent One, Who is truly Existent, is apprehended by any human being. We have in us no human organ by which we are able to envisage the Existent One, neither sense organ—for it is not sense-perceptible—nor the mind. Thus, Moses, who contemplates God (as the divine oracles say, he entered the darkness [Exod. 20:21] and figuratively representing the invisible and incorporeal essence of God), searched everywhere and sought through all things in his desire to see Him with distinct clarity and Who alone is the Good. 8 But he found no one, not even an idea that resembled what he hoped for. In despair of learning from others, Moses flies for refuge to the object of his search itself and prays, saying, "reveal yourself to me that with knowledge I may see you" (Exod. 33:13). And yet he does not attain his purpose, because the knowledge of things both material and immaterial that comes after the Existent One is considered a most ample gift for the best race among mortals. 9 For we read: "you shall see the things behind me, but my face you shall not see" (Exod. 33:23). In other words, all that comes after the Existent One, both material and immaterial, is accessible to apprehension, even if it is not already apprehended, but He alone by His very nature cannot be seen. 10 And why is it astonishing if the Existent One cannot be apprehended by the human when even the mind in each of us is unknown? For who knows the essence of the soul? The mystery, which is uncertainty, brought forth numberless contentions among the Sophists, who propound opinions contrary to each other or even totally opposed (*QG* 3.23, 27). 11 It follows that not even a proper name can be given to the truly Existent One, the Lord. Observe that when the prophet earnestly inquires what He must answer those who ask about His name, he says, "I AM He Who Is" (Exod. 3:14), which is equivalent to say "my nature is to be, and not to be spoken." 12 However, that humankind should not be in complete want of a designation for the Supremely Good, He allows them to use analogically, as though it were His proper name, the title of "Lord God" of the three natural orders: teaching, perfection, practice, whose recorded symbols are Abraham,

Isaac, and Jacob.[15] He says, "this is my eternal name," inasmuch as it belongs to our time period, not to the precosmic, "and my memorial," not a name set beyond memory and thought, and again "for generations" (Exod. 3:15), not for creatures nongenerated. 13 For it is necessary and sufficient for those who have been originated into mortality to have a substitute for the divine name in order that they may approach if not the facticity at least the name of the Supremely Good, and be ruled according to it. This is also revealed in the inspired oracle out of the mouth of the One Who is the Ruler of the whole that no proper name of the Lord has been disclosed to anyone. "I was seen," he says, "by Abraham, Isaac, and Jacob, being their God and my name of 'Lord' I did not revealed to them" (Exod. 6:3). For when the hyperbaton is placed in grammatical sequence, the meaning would be this: "my proper name I did not reveal to them," but only the one for analogical use, for the reasons already mentioned. 14 So inexpressible is indeed the Existent One that not even the ministering powers tell us a proper name. Thus, after the wrestling match that the man of practice fought in his acquisition of virtue, he says to the unseen master, "let me know your name," and He said to him, "so, why do you ask this, my name?" (Gen. 32:29); and He does not reveal His personal and proper name. It suffices for you, He says, to help yourself through my prayers, as for the names, those symbols of created things, seek them not among imperishable natures. 15 It is not difficult to understand, therefore, that the highest of all beings is inexpressible, when His Logos too cannot be expressed by us through his own name. If he is not inexpressible, He is also neither inconceivable nor incomprehensible. The words, "the Lord was seen to Abraham" (Gen. 17:1), then, should not be understood in the sense that the Cause of all extended its light upon him and appeared to him—for what human mind could be sufficient to contain the greatness of the vision? But as one of the powers with it, kingship, appears to him. For the title "Lord" is appropriate of the power and kingship.

Praem. 116–117: When God is gracious, He makes all things light and easy. He is gracious with those who are ashamed and with those who depart from incontinence to self-control, and with those who reproach their deeds of their guilty ways of life, abhor shameful images, which they imprinted on their souls. They earnestly strive to still the storm of their passions and seek to strive for a life of serenity and peace. 117 Therefore, just as God can easily emigrate in one expedition to the farthest parts of the earth and bring human beings from the limits into any place He wills, so too the mind, which was led astray everywhere for a long time, maltreated by pleasure and desire, the mistresses it honored so unduly, may well be brought back by the mercy of its Savior from pathless wild into a road, always discerning to take a straightforward flight (without return; *QG* 3.10). We are not speaking of a shameful flight, but a flight of one banished from evil to salvation, a banishment that may truly be held to be superior to a return.[16]

ANTI-ANTHROPOMORPHISM

Note

Philo stands firmly with the Greek philosophers (especially Platonists) to say that the *anthropomorphic* elements are not to be taken literally.[17]

God Has No Human Form

Conf. 98–100: When he speaks of the sensible world as the footstool of God, first, it is through this that He may show that the Cause that made it is not in what is created; then, to move beyond that, the whole universe does not set into motion at its own free unshackled will, but God, the Steersman, steers and pilots to bring to safety everything that is. Neither feet, nor hands, nor other created parts at all are absolutely an account according to the true word, "for God is not as human" (Num. 23:19). He is the only One Who leads instructions because we are not able to get outside ourselves. But we can come to terms about Him from our own experience and apprehend the conceptions about the Uncreated. 99 It is a fine saying when by way of illustration he makes known the world as it is imagined in an appearance of brick. For it seems to stand firm like a brick according to the application of the sense-perceptible, and it has been announced with a swift movement that outruns all movement in the particulars. 100 The sun during the day and the moon at night are perceived by our bodily eyes as standing still. Indeed, who does not know that the rapidity about which they are carried is unapproached, if they traverse the whole heaven in one day? In this way, indeed, the whole heaven expects also to stand still but actually revolves, although the motion is apprehended by the eye, which is itself incorporeal and closer to the divine, the eye of the understanding.

Congr. 114–115: Such too is the same for the tribute of princes chosen among the best that they had, which they offered at the time when the soul, equipped by love of knowledge and wisdom, celebrated its dedication in a holy manner, giving thanks to the God Who is his Teacher and Guide. The worshipper offers "a censer of ten gold full of incense" (Num. 7:14, 20), so that He Who alone is Wise may choose the perfume exhaled by prudence and by every virtue. 115 Whenever the perfumes seem to be pleasant in His judgment, Moses will praise them saying, "the Lord smelt a scent of sweet fragrance" (Gen. 8:21; *QE* 2.71), since "smelled" signifies "accepted." For

He, Who is not of human form, has need neither of nostrils nor of some other parts of the human organs.

Decal. 33: I may suppose that on this occasion it was a holy miracle (cf. *Mos*. 1.185), which God urged to make an invisible sound in the air, more marvelous than all instruments that joins together in perfect harmonies, not a soulless voice and not composed of body and soul like a living creature. But it is a rational soul full of clearness and distinctness, which giving shape and tension to the lower air and changing it to flaming fire, sounded forth like the breath (*pneuma*) through a trumpet an articulated sound so large, as it seems to be equally heard by the nearest and the farthest people at the same time.

Spec. 1.36: As for His divine essence, though in fact it is hard to reach and hard to apprehend, it still calls for all the inquiry possible. For nothing is better than to search for the true God, even if the discovery of Him eludes human capacity, since the very wish to learn, if earnestly entertained, produces untold joys and pleasures.[18]

GODHEAD, MONAD, DYAD

Monad

Leg. 2.3: For if something would be added to God it would be either superior or inferior or equal to Him. However, there is neither anything equal nor superior to God, and no lesser thing is assimilated to Him. Otherwise, He too would be inferior, but if He would be made inferior, He will also be perishable; to think something like that is not established by the law. Thus, God is arranged in the category of the One and the Monad, or rather the Monad has been arranged in the category of the One God (*QG* 4.118; *QE* 2.29, 94). For like time, all number is subsequent to the universe, whereas God is prior to the universe, and He is its Maker.

Deus 82–85: Similar to what was previously said is the following passage: "the Lord talked once; I have heard these two things" (Ps. 61[62]:11 LXX). For "once" is like the unmixed, for the unmixed is also a Monad and the Monad is unmixed; whereas "twice" is like mixed. For the mixed is not single, since it admits both combination and separation. 83 God, therefore, speaks of unmixed monads or units. For His word is not a beating of a loud-sounding air or mixed with anything else at all, but it is incorporeal and unclothed, and does not differ from the Monad. But our hearing is the product of two (Dyad) factors. 84 For the spirit (or breath) from the leading part, that is the faculty part, driven up through the trachea, is shaped in the mouth by the craftsman, as it were, of the tongue, and rushing out it mixes with its congenital air, and impinging on it produces in a harmonious mixing of the two. For the consonance is joined together by the different sounds in a two (Dyad), originally divided, and contains a high and a low pitch. 85 Therefore, he contrasted all beautifully the multitude of the unjust thoughts with the just One as one, numerically less, but superior in value. So, the worse should not prove the weightier when tested as in the scales, but by the power of the weight of the better in the opposite scale it might have its lightness detected and be weakened.

Fug. 164–165: But Moses through desire of knowledge lifts his head above the whole world and becomes a seeker of its Creator, asking of what sort this Being is difficult to see and so difficult to guess. Is He a body or incorporeal, or something that is above these? Is He a single nature, like a Monad, or composite Being, or what of those beings is He? And seeing that this is difficult to grasp and difficult to understand, Moses prays that he may learn about God from God Himself what God is: for he has no hope of being able to come to know this from one of those who are inferior to Him. 165 Nevertheless, he did not succeed in finding the essence of He Who Is. For "what is behind me," he said, "you shall see, but the face you shall not see" (Exod. 33:23). For it is sufficient for the wise to know what follows and all that comes after God; but he who wishes to set his vision toward the Supreme Essence will be disabled to see before the rays that beam forth around Him.

Monad and Dyad

Spec. 3.178–180: This is the reason that was often stated by many. Though I have heard another from divinely inspired men, those who think that most things in the laws are hidden symbols and unspoken truth. It was explained as follows. In the soul, just as in their families, the male part corresponds to the men, and the female part also corresponds to the women. The male soul assigns itself to God alone, as to the Father and Maker of the whole and the Cause of all things (*QG* 4.130). The female clings to the things that perish in creation, and it stretches out its faculties like a hand, so that it blindly reaches the things that comes in its way, and gives the clasp of friendship to creation with its many changes and transmutations, instead of to the divine order, the immutable and blessed, the thrice happy. 179 Therefore, naturally, it has been said expressly in the law to cut off symbolically the hand of the woman, not meaning that the body should be mutilated by the loss of a part that is very indispensable, but above it, to cut out from the soul all the godless thoughts that take for their basis all that comes into being through birth. For the genitals are a symbol of the seed sown and of the created things. 180 Following where the study of nature leads me, I will say that the Monad is the Image of the first Cause and the Dyad is of passive and divisible matter (*QE* 2.100). Thus, one who honors the Dyad before the Monad should not fail to know that he holds matter in higher esteem than God (*QG* 4.110). It is for this reason that the law deemed it right to cut off this hand, a tendency of the soul. For there is no greater impious act than to attribute to the passive element the power of the active principle.

Praem. 45–46: It is worthy to observe how this access has been obtained through an illustration. Do we see the sun, which our senses perceive, by any other thing than the sun itself? Do we see the stars by any other thing than the stars themselves? Also, is not light seen all together by light itself? In the same way, God too is His own brightness and is contemplated through Himself alone, without anything cooperating or being able to cooperate to the absolute apprehension of His existence. 46 Those diviners, who aim to discern the Uncreated and Creator of the universe, then, urge to contemplate Him from His creation, and are on the same footing as those who try to trace the nature of the Monad from the Dyad, when they should examine the Dyad from the Monad, for this is the beginning. They who are the seekers of truth envisage God through God, light through light.[19]

RELATIONSHIP BETWEEN GOD AND THE LOGOS

Note

The Stoic Logos is one of the most difficult themes in Philo's thought in his doctrine of the Logos. The Logos plays a role in Philo's theology, like the Stoics, in his cosmology, and anthropology (see Chapters 2 and 3). The divine Logos is the "instrument" (*organon*) of creation, and in Philo the Logos becomes the Image of God and the container of all the Ideas that are basic for the visible, sensible world.[20] Like other Middle Platonists, Philo incorporates the Stoic doctrine of the Logos and the Platonic framework of the supreme, transcendent God into his own interpretation of creation. He takes the Logos as the "intermediate figure" between the transcendent God (the Existent One) and the corporeal, sensible world (*kosmos aisthētos*). What is significant about God's relationship with the Logos is that God's divine Logos is the principal agent, the instrument through whom God creates, as the reader shall see in Chapter 2. The intrinsic relationship between God and the Logos is observed in Philo's famous statement in which he speaks of the Logos as a "second god" (*Conf.* 145–147). Similarly, in *On Dreams*, Philo calls God's oldest Logos "god" (*Somn.* 1.227–230).

God and Logos

Cher. 27–31: But once I heard a good word from my soul, which many times is God-possessed and concerned with prophesy where it does not know. If I can, I will say it from memory. It was said to me that God being One (*Opif.* 171) has two highest and foremost powers: goodness and authority. Through goodness He has begotten everything, and through authority He rules what has become. 28 In the midst between the two there is a third entity uniting both, Logos (*Opif.* 20), for it is through the Logos that God is Ruler and Goodness. The Cherubim are symbols of these two powers, authority and goodness; therefore, the fiery sword is the symbol of Logos. For Logos is exceedingly swift and burning hot and chiefly so the Logos of the great Cause, for it alone preceded and outran all things, having been conceived before them all, and being manifested above them all. 29 Each of the Cherubim, being intelligence, exhibits an unalloyed Image, so that, having learned about the sovereignty and beneficence of the Cause, you may visibly reap the fruits of a happy lot. For you shall also know directly about unmixed potencies, how both come together and are mixed, and how God, Who is good, manifests His honor from the beginning and also manifests His goodness from the beginning. So that you may gain virtues begotten of these potencies: friendliness and reverence toward God. When things are well with you, the majesty of the sovereign King shall keep you from high thoughts. When you suffer what you would not, you will not despair of betterment, remembering the kindness of the great and bountiful God. 30 For this reason the sword is a sword of flame, because it is necessary to closely follow reason with its fierce and burning heat, reason that ever moves with all zeal to choose noble things and to avoid evil things. 31 Do you not see that also Abraham, the wise, when he began to make God his standard in all things and leave nothing to the created, takes a copy of the fiery sword, "fire and knife" (Gen. 22:6) to divide and to consume the mortal element away from himself, and thus to fly upward to God with his understanding stripped of its trammels?

Somn. 1.62–67: The term "place" has a threefold meaning: first, that of a space filled by corporeal form; second, that of the divine Logos, which God Himself has completely filled through the universe with incorporeal potencies (*QG* 4.47, 49). For "they saw," Moses says, "the place where the God of Israel stood" (Exod. 24:10). Only in it he allowed to sacrifice, preventing them to do so elsewhere. For they were expressly questioned to go up to the place, which the Lord God shall choose (Deut. 12:5), there to sacrifice the whole burnt offerings and the deliverance offerings (Exod. 20:24), and to offer the other pure sacrifices (*QG* 2.50; *QE* 2.50). 63 According to the third meaning, God Himself is called a "place" from the fact that He contains all, but is contained by nothing whatever, and that He is a place of refuge for all, and because He is His own space, having occupied Himself and being contained in Himself alone. 64 For as for me, I am not a "place," but I am in a place, and every existing thing likewise, for that which is contained is different from that which contains it; and the Deity, being contained by nothing, its necessarily itself its own place. It bears witness to what I am saying by this oracle delivered in Abraham's case: "he came into the place which God said to him: and lifting up his eyes he saw the place from afar" (Gen. 22:3–4). 65 Tell me, did he who came to the place from afar see Him? No, it would seem that one and the same word is applied to two different things: one the divine Logos, and the other God Who was before Logos. 66 Then, he who has come from abroad under Wisdom's guidance arrives in the former place, finding in the divine Logos the sum and consummation of service. But when he has his place in the divine Logos he does not indeed reach the first "place," He Who is God, but he sees Him from afar; for it is not proper to contemplate the One God from a distance. But what he sees is the bare fact that God is far away from all creation and that the apprehension of Him is removed to a greater distance from all human understanding. 67 It may be that in this part of the text Moses has not interpreted the present "place" as an allegory on the first Cause; rather, it means something like this: "he came into the place, and looking up he saw with his eyes" the place itself to which he had come, that it was a long way off from God, Who is nameless and unutterable and cannot be reached by all forms.

The Logos as Rock

Det. 115–118: These products are legitimately nourishments of the soul sufficient to suck, as the Lawgiver says, "honey from rock and olive oil from solid rock" (Deut. 32:13). The rock displays the solid and indestructible Wisdom of God, which feeds, nurses, and rears those who yearn for an imperishable way of sustenance. 116 For this divine wisdom has become a kind of mother of all that are in the world, nursing her offspring right after they are born. But not everybody requires divine nourishment from her, but those who are found worthy of their parents. Because many of them suffered under the famine of virtue, a famine that is crueler than the destruction of grain, food, and water (*QG* 2.58). 117 The fountain of divine wisdom carries water with a gentler and softer stream, and other waters more swiftly, fast, and with fuller and stronger current. Therefore, when it runs down gently, it sweetens much as honey does; when it runs with swiftness, it comes as a voluminous matter that lights the soul like olive oil does to a lamp. 118 In another place he uses a synonym for this rock and calls it "manna," which is the Logos of God, eldest of all existences, which is called the most generic name of "somewhat," from which two cakes are made (cf. Exod. 16:31; Num. 11:8): one of honey and the other of oil. These are two inseparable and very important stages in education; at the beginning, they cause a sweetness from the principles of knowledge, and then, they cause the most brilliant light to flash from them on those who handle in no fickle and perfunctory way the subjects that they love. These, as I have said, "are caused to rise up over the strength of the earth" (Deut. 32:13).

The Logos as First-born

Agr. 51b–54: This hallowed flock He leads in accordance with custom and law, setting over it His right reason and first-born Son (*QG* 4.224), who shall take up the commission as priests of this herd like some viceroy of a Great King. It has been said elsewhere: "Behold, I AM, I send my angel before your face to guard you on the way" (Exod. 23:20). 52 Let, then, even the whole universe, the greatest and most perfect flock of God, He Who Is, say: "the Lord shepherds me, and I shall want nothing" (Ps. 23:1). 53 Let each person also say the same, not with the voice that flows through tongue and mouth, reaching over a brief stretch of air, but with that of understanding that extends and touches the ends of the universe. For it is impossible that there should be any lack of due portion, when God is the Ruler, whose wont it is to grant good things in fullness and perfection to all existing things. 54 Magnificent is the exhortation to holiness, which comes through the poet's saying. For he, unaccomplished and poor, expects to have all things else but is unable to endure the sovereignty of One. Whereas the soul that is shepherded by God,[21] having the one and only thing on which all depend, is naturally exempt from want of other things; for it worships no blind wealth, but a wealth that possesses a vision and wonders with exceeding keenness.

Conf. 146–147: If there is, by any chance, one who is not yet worthy to be called a Son of God, let him press to take his place after His first-born, the Logos,[22] who is the eldest of the angels. The Logos is the Archangel and the beginning with many names. He is called "beginning," the "name of God," "His Logos," the "human after His Image," and "He who sees" Israel. 147 Therefore, I was moved a few pages above to commend the virtues of those who affirm that "we are all sons of one man" (Gen. 42:11). If we have not yet become befitting children of God to hold in honor, we may praise His Image, the most holy Logos. For the Logos is the eldest Image of God (*QG* 2.62).

The Logos and Angels

Leg. 3.177–178: Now, the Israelites are praying to be nourished with the Word of God. But Jacob transcending even the Word of God says that he is nourished by God Himself. Jacob speaks about it this way: "the God to

Whom my fathers, Abraham and Isaac, were well-pleasing, the God Who feeds me from youth until this day, the angel who delivered me out of all evil things, bless these boys" (Gen. 48:15, 16). This beautiful expression is proper; he looks on God as feeding him, not his Word; but the angel, who is the Word, leads the way, just as Healer of ills. It is natural, for He is pleased with him to be the leader of good things; He Who Is should in His own person give the principal booms, while His angels and Words give the secondary gifts, such as protection and deliverance from evil things. 178 For this reason, I think, God grants health naturally through Himself, preceded by no disease in our bodies; but health that comes by way of escape from disease is through medical science and through the physician's skill, letting both knowledge and doctor enjoy the credit of healing. However, the truth is Himself, and He is the One Who heals through these means or without them. It is also the same with the soul. The good things, the nourishment, He himself bestows through Himself but through the agency of the angels and Words as He embraces the eradication of evils.

Deus 158–161: Therefore, he may not drink from a well on whom God bestows the unmixed rapture-giving draughts, sometimes through the service of some angels whom He has held worthy to act as cupbearer, and sometimes also by His own agency, placing nothing between He Who gives and he who takes. 159 So then, immediately, we should run through to walk by the King's road, we who hold it our duty to pass by earthly things. But the road is the King's, of which the lordship rests with no plebeian, but with Him alone who alone is the true King. 160 This road is, as I said recently, wisdom, through which alone suppliant souls can flee and find refuge in the Uncreated. For we may well believe that he who walks unimpeded along the King's road will never flag or faint, until he comes to meet the King. 161 Then, they who have arrived come to know both the King's blessedness and their own meanness. For Abraham, too, when he drew near to God, immediately he came to know himself to be earth and ashes (Gen. 18:27).

Conf. 180–182: It seems appropriate to consider this: that God is the Cause of the good things only, and absolutely nothing in Him is evil, since He Himself is the most ancient and most perfect of the existing beings; He Himself is the Good. To do the suitable work is best related to His own nature, the best of the best; indeed, the chastisement of the wicked should be assured through and by Him. 181 He is my witness by the word spoken by Jacob, who was made perfect through practice, on this account: "God who nourishes me from my youth, the angel who saved me from all evils" (Gen. 48:15–16). For Jacob, also, hereby confesses that the truly good things, which nourish virtue-loving souls, are referred to God alone as the Cause. But the part of things evil has been committed to angels—since they do not have the absolute authority to chastise. So, nothing that tends to destruction should have its origin in Him, whose nature is to save. 182 Therefore, he says, "come here! And let us come down and confound." For the impious ones, indeed, deserve to suffer from punishment and to win God's favor with His gracious and bountiful powers, and vengeance. In fact, knowing that it was beneficial for humans, He took the initiative that it should be divided by others. For while there is a need for human beings to deserve correction, the fountain of His ever-flowing gifts of grace should be kept guarded pure not only from all that is, but also from all that is deemed to be evil.

Somn. 1.140–141: Others are of perfect purity and excellence, gifted with a great and divine Spirit, and they have never felt any cravings after the things of the earth, but are viceroys of the Ruler of the universe, ears and eyes, so to speak, of the Great King, beholding and hearing all things. 141 These are called "demons" by the other philosophers, but the sacred record is accustomed to call them "angels," proclaiming a proper title (*QG* 4.33). For angels convey the bindings of the Father to His children and report the children's need to their Father.

Somn. 1.157–158: The dream revealed the Ruler of the archangels set fast upon the stairway, even the Lord. For like a chariot-driver or like a helmsman over his ship, we may conceive the Existent One standing over bodies, over souls, over deeds, over words, over angels, over earth, over air, over heaven, over sensible powers, and over invisible beings, all things seen and unseen. For the whole world depends on and clings to Himself; He guides the vast nature of creation. 158 Let no one, when he hears of His being set fast, think that anything works together with God to help Him to stand firmly. But let him account the truth signified by it to be equivalent to the statement that the sure God is the support of the firmness and steadfastness of all things, and imparts, as with the impress of a seal, to whom He may wish the power to remain unshaken. He establishes and holds it together that the system of the created things remains strongly and mightily indestructible.

Somn. 1.238–241: Why, then, do we still wonder if He is compared to angels and to men for the sake of assisting those who are in need? Accordingly, when He says, "I am the God, Who was seen by you in the place of God" (Gen. 31:13), understand that He occupied the place of the angel only so far as appeared, without changing His own real nature, with a view to the profit of him who was not yet capable of seeing the true God. 239 For just as those who are not able to see the sun's light facing east like those who are not able to see the sun itself and observe well the halo round the moon, as the light itself, so it is also the Image of God, His angel, Logos, as His very Self. 240 Do you not see how Hagar, who is elementary education, says to the angel, "are you the God Who did look upon me?" (Gen. 16:13). For being Egyptian by race, she was not befitting to see the eldest Cause. But now the mind is beginning to form mental images of the sovereign Ruler of all such potencies.

241 Therefore, He Himself also says, "I am the God," whose Image you did not behold first as me and you did not dedicate a pillar engraved with the most holy inscription (Gen. 31:13); that I am standing alone (Exod. 17:6) and that I established the constitution of all things, bringing confusion and disorder into order and array, and sustaining the "All," so that the universe rests firm and sure upon the Logos, who is My viceroy.[23]

GOD AND THE SPIRIT (*PNEUMA*)

The Spirit of God

Gig. 19–28: In such things it is impossible for the Spirit of God to remain fixed and be eternal, as the Lawgiver himself clearly shows (*QG* 4.5). For he says, "the Lord God says, my Spirit shall not abide eternally among men because they are flesh" (Gen. 6:3). 20 The Spirit sometimes remains, but it does not abide forever in all of us. Who, then, is irrational and without a soul, that never with or without his or her will he or she would never receive a conception of the best? Even the reprobate often hovers an unexpected vision of the beautiful, but to grasp it and preserve it for themselves, the reprobates do not have the strength. 21 Straightaway it is gone and removes elsewhere, having turned away from visiting migrants who move away from the law and justice, to whom it could never have come save to convict those who choose the base instead of the noble. 22 It is said that the Spirit of God means according to one sense the air that flows up from the earth, the third element that rides on the water—thus it is said in the creation account, "the Spirit of God was borne above the water" (Gen. 1:2); for the air, which is light, rises and is borne upward, using the water as its base. In another sense, knowledge is pure, in which every wise man duly shares. 23 Moses shows this by speaking of the Craftsman and Artificer of the sacred works when he says, "God called up Bezaleel and filled him with the divine Spirit, wisdom, understanding, knowledge to be minded in every deed" (Exod. 31:2, 3). Through what is said in these words we have the definition of what the divine Spirit is (*QG* 1.90; 2.28; 3.9). 24 Such too is the Spirit of Moses, which visits habitually the seventy elders that they may surpass others and to be brought to grace. They would not have truly been even elders if they had not received the portion of that Spirit of perfect wisdom. For it is written, "I shall take from the Spirit which is on you, and I will lay upon the seventy elders" (Num. 11:17). 25 But certainly do not think that this taking away comes about through severance or disjoining. But rather what happens when fire is taken from fire, for it should kindle a thousand torches, it remains the same and is not diminished or whatsoever. Such as this is what is also the nature of knowledge. All the pupils, who regularly go and have become acquainted with it, experienced evidence, and it is undiminished in any of its parts. Often knowledge improves better too, just as they declare that they draw water from the springs. For as the story goes, they then become sweeter. 26 The continuous intercourse with others entails practice and instructions and makes for the sum of perfection. If, then, it were Moses's own Spirit, or the Spirit of some other created being, destined to be distributed to so large a multitude of well-known disciples, it would be divided into so many pieces and diminished. 27 But now the Spirit, which is on him, is the Wise, the Divine, the Indivisible, the Undivided, the Clever filling all things entirely, the very Spirit that while conferring benefit remains unharmed, that though it be shared with or be added to others remains undiminished in understanding, knowledge, and wisdom (*QE* 2.7). 28 So, on this account, the divine Spirit is able to abide in the soul but is not able to remain permanently, as we have said. And why are we wondering about this? For there is nothing else of which we enjoy firm and secure possession, since human affairs swing up and down, tilt the scale on either side, and suffer vicissitudes from hour to hour.

Ios. 116–117: And the king having heard both the interpretation of the dreams, so exactly and skillfully divining the truth, and his advice to all appearance most advantageous in its foresight for the uncertainties of the invisible future, drove the associates to come closer, so that Joseph might not hear. "Sirs," he said, "shall we find men such as this one, who has the Spirit of God in himself"? 117 When they in one accord approved and applauded his words, he looked at Joseph who was standing "near," and said, "the person whom you advised to investigate is near at hand, the man of prudence and intelligence is not far distant. He for whom according to your advice we should look is yourself, for I think that God is with you in the words you speak. Come and then take the charge of my house and the superintendence of all Egypt."

Mos. 1.47–50: While such talk was in circulation, Moses retired slowly into the neighboring country of Arabia; it was safe to stay there, at the same time beseeching God to save the oppressed from their helpless, miserable plight, and to punishment as they deserved the oppressors, who had left no form of maltreatment untried, and to double the gift by granting to himself to behold both these accomplished. And God, admiring His Spirit, which loved the good and hated evil, heard the prayers, and very shortly judged the land and its doings as became His nature. 48 But while God's Spirit was intending to judge, Moses was carrying out the exercises of virtue with a clever teacher, reason, under whose discipline he exercised to fit himself for life in its best, the theoretical and the practical. He was continually opening the scroll of philosophical doctrines and discerning in the soul and entrusting them to memory never to be forgotten, and straightway brought his personal conduct, praiseworthy in all aspects, allowing not to think of it but of the truth, because that one is the object he sets before nature's right reason, the sole source and fountain of virtues. 49 Therefore, any other who was fleeing from the king's cruel wrath and had just arrived for the first time in a foreign land, who was not yet acquainted with the customs of the natives and with the precise understanding of what pleases or offends them, might have been eager to keep quiet and live unnoticed from the multitude, or else Moses might have wished to come forward in public, and by obsequious persistence court the favor of men of the highest authority and power, if none others, men who might be expected to give help and succor should some come and attempt to carry him off by force. 50 But he traveled on the road, which was the opposite road of what we should expect. He followed the wholesome impulses of his soul and suffered none of them to be to the ground. Therefore, at times, he was acting wantonly beyond his fund of strength, for he regarded justice as invincible strength, which urged him on his self-appointed task to champion the weaker.

Gig. 53–57: Therefore, we find that among the multitude, they, that is, that have set before them many life goals, the divine Spirit does not abide in them, even though it may dwell there for a short space of time. Only one sort of humans does it come to, those who, having doffed all that belongs to created being and the innermost veil and clock of false opinion, with mind disengaged and naked will come to God. 54 So too Moses built his own tent outside the encampment (Exod. 33:7). That is to say, he established his judgment immovable, and then he begins to worship God, and leading the way into the dark cloud, the invisible region, abides there while being initiated into the most holy mysteries. He becomes not only an initiate but also hierophant (one who teaches rites of sacrifice and worship) and a teacher of the secret worship (sacrifice), which he will impart to those who have their ears purified. 55 He, then, has ever the divine Spirit at his side, leading him in every righteous path, but from the others, as I have said, it quickly separates itself, from those whose span of life he has also brought to completion by a hundred and twenty years in number. For he says, "their days will be a hundred and twenty" (Gen. 6:3). 56 Yet Moses migrates from his mortal life when he has reached that same number of years (Deut. 34:7). How, therefore, can twenty years of those who are guilty be equal to that of the sage and prophet? For the moment it will suffice to say this: that things with the same name are not all alike, and often indeed have been separated altogether in kind, and that the bad may have numbers and times matched with the good since they also come as twin. But their powers may be detached from others and widely separated from each other. 57 Though the precise interpretation of these one hundred and twenty years we will hold over until we closely examine into the whole life of the prophet, when we have become qualified to initiate into its mysteries.

Mos. 2.265–266: I may say that such conjectures exist and are akin to prophecies. For the mind could not have made sharp perception if there was not a divine Spirit guiding it to the truth itself (*QG* 2.59). 266 The greatness of wonder was not only made manifest by the double nourishment and its remaining sound contrary to the usual happening, but by the combination of these two to happen on the sixth day on which the food began to be well supplied from the air; after that sixth day was to be followed by the rise of the seventh (Sabbath), which is the most sacred of numbers. Therefore, consideration will show the inquirer that the food given from heaven followed the analogy of the birth of the world. For both the creating of the world and the raining of the spoken food were begun by God on the first day out of six.

NOTES

1. Philo uses "the Existent One" (*to on*) and identifies the *ho ōn* (He Who Is [Exod. 3:14]) with the *to on* of Platonism. E.g., *Leg.* 1.99; *Det.* 160; *Post.* 21, 175; *Deus* 11, 52, 55, 69, 108, 109; *Plant.* 21, 22; *Ebr.* 107, 108; *Conf.* 95; *Migr.* 169; *Her.* 95, 229; *Mut.* 11, 27; *Mos.* 2.161; *Spec.* 1.270, 313, 344, 345; *Virt.* 34, 215; *Praem.* 56; *Prob.* 43; *QG* 1.100; *QE* 2.47.

2. E.g., *Leg.* 1.51; 2.1–3; *Opif.* 23; *Leg.* 2.2; *Cher.* 44; *Sacr.* 60, 66; *Post.* 7, 69; *Deus* 22, 60; *Plant.* 22, 31, 64, 66, 89; *Ebr.* 152; *Migr.* 40; *Congr.* 107; *Mut.* 22; *Mos.* 2.161; 2.171; *Decal.* 8, 41, 52, 60, 64; *Spec.* 1.20, 30, 34, 294; *Virt.* 65; 213, 214, 218; *Praem.* 46; *Legat.* 318; *QG* 2.10, 12, 16; *QE* 2.37.

3. *Opif.* 8, 75; *Leg.* 2.3; *Cher.* 28, 29, 99; *Det.* 55; *Deus* 110; *Agr.* 50, 54; *Plant.* 91; *Conf.* 59; *Fug.* 103; *Somn.* 1.73; cf. *Mos.* 1.111, 284; 2.88, 168; *Decal.* 41, 65; *Spec.* 1.11, 20, 22, 30, 34; 4.180; *Praem.* 41.

4. *Opif.* 100; *Leg.* 1.44; 2.1, 2, 3; 3.105; *Cher.* 97; *Plant.* 39; *Ebr.* 126; *Conf.* 181; *Her.* 93, 94, 143; *Congr.* 152; *Mut.* 31, 138, 213; *Abr.* 104, 206; *Mos.* 2.100, 168; *Spec.* 1.67, 30, 311; 2.53, 54; 3.125, 127; 4.199; *Virt.* 35; *Praem.* 44, 45; *Prob.* 20; *QG* 3.8.

5. *Leg.* 1.47; *Gig.* 2.45; *Cher.* 28, 29; *Post.* 115, 183; *Fug.* 40; *Spec.* 1.36, 53, 65, 209, 313, 344; *Spec.* 3.127; *Mos.* 2.168; *Virt.* 40, 102; *Prov.* 2.10.

6. Cf. *Spec.* 2.165; *Virt.* 64.

7. *Opif.* 172. Cf. *Decal.* 91; *Spec.* 1.308–312.

8. Cf. Frick, *Divine Providence in Philo*, 50–51.

9. *Leg.* 2.3; 3.73.

10. *Plant.* 1–8, 85–89; *Decal.* 175–178; *Prov.* 24–25.

11. The text appears here with evident alterations or with a lacuna. Although there have been several proposals to correct it by some scholars, the discrepancies and the character are conjectures; thus, it is preferable not to translate the part in question.

12. Philo understands that term *theos* (God) derives from the root *the* of the verb *theinai* (to place, to establish).

13. The text is corrupted here. I follow in the less confusing part Wendland's reconstruction and leave the rest without translation.

14. *Leg.* 1.37–38.

15. The specific texts about each Patriarch are found in Chapter 4. In numerous passages Philo reproduces the Aristotelian idea of the triple form of education: for teaching, for nature, and for practice; he understands that the allegorical personification of these paths to knowledge and to virtue are respectively Abraham, Isaac, and Jacob.

16. *Sacr.* 45–49; *Fug.* 10; *Contempl.* 78; *Prov.* 2.18–20.

17. *Conf.* 98 (Exod. 24:10); 134–140 (Gen. 11:5); *Somn.* 2.222. Aristobulus, whose allegorical interpretation is confined to the biblical anthropomorphisms, also exemplifies in lesser degree, the broader trend of Judaism to modify and remove anthropomorphism ascribed to God (Fragment 2 in Eusebius, *Prae. ev.* 8.9.38–8.10.17). Cf. Borgen, *Philo, John, and Paul: New Perspectives on Judaism and Early Christianity* (Atlanta: Scholars Press, 1987), 13. For a treatment of Philo's anthropomorphic views, see Ronald Williamson, "The Ethical Teaching of Philo," in *Jewish in the Hellenistic World: Philo.* (Cambridge: Cambridge University Press, 1989), 201–305, at 74–84.

18. *Post.* 1–4, 7–9; *Spec.* 4.51–52; *Virt.* 49–50, 95–96.

19. *Contempl.* 2.

20. Cf. Wis 7:26.

21. Cf. John 10:1–18.

22. Col 1:15–18.

23. *Post.* 89–90; *Somn.* 1.115; *Mos.* 1.66–167, 165–166.

BIBLIOGRAPHY

Frick, Peter. *Divine Providence in Philo of Alexandria.* Texts and Studies in Ancient Judaism 77. Tübingen: Mohr Siebeck, 1999.

Mackie, Scott D. "Seeing God in Philo of Alexandria: The Logos, the Powers, or the Existent One?" *The Studia Philonica Annual* 21 (2009): 25–47.

Ryu, Jang. *Knowledge of God in Philo of Alexandria.* Wissenschaftliche Untersuchungen zum Neuen Testament 2. Reihe 405. Tübingen: Mohr Siebeck, 2015.

Tobin, T. H. "Logos." Pages 348–56 in vol. 4 of *The Anchor Bible Dictionary*. Edited by David Noel Freedman. Vol 4. New York: Doubleday, 1992.

Winston, David. *Logos and Mystical Theology in Philo of Alexandria.* Cincinnati: Hebrew Union College Press, 1985.

Chapter 2

Philo's Doctrine of Creation

In this chapter the reader will encounter the complexity of Philo's interpretation of the world and how his interpretation is influenced by Plato's *Timaeus* and the traditions of other Middle Platonists' interpretations of the *Timaeus*. Philo's thinking is Jewish, but the way he expresses it is Platonic. Within the tradition of Plato's *Timaeus* Philo interprets the creation of "two worlds": the intelligible world (*kosmos noētos*) and the sensible world (*kosmos aisthētos*). In the Platonic tradition, there is the world of Ideas in God's Mind, responsible for the creation of the intelligible world, and a *demiurgos,* the craftsman, who creates the sensible world. In Philo, the reader learns that the intelligible world is the reasoning of the Architect in the Mind to create the intelligible reality and that God's Mind is the Logos, God's Image. Philo uses the Stoic Logos as the instrument and agent of creation. It is through His divine Logos that the world (the All, the whole universe) came into existence. In other words, the Logos is the idea, the archetype, the pattern for the sensible, created world. The Logos is the link between the transcendent God and the whole (*QE* 2.81).

God as the Existent One is the Creator, Maker, and absolute Ruler, who controls and governs everything in the universe. But as a transcendent Being, God has powers or potencies who assist what God has created. What is characteristic in Philo is that he consistently connects God with the mind and with solely the good; evil things are connected with other markers and the sensible world. Philo creates a sense of God's transcendence by locating the intelligible world, the divine Logos and God distant from any human apprehension. Indeed, only through the sensible, visible world are human beings capable of perceiving or conceiving the intelligible and also God's existence and presence in creation. Humanity comes to know God in the corporeal things. Philo clearly states that God is the Cause of creation, of everything that comes into existence, and that creation is God's possession and figuratively the House of God.

Philo's cosmology and his understanding of the Logos is intrinsically connected to his doctrine of providence. The Existent One is a God Who governs, cares, and provides for the world and therein. God is represented as the Giver of abundant good things only, and when Philo speaks of divine providence in relation to the created world and humanity, he establishes a connection between the goodness of God toward His creation and virtues. His famous statement in *Decal.* 52 explicitly shows this connection: as God is the source of all that exists, the virtue of piety is also the source of all the other virtues. As in his theology, there is a unity between Philo's doctrine of creation and ethics; the reader understands that virtues, including humanity, are friends of God, and the intrinsic connection of virtues with both the intelligible world and divine providence. Human beings are to give thanks to God for his beneficial gift of creation.

COSMOLOGY

Note

In the light of Plato's World of Ideas in his doctrine of creation in the *Timaeus*, Philo views the Logos also as the container of the World of Ideas. In Philo, the divine Logos is depicted as an entity or personality, an "instrument" (*organon*) *through whom* God creates the corporeal world (*Fug.* 109), a world described metaphorically as "a great city." The Logos of God is engaged in making the world (*Opif.* 24). For Philo, the world of senses is created through His divine Logos, after the creation of the intelligible world on "day one." Before the sensible world came into existence, there was the divine Logos (like *sophia* in Wisdom),[1] the incorporeal world, in the Mind of God. In Platonic terms, Philo explains that we come to know the World of Ideas—the divine Logos itself—through the human mind in the real, corporeal world, that is creation.

When relating the Logos to God's creation, the Logos plays several roles. For example, the divine Logos is God's direct force in the world: the Logos is called the commander of the world (*Leg.* 3.80; *Sacr.* 51), the governor (*Agr.* 51; *Fug.* 111; *Somn.* 1.241; cf. *QG* 2.110), charioteer (*Leg.* 3.80), and ruler (*Leg.* 3.150). Furthermore, like the Stoics, Philo ascribes to the Logos the role of director of the world's affairs (*Cher.* 35–36), the ambassador and chief messenger to creation (*Her.* 205), and metaphorically, the shepherd (*Agr.* 51–52) and the pilot of the universe (*Cher.* 36), like God.[2] In addition, in a similar way to the Stoic doctrine of the "Spirit" (*pneuma*), Philo describes the Logos as the glue that holds creation together and upwards.[3] Therefore, the Logos is not only conceived as the soul's guide to God (*Conf.* 145–147);

in Philo's cosmology, the Logos is also God's Image and fills and pervades the corporeal world, like the Stoic Spirit.[4]

Creation

Opif. 8–11: Moses, however, had not only attained the summit of philosophy but also been instructed in the many and most essential doctrines of nature by means of oracle. He recognized that it is absolutely necessary that among existing things there is an active cause and passive cause; and that the active cause, which is the mind of the universe, is the purest and unadulterated, superior to virtue, superior to knowledge, and even superior to the good and the beautiful itself. 9 The passive object, which of itself was soulless and motionless, when set in motion and shaped and ensouled by the mind, changed into the most perfect reality, namely this world. Those who declare that this world is uncreated are unaware that they are eliminating the most beneficial and indispensable of the contributions to piety, namely providence. 10 Reason demands that the Father and Maker takes care of that which has come into being. For after all, a father aims at the safety of His offspring and a maker aims at the preservation of what has been constructed, using every means at their disposal to repel all that is injurious and harmful, while desiring to provide many things that are advantageous and profitable. But there is no affinity between that which did not come into existence and the one who did not make it. 11 It is a worthless and useless doctrine, bringing about a power vacuum in this world, just like it happens in a city, because it does not have a ruler or magistrate or judge, under whom everything is regulated and controlled according to the law.

Leg. 1.21–23: "On the day in which God made the heavens and the earth and all the green of the field before it was created upon the earth and all the grass of the field before it sprang up. For God has not sent rain on the earth, and there was no human being to till the earth" (Gen. 2:4b–5). Above all, he calls this day a "book," for in as much as he is describing the creation of heaven and earth in both passages.[5] For by His own conspicuous and luminous Logos God makes both of them, which are the idea of the mind, which symbolically He calls "heaven," and the idea of the sense-perception, which by way of a figure He named "earth." 22 Moses compares the idea of the mind and the idea of the sense-perception to two fields. For the mind bears as fruit what is done in thinking, and the sense-perception what is done in perceiving by sense. What he means is something like this: before the particular and individual mind there exists a certain idea as an archetype and pattern of this; and again, before the particular sense-perception, a certain idea of sense-perception exists related to the particular as a seal, making impressions of forms. So too, before individual, intelligible objects came into being, there existed as a genus the intelligible itself, by participation in which the other intelligible objects are named; and before the individual sense-perceptible objects came into being, there existed as a genus the sense-perceptible itself, by sharing in which the other sense-perceptible objects came into being. 23 He calls the intelligible object of the mind "green of the field." For just as the green things of the field spring up and bloom, so too the intelligible object is a growth springing from the mind. Before, then, the particular intelligible object came into being, He produces the intelligible itself as a genus, which He rightly calls the "All." For the particular intelligible object, being incomplete/imperfect, is not the All, but the intelligible itself as a genus is so, since it is a complete whole.

Deus 106–107: For how great must we suppose Him to be, who shall be judged worthy of grace with God? I understand that hardly the whole world could attain to this, and yet this world is the first and the greatest and the most perfect of God's works. 107 Perhaps, then, it would be better to accept this explanation: that the man of worth is zealous in inquiring and eager to learn, and in all his inquiries he found this to be the highest truth, that all things are the grace or gift of God: earth, water, air, fire, sun, stars, heaven, all animals and plants. But God has bestowed nothing on Himself, for He needs nothing, but He has given the world to the world and its parts to themselves and to each other, and also to the All.

Ebr. 106–108: He points in these last words, I think, to the whole of creation, heaven, earth, water, spirit, animals, and to plants alike. To each of them, he who has braced the activities of his soul stretching toward God and who hopes for assistance from Him alone would suitably say: "I shall take nothing from aught of your creatures, nor the light of day from the sun, nor the light of night from moon and from the other stars, nor rain from the air and from the clouds, nor drink and food from water and from the land, nor sight from the eyes, nor hearing from the ears, nor smell from the nostrils, nor taste from the juices of the palate, nor speech from the tongue, nor giving and receiving from the hands, nor moving forwards and backwards from the feet, nor respiration from the lungs, nor digestion from the liver, nor from the other inward parts the function proper to each, nor their yearly fruits from the trees and seedlings. But I shall take them all from the only Wise who has stretched His beneficent power to every whither, and through them He succors me." 107 Therefore, he who is able to have a vision of the Existent One knows Him Who is the Cause, Who honors the things of which He is the Cause only as second to Him. He will use no words of flattery, yet He acknowledges what is their due; this acknowledgment is completely just. I shall take nothing from you, but I will take from God, the Possessor of all, but perhaps I will take through you. For you have been made servants to His undying acts of grace.

108 But the one with no discernment, whose understanding, by which alone the Existent One can be comprehended, is blinded, has never anywhere seen Him, but is shown to him in the corporeal and sensible things of the world. He believes that He is the Cause of all that comes into existence.

Decal. 52–53: We must consider with all precision of the commandments (*QG* 4.65), making none of them subordinate to each other. The noblest Source of all that exist is God, and piety is the source of virtues. It is very necessary that these two should be first discussed. . . . 53 They have deified the four principal elements, earth, water, air, and fire, and others, the sun, moon, planets, and fixed stars (*QE* 2.75–77); others again heaven by itself; and others the whole world. But the highest and the most ancient, the Begetter, the Ruler of the great city, the Commander in Chief of the invisible host, the Pilot who always steers all things in safety, Him they have hidden from sight by the misleading titles assigned to the objects of worship mentioned above.

Spec. 1.34–35: Then, he, who comes to the truly great city, this world, beholds the hills and plains teeming with animals and plants and rivers, carrying natural springs and winter torrents, and the seas with their expanses, and the air with its happily tempered phases, the yearly seasons passing into each other. Then he also beholds the sun and moon, ruling the day and night, and the other heavenly planets and fixed stars, and the whole revolution of the stars of heaven. Must he not naturally but rather constrained admit necessarily the conception of the Maker and Father and Ruler? 35 For none of the works of human arts is self-made, and the highest work and the greatest knowledge is shown in this universe. Thus, the universe has been fashioned by one of excellent knowledge and absolute perfection. In this way, we have received the conception of the Existent God (*QG* 2.64).

The Cause of Creation

Migr. 180–181: Moses seems to impart the connection and affinity in the parts of the All to be one and to be one created world; for if it has come into being and is one, it stands to reason that all its completed several parts have the same elementary substances for their substratum, on the principle that interdependence of the parts is a characteristic of corporeal things that hold together in unity. 181 But Moses differs in opinion about God. For neither the universe nor the soul of the world is the first or primal God, neither the stars nor the revolutions are the primary causes of the things that happened to human beings. But this universe is kept together by an invisible power, which the Craftsman has made to reach from the end of the earth until heaven's furthest bounds, providing that what was well bounded should not be loosened. For the powers of the universe are unbroken bonds.

Abr. 120–123: No one, however, should think that the shadows can be expressly spoken of as God. The use of a name is only made clear to a visible image of an action, since the real truth is not so. 121 But it is as anyone, who is standing nearest to the truth, would say that the central truth is held by the Father of the universe, Who is called "Lord" in the sacred Scriptures, He Who is the Existent One. While on either side of Him are the senior potencies of the Existent and are nearest to Him, the creative and the kingly. The creative title is called God, for this established and ordered the universe; while the kingly title is called Lord, for it is the fundamental right of the Maker to rule and control what He has brought into being. 122 Therefore, the central Being, keeping guard over each of His potencies, gives to the mind the ability to see, a vision sometimes of one, sometimes of three: of One (unit), when the mind is highly purified by good fortune and passing beyond not merely the multiplicity of other numbers, but even the Dyad, which is next to the unit presses on the ideal form, which is free from mixture and complexity, and being self-contained needs nothing more; of three, when not yet initiated into the great mysteries, it is still a votary of the minor rites and unable to apprehend the Existent One alone by itself and apart from all else, but only through its actions, which is either creative or ruling. 123 Thus, this is, as they say, a second-best voyage,[6] yet all the same there is in it an element of a way of thinking such as God approves. But the former state of mind takes no part in the approved way of thinking. This is in itself the approved way of thinking of the One who is highly favored; it is the truth, higher than a way of thinking, more honorable than everything that is thought.

Spec. 1.210–211: So too it is with what follows: when you wish, my mind, to give thanks to God for the created world, show gratitude for the creation of the universe, for the whole and for its principal parts, thinking of them as the limbs of a living creature of the utmost perfection. I say, such parts are heaven, the sun, the moon, the planets, and the fixed stars; then again the earth and living creatures and plants on it; then, the sea and the rivers, both spring-fed and winter courses, and all in them; then, the air and its phases, for winter and summer, spring and autumn, those seasons, which recur annually and are also highly beneficial to our life, are different conditions in the air that changes for the preservation of sublunar things. 211 And if you give thanks for human beings, do not only for the genus but also for its species and most essential parts: for men, women, Greeks, Barbarians, for dwellers on the mainland, and those whose lot is cast in the islands. And if it is for one man, divide the thanksgiving as reason directs, not into every tiny part of him down to the very last, but into those of primary importance: first of all into the body and the soul of which he is composed, then into speech, mind, and sense-perception. For each of these will by itself be not unworthy to obtain audience with God.

Spec. 3.189–191: The mind, having discerned through the faculty of sight, what through itself is not possible to apprehend, did not simply stop short at what it saw, but eager by its love of knowledge and beauty and admired by the sight, came to the reasonable conclusion that these were not put together automatically by unreasoning movements, but by the Mind of God, Who is rightly called Father and Maker. They are also not infinite but are bounded by one universe, walled in like a city by the outermost sphere of the fixed stars; also that the Father, who begat them by the Law of Nature, cares for what has come into existence, His providence watching over both the whole and the parts (*QG* 4.205). 190 Then next was to inquire what is the substance of the visible world; if its constituents are all the same in substance, or are some different from others; how are the elements of which each particular part has been formed different from others; what have been the causes through which they came into being; what are the properties which held them together, and if these forces are either corporeal or incorporeal. 191 What name can be given to research into these matters but philosophy? And what fitting name is more appropriate than philosopher to the one who is the investigator? To consider a study to know God and the universe, embracing all that is therein, both animals and plants, and the intelligent patterns, and also the works that they produced for sense to perceive, and the good and evil qualities in each of the created things, exhibits a disposition that is proper of the one who loves learning and contemplation and is a true lover of wisdom (*QG* 4.143; *QE* 2.21).

Spec. 4.187: For this is to follow God, since He is able to do both but wills the good things only. He has shown both in the creation of the world and in the ordering of the world (*QG* 3.39). He called the things that did not exist into existence and produced order from disorder, qualities from things devoid of quality, similarities from dissimilarities, identities from the different, fellowship and harmony from the dissociated and discordant, equality from inequality, and light from darkness. For He and His beneficent powers always make it their business to transmute the faultiness of the worse wherever it exists and convert it to the better.

Prov. 2.43–45: Later again he says, winds and rains were made by God, not as you supposed, to do outrageous harm to voyagers and husbandmen, but to benefit our race as a whole. For He purges the earth with waters and the moon country with all the spirits (*QG* 2.8). He gives sustenance, growth, and maturity to both animals and plants. 44 If these at times hurt the sailors who travel by sea out of season or farmers of the land, there is nothing wonderful. For these are a small fraction of the human race, and His care is for all the human race. So then as the course of training in the gymnasium is drawn up for the benefit of the pupils, but the gymnasiarch sometimes to suit civic requirements makes a change in the arrangement of the regular hours whereby some of those under training lose their lesson, so too God, Who takes care of the whole world as like a city, does sometimes create wintry summer and spring-like winters for the benefit of the whole world, even though some shipmasters or workmen of the land are bound to suffer loss through the irregular way in which they occur. 45 Therefore, the interchanges of the elements out of which the world was established and now consists of He knows to be a vital operation and produces them in an unhindered succession. But the frost, the snowstorms, and other similar phenomena follow the cooling of the air, as thunders and lightnings arise from the clashing and friction of clouds. None of these are according to providence, but the rains and winds are the causes of existence, and sustenance and growth to all things, which are upon the earth, and these phenomena are the natural consequences of those others.[7]

THE LOGOS'S ROLE IN CREATION

The Divine Logos

Opif. 24–26: If one would wish to use mere expressions, he would say that the intelligible world is nothing else than the *Logos of God*, who is actually engaged in making the world.[8] For the intelligible city, too, is nothing else than the reasoning of the Architect as He is actually engaged creating the intelligible city. 25 This is the doctrine of Moses, not my own. When he describes the origin of the human being in what follows, he explicitly declares that the human being was distinctly formed after the Image of God (Gen. 1:27; *QG* 2.56; 4.115). Now, if the part (that is, the human) is an image of an Image, it is evident that this is also the case of the whole. But if the all sense-perceptible world, which is greater than mankind, is a copy of the divine Image, it is also evident that the archetypal seal, which we assert to be the intelligible world, would itself be the model, and archetypal Idea of the ideas, the Logos of God. 26 When Moses says, "in the beginning God made the heavens and the earth," he does not take the term "beginning," as some people think, in a temporal sense. For there was no time before the world, but rather time came into existence either with the world or after it. When we consider that time is the extension of the world's movement, and that there could be any movement earlier than the thing that moves but must necessarily be established either later or at the same time, then we must necessarily conclude that time too is either the same age as the world or younger than it.

Leg. 3.95–96: Whence, God shall call on Bezaleel by name, and proclaim that He has given him wisdom and knowledge, as well as He will appoint him maker, chief artificer of all the works of the Tabernacle, that is of the soul

(Exod. 31:2–3), He has pointed no work to Bezaleel's, even if he receives some commendation. Thus, we must say that here too we have a form that God has carved on the soul of the approved character as on the tested coin. What, then, the character is we shall know if we shall ascertain accurately the first meaning of the name. 96 Bezaleel means "in the shadow of God"; but God's shadow is the Logos of God, which He used like an instrument to make the world. Though this shadow, what we may describe as the representation, is in turn the archetype for further creations. For just as God is the pattern of the Image, to which the name "shadow" has now been given, so does the Image become a pattern of other beings, as Moses made clear at the beginning of the law-giving by saying, "and God made human being after the Image of God" (Gen. 1:27), implying that the Image has been made as a representation of God, but that human being was made after the Image, which had acquired the force of a pattern.

Fug. 97–99: He persuades to run swiftly and to draw tight without adequate breathing upwards to the divine reason, who is a fountain of wisdom, so that he may draw from the stream and find eternal life instead of death. Thus, one who is not as speedy it directs to the power that Moses gives the name "God," since by it the universe was established and ordered. It urges him to flee for refuge to the creative power, knowing that to the one who has grasped that the universe has come into being acquires a great good, the knowledge of its Creator, which directly persuades to love what has been created, of which He is the Cause. 98 Thus, one who is not ready flees for refuge on kingly power, for fear of the ruler has forced to obedience; also, if a father has no kindness for the child, he admonishes chastening with force. For him, who fails to reach the goals just mentioned, because he considered them too distant, another set of goals has been fixed nearer by powers that are indispensable, the gracious power, the power that assigns duties, and that which forbids offenses; those in fact which are indispensable. 99 For he who has assumed beforehand that God is not inexorable but kindly, owing to gentleness of nature, even if he should at first sin later repents in the hope of forgiveness. And he who has taken a thought that God is Lawgiver will be obedient to all injunctions and will attain happiness, while the last of the three will find a last place for refuge, turning away from all evils, even if he obtains no share of God's principal goods.

Mut. 115–116: God Who takes care of His own flock has at hand numerous gifts, sheep and goats, for those who are obedient and do not rebel. In the Psalms there is a song that praises in this way: "the Lord is my shepherd, and nothing shall be lacking to me" (Ps. 23:1). 116 Therefore, we should learn likewise that the mind, which has the divine Logos for its shepherd and king, will ask of his seven daughters, why have you arrived at today with such a speed and so eagerly? (Exod. 2:18). For at other times when you visited the sensible objects, you remained for a long time out there almost refusing to return, as you were greatly enticed by them. But now, something or other has induced you to come back with this unwonted eagerness.

Plant. 9–10: This is the Logos, extending himself from the center of its furthest bounds and from its extremities to the center again, runs nature's unconquered course joining and binding all its parts. For the Father, Who created the Logos, made an unbroken bond of the universe. 10 Therefore, nothing in the whole earth can naturally be dissolved by all the water contained within its bosom-like hollows; nor fire shall be quenched by air; and nor air shall be ignited by fire. The divine Logos marshals himself between, like a vowel amid consonants, that the whole may produce a harmony like that of literary art.[9] He mediates and moderates the threats of the opposites through a conciliatory persuasion.[10]

THE CREATION OF "TWO WORLDS"

Creation of the Intelligible World

Opif. 29–31: First, then, the Maker made the incorporeal heaven (*QG* 3.42), the invisible earth, and the form of the air and of the void. To the former He assigned the name "darkness," since the air is black by nature, to the latter the name "abyss," because the void is indeed full of depths and gaping. Next, He made the incorporeal being of water and of spirit (Gen. 1:2), and as seventh element and last of all light, which once again was incorporeal and was also intelligible pattern of the sun, and all the luminaries, which were established to give great light to the stars in heaven. 30 Moses gave a special privilege to the Spirit and light. He called the former Spirit of God, because the spirit is the most important for life and God is the cause of life. Light he describes as exceedingly beautiful (Gen. 1:4), for the intelligible light in its brilliancy and radiance is greater than the visible, I believe, just as much as the sun surpasses darkness, day surpasses night, and mind (the means for judgment), which gives leadership to the entire soul, surpasses its sensible sources of information, the eyes of the body. 31 That invisible and intelligible light has come into being as an image of the divine Logos, which communicated its beginning. It is a star above the heavens, a source of the sense-perceptible stars. It would not be off the mark to call it "all-brightness," from which the sun and the moon, the other planets, and fixed stars draw the illumination that is fitting for them in accordance with the capacity they each have. That spotless and pure gleam hast its brightness dimmed when it begins to undergo a change from the intelligible to the sense-perception (*QE* 2.56–60), for none of the objects in the sense-perceptible realm is absolutely pure.

Opif. 36–37: Then, when the incorporeal world had been completed and further established in the divine Logos, the sense-perceptible world began to be formed after the pattern of the incorporeal. As first of its parts, which now indeed was also the very best of all, the Craftsman proceeded to make heaven, which He called firmament as it is corporeal. For the body is by nature solid, because it is extended in three directions. What other conception of what is solid and bodily is there than that which has been extended in all directions? Similarly, therefore, he set the sense-perceptible and corporeal heaven against the intelligible and incorporeal counterpart and called it firmament. 37 Then, He immediately named it heaven, an apposite and highly appropriate title, either because it is the boundary of all things, or because it came into being as first of the visible things. After what comes into existence, He also names the day second, attributing the entire extension and measure of a day to heaven, on account of both the value and honor in the sense-perceptible things.

Opif. 16–18a: For God, because He is God, assumed that a beautiful copy would never come into existence produced without a beautiful pattern, and that none of the objects of sense-perception would be without fault, unless it was modeled on the archetypal and intelligible idea. When He wished to construct this visible world, He first marked out the intelligible world, so that He could make use of the incorporeal and the most God-like paradigm and so produce the corporeal world, a younger likeness of an older model, which would contain as many sense-perceptible objects as there were intelligible objects in that other one. 17 To state or think that the world constituted of the ideas exists in some place is not permissible. How it has been constituted we will understand if we pay careful attention to an image drawn from our own world. When a city is founded, in accordance with the high ambition of a king or a leader, who has laid claim to supreme power and, outstanding in his conception, adds further adornment to his good fortune, it may happen that a trained architect comes forward. Having observed both the favorable climate and convenient location of the site, he first designs within himself a plan of virtually all the parts of the city that is to be completed: temples, gymnasia, town-halls, marketplaces, harbors, docks, streets, constructions of walls, the establishment of other buildings, both private and public. 18 Then, taking up the imprints of each object in his own soul like in bee-wax, he carries around the intelligible city as an image in his mind. Summoning up the representations by means of his innate power of memory and impressing their features even more distinctly on his mind. And he begins, like a good craftsman, to construct the city out of stones and timber, looking at the model and ensuring that the corporeal objects correspond to each of the incorporeal ideas.[11]

Creation of the Sensible World

Opif. 129–130: Concluding his account of creation with a summarizing statement, Moses says: "this is the book of the origin of heaven and earth when they came into existence, on the day that God made the heavens and the earth, and all the green of the field before it came into being on the earth and all the grass of the field before it sprang up" (Gen. 2:4–5). Does he not clearly present here the incorporeal and intelligible ideas, which are in fact the seals of the completed products perceived by the senses? For before the earth became green, this green itself was present in the nature of things, he says, and before grass sprang in the field, there was not visible grass. 130 We must understand that for each of the other things that the sensible objects judge, original forms and measures also preexisted, by means of which all things that come into existence are formed and measured. For even if he does not accomplish everything in accord with the partial things all together, being as concerned as anyone ever was to attain brevity of speech, nevertheless the few things mentioned are indications of nature of the whole of reality, which brings none of the things that are sense-perceptible to completion without an incorporeal pattern (*QE* 2.33).

Fug. 188–190: Such are the children of the middle sources, and we might consider the child of folly, in respect to what the Lawgiver has spoken in these terms: "whosoever shall have slept with a woman during her menstruation has unclosed her spring, and she has enclosed the flow of her blood; let them both be put to death" (Lev. 20:18). He gives to sense-perception the name woman, suggesting mind as her husband. 189 Sense-perception is "in separation," although it is "sitting a long way off," when having forsaken mind, her lawful husband, she plants herself on the objects of sense-perception that snare and corrupt, and passionately he embraces them one after another. Therefore, at such a time, if mind goes to sleep when he ought to be awake, "he has unclosed the spring" of sense-perception; that is, he unclosed himself—for he himself was, just as he said, the spring of sense-perception. This means that he has exposed himself, unfortified, very vulnerable to the plots of his enemies. 190 Moreover, she too "unclosed the flow of her blood"; for every sense in its flow towards the external object of sense-perception is covered over and drawn in when controlled by reason but is left destitute when widowed of an upright ruler. As it is the most grievous evil for a city is to be without walls, so too, it is for a soul to be without a protector.

Somn. 1.27: With respect to sense-perception, also, we are not created blind and dim-sighted, but we are able to say that that is divided into fivefold division, and that each part has its organs fashioned by nature: eyes for seeing, ears for hearing, nostrils for smelling, and for the others the organs in which they fit; these are angels, intellects, that proclaim colors, shapes, sounds, characters of scents and savors of material bodies and their qualities; and that they are bodyguards of the soul, making known all that they have seen or heard. . . .

Somn. 1.41–44: Let us examine the things that follow, what the "Haran" is and why one who goes away from the well comes to it (Gen. 28:10). Haran is, then, as it appears to me, a kind of mother city of the objects of the sense-perception. Sometimes, it is interpreted as "dug" and other times "holes" of the objects of sense-perception, making clear that both names mean one thing. 42 For our body has been "dug" out to furnish the organs of the senses, and each of the organs has been constituted a kind of "dug-out" of each sense, in which it has been begotten to lurk in a hole. Therefore, whenever someone from the well, which is called an "oath" as it were from a harbor, of necessity he arrives at Haran immediately. Withdrawing from his journey from the place of knowledge, infinitely great as it is in extent, without any guide, he receives according to necessity. 43 For our souls, Haran moves often from itself stripping itself of the entire corporeal burden and escaping from the multitude of the senses of sense-perception; and the soul often does it again when clad in these wrappings. Thus, what is apprehensible by the intellect only is the lot of its unclad movement, while the objects of sense-perception are among the body. 44 Therefore, if someone is absolutely incapable of holding intercourse with the understanding by itself, he finds in sense-perception a second-best refuge; and a man who has been balked of the things of the intellect is swept down immediately to those of sense-perception. For those who have failed to make a good voyage under the sails of the sovereign mind can always fall back upon the oars of sense-perception.[12]

Potencies of God/Powers of God/The "Others"

Deus 109–110: We must observe that he says that Noah was well pleasing to the potencies of the Existent One, to the Lord and to God (Gen. 6:8; *QE* 2.63),[13] but Moses to Him, Who is attended by the potencies and without them only His existence is conceived. For it is said speaking in the person of God, "you have found grace with me" (Exod. 33:17), in which He shows Himself as Him Who has none other with Him. 110 Then, according to Moses, through His own agency alone does He Who Is judge as worthy the highest wisdom, which was but a copy of that, the wisdom which is secondary and of the nature of species. He judges as worthy through the subject powers, as which is also Lord and God, Ruler and Benefactor.

Conf. 171–173: . . . Thus, let us consider what these considerations are: God is One; He has around Him unspeakably many potencies all assisting and saving everything that was created, and among them are included the chastisers. Now the chastisement is not hurtful; rather, it is a prevention and a correcting of sins. 172 Through these potencies the incorporeal and intelligible world was brought forward, the archetypal of this phenomenal world; the intelligible world was framed in invisible ideal forms, as this is in visible bodies. 173 Therefore, the nature of each of these two worlds has struck the minds of some, that they have deified not only the whole, but also the most beautiful parts, the sun and the moon and the whole heaven, which some have felt no shame calling them gods.

Fug. 69–72: Therefore, the Father of the universe is holding a conversation with His powers, to whom He allowed to fashion the mortal portion of our soul by imitating the skill shown by Him when He was forming the rational part in us, deeming it right that the leading part in the soul be the work of the Sovereign, and that the subject part be the work of the subjects. 70 He employed the powers that are associated with Him not only for the reason mentioned, but because the man's soul alone is intended to grasp the conceptions of evil things and good things, and to make use of one sort or the other, since it is not possible to use them both. Thus, God deemed it necessary to assign the cause of evil things to other makers, and the cause of good things to Himself alone. 71 Therefore also the prior expression "let us make man" as though more than one were to do it, there is used afterwards an expression pointing to only one, "God made the man" (Gen. 1:27). Of the true man, who indeed is purest mind, one, and the only God is the Maker; but there is a great number of those who have produced what is commonly called human and is a mixture with sense-perception. 72 That is why the human in the special sense has been mentioned with an article; for it says, "God made *the* man," that reasoning faculty, incorporeal, and unmixed. But the other expression has no article added; for the expression "let us make man" exhibits that the human is woven out of irrational and rational nature together.

Mut. 29–34a: Akin to these is also the creative power, which is called God. Through this power the Father, who is Creator and Maker, established all things, so that the expression "I am your God" is equivalent to "I AM the Maker and Artificer." 30 And the greatest gift is to obtain from Him the same chief Artificer, Who is also the tutelar Deity of the whole world. Because He did not form the soul of the bad person—for wickedness is an enmity to God (*QG* 4.237, 240, 243); and in framing the soul, which is in the middle stage, he did not make it through Him alone, according to the holiest Moses, since this soul was surely destined to receive like a wax the different qualities of noble and base. 31 It is said, thus, "let us make human after our image" (Gen. 1:26), so that as the wax received the bad or the noble impress it should appear to be the handiwork of others or of Him Who is the Artificer of the noble things and good things alone. Thus, surely he is a man of goodness, to whom He says, "I am your God," for he has God alone for his Maker without the assistance of others. 32 At the same time, indeed, Moses teaches the doctrine and often lays down the instruction that God is the Craftsman of the good and wise things only. And all that company have voluntarily stripped for themselves the external possessions, which are abundant, but further have despised things dear to the flesh. 33 For they are in good and vigorous condition and contend in battle using the body as a menace to the soul, and they also turn pale, wasted, and withered, so to speak, are the children from discipline. They have made the bodily muscles serve the powers to the soul and, in fact, are resolved into a single form, that of the soul, and become unbodied minds. 34a Thus, the earthly element is naturally destroyed and dissolved, when the mind in all its parts prefers to be well pleasing to God.

Somn. 1.185–188: Therefore, he cried out, "this is not" (Gen. 28:17); this that I supposed, "that the Lord is in the place" (Gen. 28:16). For according to the true reckoning He contains, but He is not contained. But this that we can point out and see, this world of sense-perception is nothing other than a house of God, that is, one of the potencies of the Existent One, that is, the potency corresponding to His goodness. 186 The world, which he named a "house," is also addressed as a "gate of" the true "heaven" (Gen. 28:17). What is this? The intelligible world constituted of forms in Him who was appointed in accordance with the divine Logos cannot be apprehended other than through the analogy of this sensible and visible world. 187 For neither is it possible to form an idea of any other incorporeal thing among existents except by taking one's start from corporeal objects. From their state of rest came the conception of place, from their motion, time, whereas points, lines, and superficies, in short, limits, from what covers their exterior like a garment. 188 For it was by analogy with the sensible world that the intelligible world was conceived; for the sensible world is something like a gate into the intelligible world. For as those who wish to see our cities enter through gates; thus, many who wish to apprehend the incorporeal world are introduced by the appearance of the visible world. The world, whose essence is perceptible only by the mind, apart from any sight whatever of material forms, that is only through the archetype forms present in the world, which was fashioned in accordance with the Image beheld by himself without shadow, that the world will change its name, when all its walls and every gate have been removed so that no one will see it derivatively but behold its unchanging beauty by itself alone, through a sight ineffable and indescribable.[14]

THE WORLD/COSMOS/UNIVERSE

The Nature of the World (the World of Becoming)

Opif. 12–13a: But the great Moses considered the uncreated to be a totally different order from that which was visible—for the entire sense-perceptible world is in a process of becoming and change and never remains in the same state. So, to what is invisible and intelligible he assigned eternity as being akin and related to it, whereas on what is sense-perceptible he ascribed the proper name "beginning." Since, thus, this universe is both visible and sense-perceptible, it must necessarily also be generated. Hence, Moses was not off the mark in also giving description of its becoming, thereby speaking about God in a truly reverent manner. 13a He says that the world was created in six days, not because He was in need of a length of time (for God surely did everything at the same time, not only in giving commands but also in His thinking), but because things that come into existence required order.

Plant. 15–16: For even as in women and all womankind it pours forth a fountain of milk when the time to deliver draws near, that they may provide necessary drink of a suitable nourishment to their offspring. In the same way did the Creator bestowed on earth, the mother of living land animals, plants of all sorts, to the end that the newborn might have the benefit of nourishment not foreign but akin to them. 16 Also, while He fashioned the plants heads downwards, fixing the heads in the portion of the earth where the soil lay deepest, He raised from the earth the heads of the animals that are without reason and set them on the top of a long neck, placing the fore feet as a support for the neck.[15]

The View of Creation

Cher. 120–125: In relation to each other all created beings rank human beings of longest descent and highest birth; all enjoy equal honor and equal rights, but to God they are aliens and sojourners. For each of us has come into this world just as into a foreign city, in which before our birth we had no part; and coming into the world, he dwells temporally until he has exhausted his appointed span of life. 121 There is another lesson of wisdom that he teaches in these words, that legitimately God is in the true sense One citizen, and also each created being is an alien, and those whom we call citizens are so called only by a license of language. But to the wise men, it is a gift that when compared with God, the only Citizen, they are counted as aliens and sojourners. With respect to those who are foolish men, there is no wise man who becomes a stranger or sojourner in the city of God; but we see him in exile and nothing more. A lesson too He has proclaimed to us in such a doctrine when he says, "the land shall not be sold at all" (cf. Lev. 25:23; Deut. 21:14). No word of the seller there, that he, who has access to the mystery of nature, shall benefit in the quest of knowledge. 122 So, looking around, you shall see that all men, those who are said to bestow benefits sell rather than give, and those who seem to us to receive them in truth buy. The givers are seeking reward, praise, or honor as their exchange and look for the repayment of the favor, and under the name of gift, they in real truth carry out a sale. Since the seller's way is to take something for what he offers; and those who receive the gifts study to give back and they do so as opportunity offers; thus, they do act as buyers. For these buyers know well that receiving and paying go hand in hand. 123 But God is not a salesman, who lowers the price of His possessions, but a free Giver of all things, pouring forth eternal fountains of free bounties, and seeking no return. For He Himself is neither in need of anything nor is any created being able to give back His gift (*QG* 2.11). 124 Therefore, having come to acknowledge that all things are God's possessions on the strength of true reasonings and testimonies, which none may convict of false testimony, for the oracular responses are registered in the secret books of Moses; these are witnesses; so, we must make our protest against the mind, which thought the offspring engendered by union with sense his own possession, called it Cain, and said: "I have gotten a man through God." Even in these last two words he went astray. 125 Why in the world? Because God is the Cause, not the instrument, and that which comes into being has come into existence through an instrument, though by a Cause (*QE* 2.118). For to bring anything into being needs all these to come together: the "by which," the "from which," the "through which," the "through whom." And the "by which" is the Cause, and the "from which" is the matter, and the "through which" is the instrument, and the "through whom" is the Cause.

Deus 108: He has given His good things in abundance to the whole and its parts, not because He judges anything worthy of grace, but looking at His eternal goodness and thinking that to benefit was incumbent on His blessed and happy nature. So that if someone would ask me, what was the cause of the creation of the world? I will answer what Moses has taught: that it was the goodness which is the oldest of His graces and is the source of others.

The Four Elements

Gig. 6–9: "And seeing the angels of God the daughters of human beings that they are beautiful, they took to themselves women from among all those whom they chose" (Gen. 6:2). Those whom the philosophers designate "daemons,"[16] it is customary of Moses to call them angels, and they are souls that fly in the air. 7 No one might assume that what has been said here is a myth. For the universe must be animated through and through and each of the most important divisions of the elements encompasses the life forms that are akin to it. The earth contains the land creatures, and the sea and the rivers those that are aquatic, fire the things fire-engendered[17]—especially according to an account, these things are located in Macedonia—and heaven the stars. 8 For these stars are also souls both uncompounded and divine throughout, and thus, they move in a circle, a motion most akin to the mind. For each of their minds is a purest mind. Therefore, too, the element of the air has to be filled with living beings, though these are invisible to us, since even the air itself is not visible to our senses. 9 Yet as our vision is incapable of forming images of souls in the air, the elements must be apprehended by the mind, so that the like may be perceived in conformity with those with which it is similar.

Plant. 120–122: . . . For the roots of the All, out of which the world grows, are four: earth, water, air, and fire. 121 The annual seasons are equal in number, winter and summer, and those that come between, spring and summer. Since it is the first of all numbers produced by squaring another number, it is in right angles that it presents itself to view, as is made evident by geometrical figures. And right angles are clear patterns of rightness of reasoned thought, and right reason is an ever-flowing spring of virtue. 122 Again, the sides of the four angles are necessarily equal, and equality begets justice, which is a leader and queen of the virtues. Indeed, it shows that this number is a symbol of equality and justice and every virtue without the other numbers (*QE* 1.6, 15).

Her. 281–283: Some have surmised that the "fathers" are meant to be names for the four principles and powers from which the world has been framed: that is, earth, water, air, and fire (*QE* 2.85–87). For each thing that has come into existence, they say, is suitably resolved into these. 282 Just as names and words and all parts of speech are composed of the "elements" in the grammatical sense are again resolved into the same end, so too each of us is composed of the four elements, borrowing small fragments from the substance of each, and he repays the loan when the appointed time-cycles are completed (*QE* 2.51). The dry in him is rendered to the earth, and the wet in him to water, and the cold to the air, and the warm to fire. 283 These things belong to the body, but the soul, whose nature is both intellectual and celestial, will reach the purest ether to find the Father. The fifth substance, as the ancient ones said, is a substance that moves in a circle and has a different and superior quality from the four elements. Out of this it is thought that the stars and the whole heaven have been created and deduced as a natural consequence. We must note that the human soul is also a fragment.[18]

God's Providence

Deus 29–31: For a human being it is impossible to foresee the future events or the judgments of others, but to God as in pure sunlight all things are manifest. For already He has pierced into the recesses of the innermost souls and what is invisible to others is clear as daylight to His eyes. He uses the forethought and providence, virtues peculiar to his own, and He does not allow anything to escape and to go outside His comprehension. For to Him nothing is uncertain or unseen nor even about the future. 30 No one doubts that the parent must have knowledge of his offspring, the craftsman of his handiwork, and the steward of things entrusted to his stewardship. But God is in very truth the Father and Craftsman and Steward of all in heaven and in the universe. The future events are overshadowed by the darkness of the time that is yet to be at different distances, some near, some far. 31 But God is also the Creator of time. For He is also the Father of time's father, that is of the universe, whose motion he has made the origin of the former. Thus, time holds in relation to God the position of a grandson. For this world is the younger son of God because it is perceptible. The elder son, the intelligible world, He assigned the place of firstborn and determined that it should remain by His side.

Ebr. 199: When some propose the universe is infinite, others that it is finite, and some declare it to be created, others say it is uncreated; when some refuse to connect it with a ruler or governor, but assume it to be dependent on the automatic action of a nonrational force, others postulate a marvelous providence and care for the whole and each of its parts exerted by God, Who guides and steers it and makes safe its steps. . . .

Fug. 101–105: The divine Logos, who is high above all these, is not near the visible outward appearance, being like to no one of those resembling objects of sense-perception, but he himself is the Image of God, the chiefest of rulers of all the beings intellectually perceived, placed nearest, with no intervening distance from the only One, Who is without deceit, with no image of Him; for it says, "I will talk with you from above the mercy seat, between the two Cherubim" (Exod. 25:21). Just as the Logos is a charioteer of the powers, He Who talks is seated in the chariot, giving directions to the charioteer for the right wielding of the reins of the universe. 102 Therefore, he who has shown himself free from even unintentional offense, intentional is not to be thought of, having God Himself as his portion (Deut. 10:9), shall settle in Him alone. But those who have fallen, not from divine providence but against their will, shall find refuges that have been mentioned, so abundantly and richly provided. 103 Now, of the cities for refuge, three are beyond the river (Num. 35:14); they are far removed from our race. Which ones are these? The Logos of the Ruler and His creative and kingly power; for in fellowship with these are heaven and the whole universe. 104 But those that are close to us and reach the perishable race of human beings, the only race that sin has befallen, are the three within—the gracious power, the power that enjoins things that are to be done, and that which prohibits those who are not to be done; for these reach us closely. 105 For what need does the prohibition have to those who intend to do no wrong? What need does the prescription have to those whose nature is exempt from failure? And what is the need for the recourse to the gracious power for those who will commit no sin at all? But our race stands in need of those powers through and through to be disposed by nature to have an inclination both to voluntary and involuntary sins.

Spec. 2.198–199: Although the sound of their voices is not openly heard at all, they shall speak loud and clear. They, who abstain from food and drink after the ingathering of the fruits, cry aloud with their souls and say these words: "we have gladly received and are storing the graces of nature, though we do not ascribe a perishable cause to any of our preservation, but to God the Begetter and Father and Savior of the world and all that is in the world, Who also has the power and right to nourish us and maintain us by means of these or without these. 199 At least see, then, as well how the many thousands of our forefathers when they passed through all the barren and pathless desert, were sustained continually for forty years, the life of a generation; how He cut open first fountains and then He provided abundant drink for their use; how He rained food from heavens, neither more nor less than what sufficed for each day, that they might use what they needed without storing anything, nor selling to soulless stores their hopes of His goodness, something of which they might have been accustomed to do. But taking little thought of the supplies received they marveled at the Supplier and honored Him with the hymns and benedictions that are His due."

Praem. 40b–44: He Is, which can be apprehended under a name of His existence, is not apprehended by all or not in the best way. Some distinctly declare that the Godhead is not divine; others hesitate and fluctuate as though unable to say whether there is or not. Others whose notions about the conception of the reality or the existence of God are derived through habit rather than thinking from those who brought them up, believe themselves to have successfully attained to reverence, but they have inscribed the reverence toward God (that is piety) with superstition. 41 If there are, again, others who have had the strength through knowledge to envisage the Maker and the Ruler of all have this phrase advanced from down to up. Passing into the world as a well-ordered city, they have also beheld the earth standing fast, highland and lowland full of sown crops, trees, and fruits, and of all sorts of living animals to boot; also spread over its seas and lakes and rivers, both natural springs and winter torrents. They have also seen the air and the good temperatures of the winds, and the changing harmonies of the yearly periodic winds, and over all the sun and moon, and planets and fixed stars, and the whole heaven set in order after the houses' armies, the true universe in itself revolving within the universe. 42 Being marveled and struck by amazement they arrived at a conception according with what they beheld, that surely all these beauties and this transcendent order have not come into being automatically but by the Maker and Architect of the world; also, that absolutely there is a necessary providence (*QG* 3.43). For it is a Law of Nature that a Maker should take care of what has been created. 43 These are admirable persons and superior to all others. They advanced, as I said, from down to up by such a sort of a heavenly ladder and by reason and reflection aimed at the Maker from His works. But those, if such there be, who were able to apprehend Him through Himself conceive the desire to behold the divine without the cooperation of any reasoning, must be recorded among those who are regarded as holy and genuine worshippers and friends of God. 44 Among them is he who in the Chaldean (or Hebrew) language is called by the name Israel, and in Greek the God-seer who sees not His real nature, for that is impossible, as I said, but that He Is. He has perceived this knowledge not from any other source, not from things on earth, not from things in heaven, not from the elemental principles, nor combinations of elements mortal and immortal, but from Him alone Who has willed to reveal His own existence to those who come to seek protection.

Prov. 2.52–54: Just then, as the sun and the moon have come into being by providence, so too, all the heavenly bodies, even though we are unable to trace the natures and powers of each of them. 53 Earthquakes and pestilences and thunderbolts and such as these, they are said to be sent by God, but the truth is that they are not; for absolutely nothing evil is caused by God and these things are generated by changes in the elements, not by the preliminary works of nature, but by sequels of her essential works, attendant circumstances to the preliminary. 54 If some people of a finer character participate in the damage that they cause, the blame must not be laid on God's ordering of the world; for in the first place, it does not follow that if some people are considered good by us they are truly such, for God judges by standards that are more accurate than by those that the human mind employs. Secondly, providence may be found to observe upon the most important things in the world, just as in the kingdoms and commands of army it pays regards to cities and troops, not to some chance individual of the obscure and insignificant kind.[19]

NOTES

1. *Wis.* 6:22–10:21.
2. *Opif.* 46; *Her.* 228.
3. *Her.* 188; *Fug.* 112.

4. *SVF* 2.416, 1021, 1033.

5. This can be explained as follows: in the book ("this is the book of creation") and in the (seventh) day ("the day in which He created heaven and earth").

6. A proverbial expression (see *Somn.* 1.44).

7. *Migr.* 134–138; *Somn.* 1.76.

8. *QG* 3.15, 30; 4.59, 61, 196; *QE* 2.89–90, 110–111, 120, 124.

9. The text as it is in the manuscripts is unintelligible; therefore, translations here are conjectures.

10. *Opif.* 29–31; *Conf.* 41–43, 96–97; *Migr.* 102–105, 174–175; *Her.* 234–236; *Fug.* 100–105, 137–139; *Somn.* 1.189–193.

11. *Plant.* 41–42; *Ebr.* 133–136; *Her.* 66–67; *Mut.* 267–269.

12. *Leg.* 1.25–27; 2.7–8; 3.200–202; *Post.* 132–139; *Agr.* 80–84; *Migr.* 118–119, 187–189, 190–191.

13. Philo understands the term "Lord" as the sovereign and divine power or potency, and the term "God" alludes to His providential and beneficial potency as in *Plant.* 86–88.

14. *Her.* 165–166, 312; *Fug.* 67–72; *Abr.* 120–123.

15. *Cher.* 124–127; *Aet.* 37–41, 69–70.

16. The daimones were in the Greek mythology inspired beings, intermediary spirits between the deities and human beings.

17. Aristotle, *History of the Animals* 5.552.

18. *Congr.* 116–117; *Somn.* 1.15–24; 2.115–116; *Aet.* 107–110.

19. *Her.* 58–60; *Aet.* 51.

BIBLIOGRAPHY

Mackie, Scott. "Seeing God in Philo of Alexandria: The Logos, the Powers, or the Existent One?" *The Studia Philonica Annual* 21 (2009): 25–47.

Radice, Roberto. "Observations on the Theory of the Ideas as the Thought of God in Philo of Alexandria." *The Studia Philonica Annual* 3 (1991): 126–34.

Runia, David T. *Philo of Alexandria and the Timaeus of Plato*. Leiden: Brill, 1986.

Runia, David T. *Philo of Alexandria on the Creation of the Cosmos According to Moses: Translation and Commentary*. Philo of Alexandria Commentary Series 1. Leiden: E. J. Brill, 2001.

Sterling, Gregory E. "Dancing with the Stars: The Ascent of the Mind in Philo of Alexandria." Pages 155–66 in *Apocalyptic Literature and Mysticism*. Edited by Pieter G. R. de Villiers et al. Ekstasis: Religious Experience from Antiquity to the Middle Ages. Berlin: Walter de Gruyter, 2018.

Tobin, Thomas H. *The Creation of Man: Philo and the History of Interpretation*. Catholic Biblical Quarterly Manuscript Series 14. Washington, DC: Catholic Biblical Association of America, 1983.

Tobin, Thomas H. "Logos." Pages 348–56 in vol. 4 of *The Anchor Bible Dictionary*. 6 vols. Edited by David Noel Freedman. New York: Doubleday, 1992.

Chapter 3

Philo's Anthropology

Similar to his cosmology, Philo's doctrine of anthropology is interpreted within Plato's *Timaeus* and his understanding of Genesis 1 and 2. In his interpretation, mainly influenced by the Platonist and Stoic traditions and interpretations, the creation of two humans is interpreted as the intelligible human and the sense-perceptible human. On the one hand, the latter human is created according to the Image of God and in His likeness (Gen. 1:26–27); this human is identified as incorrupt, immortal, perfect, imperishable, and neither male nor female. The interpretation of the intelligible human is described in Middle Platonic categories. On the other hand, this intelligible human is the paradigm, the archetype for the creation of the sense-perceptible or sensible human. This human, who is inferior to the first human created in the Image of God, is material, corrupt, perishable, mortal, and male and female (Gen. 2:7). Philo's interpretation of the sense-perceptible human is governed by the Stoic tradition, in that through the Spirit of God, the human becomes a living being. His anthropology is clearly dualistic: one human interpreted Platonically (Image), and another human interpreted Stoically (Spirit).

For Philo, human beings hold a special place; they are the borderline between the mortal and immortal (see Chapter 6). God as the Creator and Maker forms living creatures and bestows on the human soul, the mind, which is the highest faculty in the human. In this chapter the reader notices that Philo's anthropology and the differences of the two humans are explained using philosophical language, particularly in line of the *Timaeus,* e.g., Spirit, Image, Mind, Reason (Logos), and within the philosophical ethical systems of Plato, Aristotle, and Stoics, e.g., virtues, vices, and passions. The nature of human beings is composed of both rational and irrational, or nonrational, and the human of the earth is composed of soul and body (*QG* 4.189, 215, 218). The rational and immortal human being is associated with virtues, and he describes the good qualities of humans as the noblest of things. His interpretation of the differences between both humans is, indeed, ethical in character;

it is in this ethical context that Philo speaks of flesh in connection with passions, pleasure, and effeminacy, and in opposition to the knowledge of God.

As Philo moves on describing his view of human beings and their nature, he makes a radical contrast between man and woman, between sense-perception and the mind interpreted in a context of ethics. Like the mind, the human soul is related to Logos, and it is described as masculine, perfect, fatherly, and active. Philo is consistently clear in interpreting the differences between man and woman (male and female). In his description of the different gifts and qualities between male and female, Philo asserts that male is rational, active, connected with reason, wisdom, and the mind, perfect, incorruptible, and associated with the civic life (*QG* 3.46). The female, on the contrary, is passive, irrational, ordinary, instructive, learning, and associated with the domestic life only. His understanding of both genders is also socially established in his exhortation to proper appearance and behavior of man and woman interpreted ethically and giving priority to the male gender. Interestingly, in this chapter the reader will learn that Sarah, the Matriarch of Israel, and Leah are a representation of virtue.

Philo also offers themes related to human nature, such as parenthood, prophecy, education, and sex. I have included these topics/themes in the sourcebook because they will certainly enlighten the way Philo perceived human beings in other facets and his ethical outlook of his anthropology.

HUMAN NATURE

Note

While God is the cause of the world's becoming, He is also the cause of the creation of humanity. Similar to the creation of the "two worlds," Philo also provides an account of the "double creation of man": the intelligible human and the sense-perceptible human. The creation of the former is likewise in the Mind of God and has the characteristics of an intelligible, heavenly human. This human who is formed in God's Mind as a paradigm of the earthly human, who is male and female, is composed of body and soul, and by nature corruptible. Philo says that the creation of the intelligible human was "after the Image of God," the "image" who is the Logos of God (*Opif.* 24–25).[1] In Philo's interpretation of Gen. 1:26–27 in *Opif.* 69–75, he presents a Platonic description of the creation of the human where there is no figure of the Logos.[2] That is, the intelligible human is an Image of God. In *Opif.* 24–25, however, there is a small yet crucial difference in that human is created as the image of an Image, that is the Logos.

This is how it works in Philo's mind: man is an image of the Logos, who is the Image of God.[3] The major characteristics or qualities of this human, who is distinct from the sense-perceptible human, are that this human is intelligible, an idea, type, seal, incorporeal, neither male nor female, and by nature incorruptible (*Opif.* 134–147). Just as the incorporeal world is the manifestation of the World of Ideas or the divine Logos, the creation of the intelligible human is the copy of the divine image, who is the very Image of God. The creation of the sense-perceptible human as clearly distinct from the intelligible human (Gen. 1:26–27) is found in Philo's interpretation of Gen. 2:7 (Gen. 1:17) in *Opif.* 134–147. This is how Philo's "double creation of man" works:[4] while the human in Gen. 1:26–27 is the creation of the human after the Image of God and possesses attributes belonging to the intelligible world (e.g., incorporeal, immortal . . . a kind of idea or genus or seal, and who is perceived by the intellect), the corporeal sense-perceptible human is molded by the inbreathing onto the human being's face the breath of life or divine Spirit (*Opif.* 134). The phrase "into man's face" means for Philo the human's soul or the human mind.

   Viewed within the philosophical spectrum, Philo's reinterpretation of Gen. 2:7 is a Stoic description of the creation of the sense-perceptible human.[5] This human is composed of earthly substance and divine Spirit, has both body and rational soul, is male and female, and is mortal. For Philo, the human mind is the master ruler of the body and soul,[6] and in terms of the spiritual world, the human mind is the heavenly element in the human body, the soul of the soul.[7] Then the nature of the first human on earth is composed of body (earth) and rational soul (the most God-like of images). This earthly human comes into existence by being inbreathed into the face (*Opif.* 139). Philo explains philosophically that the mind or rational soul as the Logos of God has come into being as a fragment or effulgence of the blessed nature (*Leg.* 1.39–40; 3.161).[8] Furthermore, the structure of the sense-perceptible human (the human being born from the earth) is intrinsically connected with the entire world in the sense that this human possesses the four elements of earth air, water, earth, and fire (*Opif.* 145). Certainly, Philo is familiar with and follows the four elements of this world, which are the standard four of the ancient world.[9] In this regard, Philo tells us that the earthly human "bears about within himself, like holy images, endowments of nature that correspond to the constellations" (*Opif.* 82). Human beings also have the capacities for sciences and arts, knowledge, and the noble lore of virtues.

Human Beings

Opif. 66–69: For this reason, as the first of all the creatures that have life, He produced fishes, which share in more of the substance of body than soul. In a sense they both are and are not living beings. They move, yet they do not really have soul. The soul-principle has been sown in them in order to preserve their bodies, just like they say salt is put in meat, so that it will not easily go bad. After the fish come the birds and land animals. These are already perceptible things, and in their makeup, they reveal more clearly through the characteristics of being ensouled. And above all, as was said, He produced the human being, whom He endowed with a mind as special gift, a kind of soul of the soul, just like the pupil in the eye. Indeed, those who examine more scrupulously the nature of things call this the eye of the eye. 67 At that time, therefore, all things were constituted at the same time. But even though everything was constituted together, it was still necessary that the ordered sequence should be outlined in an account, because in the future beings would originate from each other. When individual beings come into existence, the following ordered sequence takes place: nature begins with what is most insignificant and ends with what is best of all. Let's see what this sequence is. The seed is the starting point in the first cause of living beings. It is common knowledge that the seed is something very insignificant, similar to foam. But when it is deposited in the womb and has established itself there, it immediately obtains movement and is turned directly into natural growth, which is superior to seed, since movement is superior to quietude in the realm of becoming. But the Artificer is unique, the Master, or to say it more accurately, like a blameless art, molds living beings by distributing the moist substance to the limbs and organs of the body, and the spiritual substance to the faculties of the soul, namely the principle of growth and sense-perception. The faculty of reasoning should be set aside for the moment on account of those who affirm that, as something divine and eternal, it enters the living being from the outside. 68 Then, nature started from the insignificant seed, and it ended with what is most precious, the constitution of an animal and of a human being. The same was also the case when everything came into existence. When the Maker decided to form living beings, the first in the ordered sequence were pretty insignificant, namely the fishes, while the last were the best, human beings. The other things are situated in between the extremes, being superior to the first group but inferior to the other, namely land animals and birds of the air. 69 After all these other creatures, as it was said, the human being has come into existence, after the Image of God and after His likeness (Gen. 1:26). Certainly, for nothing earth-born bears a closer likeness to God than the human being. Let no one represent this likeness from the characteristics of the body; for God does not have a human form, and the human body is not God-like. But it has been said that the term *image* has been used here with regard to the director of the soul, the mind. On that single mind of the whole, as on an archetype, the mind in each individual human being was fashioned. In a fashion it is a god of the person who carries and enshrines it as a divine image. For it would see that the same position that the Great director holds in the entire world is held by the human mind in the human being. It is itself invisible, yet it sees all things. Its own nature is unclear; yet it comprehends the natures of other things.

Opif. 131–133: Holding on to the sequence of creation and to the sequence of thought and preserving what goes before and comes next, he says: "a spring went up out of the earth and watered all the face of the earth" (Gen. 2:6). Other philosophers say that the entire water is one of the four elements, from which the world was made. Moses, who observes and comprehends distant objects right well with keener eyes, regards the great sea to be an element, a fourth part of the entirety of things, which those who came after him called "the ocean," considering the seas that we traverse as having the size of harbors. He distinguished the sweet drinkable water from the seawater. He apprehended it to the land and understood it to be a part of it and not of the sea, for the reason mentioned earlier, so that the earth would be bound and held together by a sweet quality of a unifying glue. For if it had been left dry earth, without spreading the moisture in and penetrate through its pores by multiple divisions, it would have been broken. But now it is held together, and it is also preserved through the faculties of the Spirit, that unifies it, and through the power of the moisture, that does not allow it to dry up and be broken into small and large pieces. 132 This is one explanation, and I must also speak about another that aims at the truth like a target. Nothing of what grows on earth can gain its structure without moist substance; and this is revealed by the deposition of seeds. Then, either it is wet, as in the case of animals, or it does not grow without moisture, as in the case of plants. From this is clear that what has been spoken about the moist substance is part of the earth that gives birth to all things, just as in the case of women there has to be the menstrual flow. For it is said by men of science that this is the bodily substance of new fetuses. 133 What I now shall state is in harmony with what has been said so far. Nature has equipped every mother with the necessary bodily part in the form of breasts and has prepared nourishment in advance for the child that will be born. The earth is also like a mother. For this reason, the first human beings decided to call her Demeter, combining the words for mother and earth. For as Plato has said (*Menexenus* 238A), it is not earth that imitated woman, but rather woman has imitated earth (*QG* 1.52). For the true poets were used to call her "universal-mother," "fruit-bearing," and "giver of all," because she is the cause of everything created and of the conservation of animals and of plants alike. Therefore, nature gave the earth, as the eldest and most fertile of mothers, with flowing rivers and springs like breasts, so that it could both water the plants and provide an abundant supply of drink for all living beings.

Leg. 1.88–89: "The Lord God took the human whom He had made and placed him in the garden to work and to guard it" (Gen. 2:15). "The human whom God made" differs, as I have said, from the one that "was molded."[10] For the "molded" intellect is earthlier, but the one "made" is more immaterial, having no share in perishable matter, possessing a purer and more unalloyed constitution. 89 Thus, God takes this pure mind and does not allow it to go outside of Himself. And having taken it, He sets it among the firmly rooted and growing virtues, so that he may till and guard them (QG 4.28). For many, after they become practicers of virtue, in the end changed course. But to the one whom God provides with secure knowledge, He bestows both advantages: that of practicing virtues, and also that of never departing from them but always preserving and guarding each of them. Therefore, "working" stands for practicing, and "guarding" stands for remembering.

Det. 83–85: Therefore, to the faculty that we have in common with the irrational creatures, blood has been given as its essence (*QG* 2.59); but to the faculty that emanates from the fountain of reason obtains the Spirit as its essence; not moving air, but as it were an impression stamped by the divine power that Moses calls "Image," thus indicating that God is the Archetype of the rational existence, and the human is a copy and likeness. By "human" I mean not the living creature with two natures, but the highest form in which life shows itself; this has been called the "mind" and "reason." 84 This is why he says the blood is the life of the flesh, knowing that the nature of the flesh has received no share of mind but partakes of the life as the whole of our body does; though he names human's life "breath," giving the title of *human* not to the composite mass, as I have said, but to that God-like creation with which we reason, whose roots He caused to reach even to heaven and come forth from the outmost circles of what are called fixed stars (Plato, *Tim.* 90A). 85 For God made human, alone of the things on the earth, a heavenly tree, fixing on the ground the heads of all others—for all have their heads down (*Tim.* 91E); and He lifted upward the human's head, so that he may have nourishment celestial and imperishable, not earthly and perishable. For this reason, He removed the part of our body least capable of sensation as far as possible from our reasoning faculty and planted our feet firmly to the earth, but our senses, which are satellites of the mind, He banished to a distance furthest from the ground, and bound them to the circuits (*Tim.* 90D) of air and heaven, which are imperishable.

Deus 45–48: In all these ways living animals surpass plants. Let us now see where the human has been made superior to other living creatures. He has received selected understanding according to a prerogative accustomed to apprehend the natures of all material objects and of things in general. For sight holds the leading place in the body, and the quality of light the leading place in the universe; also in us the dominant element is the mind. For the mind is the sight of the soul, illumined by rays peculiar to itself, 46 through which the vast and profound darkness, poured upon it by ignorance of things, is dispersed. This branch of the soul was not from the same elements of the world, out of which the other branches were brought to completion, but allotted something better and purer, the substance out of which the divine natures were fashioned, 47 for it is the mind alone that the Father who begat it deemed worthy of freedom, and loosening the bonds of necessity, allowed it to range free, and of that power of volition that constitutes his more intimate and fitting possession presented it with such a portion as it was capable of receiving. For the other living creatures in whose souls the mind, the element that sets apart for freedom, has no place, have been committed under the yoke and bridle to the service of human beings, as slaves to masters. But the human being, possessed of a spontaneous and self-determined will, whose activities for the most part rest on deliberate choice, is with reason blamed for what he does wrong with intent, praised when he acts rightly of his own will. 48 In the others, the plants and animals, no praise is due if they are fruitful, nor blame if they fail to be productive. For their movements and changes in either side come to them from no deliberate choice or volition of their own. But the human soul alone has received from God the faculty of voluntary movement, and in this way, he has been made especially like to Him. . . .

Conf. 176–179: Therefore, this outline was precisely needed as a premise. The nature of living beings was primarily divided into two opposite parts: the irrational and rational. The rational is also divided into two species: the mortal and immortal. The mortal being that of human beings, and the immortal of the incorporeal soul, which ranges through the air and sky. 177 These are immune from wickedness, the uncontaminated and happy inheritance obtained from the beginning, and they have not been imprisoned in that dwelling place of endless calamities, the body. This immunity is shared by unreasoning natures, because, as they have no gift of understanding, they are also not guilty of wrongdoings willed freely as a result of deliberate reflection. 178 The human is almost the only being, who having knowledge of all the good and evil things (*QE* 2.19), often chooses the bad things and shuns the things worthy of attention; therefore, he stands apart as convicted of deliberate and aforethought sin. 179 Therefore, it was right that when the human being was formed, God assigned a share to the one who belonged to Him saying: "let us make man," so that the human's right actions might be attributed to God, but his sins to others. For it seems to be unfitting to God the Ruler of all that in the rational soul the path that leads to vice should be of His making; for this reason, He delegated the formation of this part to His inferiors. The work of forming the voluntary element had to be accomplished in order to balance the involuntary and render the whole complete.[11]

Legat. 196: Perhaps these things are sent to test the present generation, to test the state of their virtue, and if they have been educated to bear the terrible misfortunes with a resolution that is fortified by reason and does not collapse at once. Everything that human beings can do is gone and can go away. But let our souls retain the hope in God our Savior, Who has often saved the nation from being helpless and pathless.[12]

Life-Creating and the Divine Spirit

Opif. 134–136a: After these he says that "God formed human by taking clay from the earth, and breathed into his face the spirit of life" (Gen. 2:7). By this also he shows very clearly that there is also a vast difference between the human formed and the human that came into existence first after the Image of God. For the human that was formed is an object of sense-perception, partaking already of such quality, consisting of body and soul, man or woman, by nature mortal. But the one that was after the Image is an idea, or genus, or seal, intelligible, incorporeal, neither male nor female, by nature incorruptible. 135 It says, however, that the formation of the individual human, the object of sense, is a composite one, a makeup of earthly substance and of divine Spirit. For it says that the body has come into existence through the Artificer taking clay and molding out of it a human form, but that the soul was originated from nothing created whatever, but from the Father and Ruler of all things. For that which He breathed in was nothing else than a divine Spirit that migrated hither from that blissful and happy existence for the benefit of our race, to the end that, even if it is mortal in respect of its visible part, it may in respect of the part that is invisible be rendered immortal. Hence, it may be properly said that the human is the borderline between mortal and immortal nature, partaking each so far as is needful, and that the human was created at once mortal and immortal, mortal in respect of the body, but in respect of the mind immortal. 136a That the first human, who was created from earth, is the whole of our first race and seems to me that this human is the most excellent in both soul and body. This human greatly excels all those who came after him in the transcendent qualities of both alike; for this human was truly a beautiful and good being.

Opif. 139: That the human was also the noblest, in respect to his soul, is obvious. For it is fitting that for its constitution God used no other pattern belonging to the realm of becoming, but only, as I said, His own Logos. For this reason, Moses says that the human has come into existence in the likeness and imitation of this Logos, being breathed into the face, which is the place of the senses. By means of these the Creator of the world gave soul to the body. He established the chief reason in the directive part (that is reason) to be guarded by senses for the apprehension of colors and sounds and tastes and smells and related sensations. Reason through itself alone without sense-perception was unable to grasp them. The representation of a beautiful pattern must be beautiful itself. The Logos of God is even superior to the beauty that is beauty as it occurs in nature. It is not adorned with beauty, but if the truth be told, it is itself beauty's pre-eminent adornment.

Virt. 203–205: But why is it to mention these while passing over the first human born from the earth? Because of nobility of birth, he is comparable to no other mortal, having been molded by divine hands into the figure of a human body with a perfect skill of the molding art, and deemed worthy of a soul coming not from anything already in creation, but from God breathing into him as much of his own power such as mortal nature was able to receive. Was this not a surfeit of nobility, which cannot be brought into comparison with any others whose names are held in acclaim? 204 For their fame derives from the prosperity of their ancestors—and they were men, forefathers, mortal, and corrupt creatures—and their accomplishments were mostly uncertain and short-lived. But his Father was not mortal but the eternal God. 205 Being in a way His image on account of the ruler in his soul, the mind, it was proper to keep that image undefiled by adhering as far as possible to the virtues of his Creator. When the opposites were set before him to choose or avoid, good and evil, honorable and shameful, true and false, he quickly chose the false and shameful, and the evil things, disregarding those that are good and honorable and true, on which account he, in a natural consequence, exchanged immortality for mortality, and forfeiting blessedness and happiness, promptly changed to a life of pain and misery.

Opif. 144: Who else would these be than the rational and divine natures, some of whom are incorporeal and intelligible beings, while others have bodies of the kind that the stars in fact possess? Consorting and living with these beings, the first human surely passed the time in unmixed well-being. He was a descendant of and closely akin to the Ruler, because the divine Spirit had flowed into him in ample measure, and so all his words and actions were undertaken in order to please the Father and King (*QE* 2.66), in whose footsteps he followed along the highways that the virtues mark out, because only those souls are permitted to approach Him Who considers the goal of their existence to become like God, Who brought them forth.

Leg. 1.33–42: One might ask: why did God think the whole earth and body-loving mind worthy of the divine Spirit at all, but not the mind brought into being after the idea and after His own Image? Second, what does "he inbreathed" mean? Third, why is breathing "into the face"? Fourth, why, although he knows of the word "Spirit" when he says, "and the divine Spirit was born above the water" (Gen. 1:2), he now mentions "breath" (*pnoēs*) but not "Spirit" (*pneumatos*)? 34 In reference to the first question, then, it should be said that God, since He is bountiful, bestows freely good things on all, even on those who are not perfect, encouraging them at the same time to a participation in and a zeal for virtue (*QG* 4.223), and showing His own extraordinary wealth, that it suffices even for those who will not be greatly benefited from it, He also shows this very clearly in other instances. For when He rains down on the sea, and pours forth springs in the most deserted places, and waters the poor and rough and barren soil, causing rivers to overflow with floods, what else does He show but the surpassing greatness of His own wealth and goodness? This is the motive why He fashioned no soul barren of goodness, even though the practice of it is impossible for some. 35 A second thing that should be said is this: He wishes to propose positive ordinances. One, then, into whom true life had not been breathed but who was without experience of virtue, when punished for his transgressions, he would have said that he is unjustly punished, for that it was through lack of experience of the good that he was tripped up in respect of it, and that the culprit is the one who had breathed into him no conception of the good. Perhaps he will even declare that he does not sin at all, as indeed some say that the involuntary acts and acts done in ignorance do not count as wrong deeds. 36 Indeed, "he inbreathed" is equivalent to "he inspired" or "he gave life to" the soulless. For may we not be infected with such great oddness as to believe that God uses organs such as a mouth or nostrils for inbreathing. For God is entirely without qualities and not only anthropomorphic—not in the form of human—yet the expression shows something even more in accord with nature (*QG* 1.42). 37 For there are necessarily three things: what breathes into, what receives it, and what is breathed into it. What breathes into, then, is God; what receives it is the mind; and what is breathed into it is the breath/Spirit. What, then, should we conclude from these premises? A union of the three happens, when God extends the power that comes from Himself through the mediant breath/Spirit until it reaches the external object. And for what purpose other than that we may thus obtain a conception of Him? 38 For how could the soul have conceived of God, if He had not breathed into it and powerfully grasped it? For the human mind would not have dared to soar so high as to apprehend the nature of God, if God Himself had not drawn it up to Himself, in as far as it was possible for the human mind to be drawn up and stamped it and keeping with the powers within the scope of its understanding. 39 "He breathes into the face" means something both physically and ethically. Physically, because He fashioned the senses in the face; for this part of the body is especially ensouled and breathed into. But ethically the meaning is as follows: as the face is the dominant part of the body, so is the mind the dominant part of the soul. God breathes into this alone, but He does not see fit to do so with the other parts, the senses and the organ for speech and that for reproduction. For these are secondary in capacity. 40 By what, then, were these also "breathed into"? Clearly by the mind. For the mind imparts to the nonrational part of the soul a share of what it received from God; so that the mind is, so to speak, God of the nonrational part. Similarly, he did not hesitate to speak of Moses as "a God to Pharaoh" (Exod. 7:1). 41 For of the things that are brought into being both by God and through Him; but others are brought into being by God and not through Him. Therefore, the best, most excellent things have come into being both by God and through Him. For example, he will say, "God planted a garden" (Gen. 2:8). The mind is one of these things. But what is devoid of reason (the irrational part) has come into being by God but not through God, but through the reasoning (the rational) part, which rules and governs in the soul. 42 He speaks of "breath" (*pnoēs*) but not "Spirit" (*pneumatos*), since there is a difference between them. For "Spirit" is conceived of in terms of strength and vigor and power, but "breath" is a kind of breeze and a mild and gentle vapor (*QG* 1.5). One might say that the mind brought into being after the Image and the idea partakes of Spirit; for its reasoning faculty possesses the same strength, but that the intellect brought into being out of matter partakes of a light and less substantial breeze, as of some fragrance, as comes from spices. For if they are preserved and not burned for incense there is still a sweet scent coming from them.

Plant. 17–22: But for the constitution given to the human was obtained by lot, and by turning the eyes of the other living creatures downwards, he made them incline to the earth beneath them. The eyes of the human, on the contrary, He set high up, that he might look at heaven, as the old saying said: it is a heavenly plant not terrestrial (Plato, *Tim.* 90A). 18 But others, by saying that our mind is a portion of the ethereal air, have claimed for the human a kinship with the upper air; the great Moses likened the fashion of the reasonable soul to no created thing, but he averred it to be a genuine coinage of that dread Spirit, the divine and invisible One, signed and impressed by the seal of God, the stamp of which is the eternal Logos (*QE* 2.117). 19 For he says, "God inbreathed into his face the Spirit of life" (Gen. 2:7); so that, it cannot but be that he that receives is made in the likeness of Him Who sends it forth the Spirit. Respectively, he also says that the human has been made after the Image of God (Gen. 1:27), certainly not after the image of anything created. 20 Therefore, it followed as a consequence of human's soul having been molded after the image of the archetype, the Logos of the first Cause, that his body was made erect to raise up his eyes to heaven, the spotless portion of the "All," that by means of that which could see the human might clearly apprehend that which he could not see. 21 Since, then, it was difficult for anyone to discern how the understanding tends toward the Existent One, except for those only who were led by Him. For each one knows what he has himself experienced as no other can know it. Especially, He endows the bodily eyes with the power of the incorporeal, and so makes them a distinct representation of the invisible eye. 22 For when the eyes formed out of perishable matter, obtained such a height as to travel from the earthly region to the far heaven, that is so far away, and to touch its limits, how vast must we deem the flight in all directions of the eyes of the soul? Which, by a great distance yearning to clearly perceive the Existent One, gives the soul wings to stretch not only to the furthest upper heaven, but to overpass the boundaries of the entire universe and speed toward the Uncreated.[13]

Plant. 43–45: It is not, therefore, that we must raise the question to know why there were brought into the ark, which was built at the time of the great flood, all the kinds of wild animals, but into the Garden of Eden no kind at all. For the ark was a symbol of the body, which for necessity therefore contained all the most savage and ferocious evils of passions and vices, whereas the garden of Eden was a symbol of virtues. And virtues receive nothing wild that is irrational. 44 And having observed closely that the human who was not formed after the Image, but after the one who was molded, the Lawgiver says that this human was introduced into the Garden of Eden. For the man inscribed with the Spirit, which is after the Image of God, does not differ a whit, as it appears to me, from the tree that bears the fruit of immortal life; for both humans are incorruptible and deemed worthy of the most central and the most leading portion, that is the mind. For the Lawgiver says that the tree of life is in the middle of the Garden of Eden (Gen. 2:9). And there is no difference between the human fashioned out of the earth and the earthly composite body. He has no part in a nature simple and uncompounded, whose house and courts only the self-trainer knows how to occupy, even Jacob who put before us as "a plain man dwelling in a house" (Gen. 25:27). The earthly man leads with much wondering, shaped and concocted of elements of all sorts. 45 Hence, it was expected that God should plant and set in the Garden of Eden, or whole universe, the middle or neutral mind,[14] played upon by forces drawing it in opposite directions and given the high calling to decide between them, that it might be moved to choose and to avoid; if it welcomes the better, it has used immortality and good repute, and if it welcomes the inferior, it finds blamable death.

THE MIND

The Nature of the Mind

Leg. 3. 236: . . . For the mind that is a eunuch and a chief cook, dealing not only with the simple pleasures but also with excessive ones, deserves the title of eunuch as one who is unable to produce wisdom, seeing that he serves as eunuch none other than Pharaoh, the dispenser of noble things. Keep in mind that according to another view to become a eunuch would be a good thing if our soul is able to escape from wickedness and unlearn passion.

Gig. 58–61: Now "the giants were on the earth in those days" (Gen. 6:4; *QG* 1.92). In the same way, some may think that the Lawgiver is alluding to the myths of the giants by poets; but indeed, the invention of myth is the thing most foreign to him and deems it right to follow on the steps of truth itself. 59 Therefore, he has expelled from his own commonwealth the painting and sculpture, for all their glorious and nice artistry, because their crafts easily lead to deceive the nature of truth to bear false witness through the eyes to the souls. 60 Therefore, in no way is he introducing a myth about giants, but he is willing to show you that on the one hand, some human beings are earth-born, and on the other hand, some human beings are heaven-born; and some human beings are God-born. The earth-born are those who are hunters of the pleasures of the body, who are preoccupied with their enjoyment and indulgence and provide the things that contribute each. The heaven-born are craftsmen, wise, and eager to learn knowledge. For the heavenly element in us, the mind (for every heavenly being also constitutes a mind) practices the encyclical branches of education and other art of every description, sharpening and exercising, and practicing itself, and rendering itself acute in all those matters that are objects of the realm of the intelligible. 61 But the men and prophets of God are priests, who did not design to obtain membership in the universal commonwealth and to become world citizens and have transcended the sense-perceptible world and migrated to the intelligible world and dwell there enrolled as citizens of the commonwealth, which is of imperishable and incorporeal Ideas (*Opif.* 4).

The Mind and the Human

Her. 232–236: Our mind is indivisible in nature. The irrational part of the soul is divided into six parts, which the Craftsman formed into seven parts: sight, hearing, taste, smell, touch, voice, and productive intellect (*QG* 4.230). The rational part is really called the mind and remains undivided; He followed the analogy of the whole heaven. 233 For also there in the outermost sphere of the fixed earth is kept indivisible, and the inner sphere of six parts is cut down to render seven circles of what we called the wandering stars. I think, the soul as being in human beings what the heaven is in the universe. Thus, the two reasoning and the intellectual natures, one in the "human" and the other in the "All," prove to be integral and undivided. Therefore, it is said, "He did not divide the birds." 234 Our mind is similar to a dove, since the animal is domestic and natural, while the turtledove is the figure of the mind, which is the model of ours (*QG* 2.44). For the Logos of God is the lover of the wild and solitary; it does not mix with the crowd or mob of those that have come into being and have come to perish. But, its wonted resort is ever above, and its study is to wait on one and only attendant. Therefore, the two natures are indivisible: the reasoning power in us and the Logos of God above us are indivisible, yet they divide other things without number. 235 The divine Logos separated and distributed all that is in nature. Our mind received both intelligible and material things, which the mental process brings within its grasp, divides them into an infinity of infinite parts and never ceases cleaving them. 236 This is the result of its likeness to the Maker and Father of the universe. For God is unmixed, absolute, the most indivisible commander Ruler in the whole world, which has come into being, the Cause of mixture, infusion, division, and consists of many parts. Similarly, these two that are made alike, the mind within us and the mind above us, indivisible and undivided in existence, are able to divide and to distinguish vigorously each of the things created.

Spec. 1.335c–336: . . . This mind is the discoverer of the mechanical and the finer arts. 336 This mind trained and brought letters, numbers, music, and the whole range of the school studies, and increased them to the goal. This mind also brought forth philosophy, the greatest good, and through each of its parts benefited human life: the logical for the benefit of infallible interpretation, and the ethical for the correction of human character, and the physical for knowledge of heaven and universe. However, beside these they say that they collect and bring a vast amount of praises to the mind with the same effect as those already mentioned, with which we have no occasion to trouble ourselves now.

Prob. 45b-46: Those in whom anger or desire or any other passion, or again any insidious evil holds power, are entirely slaves; and many who live by means of the law are free. 46 And right reason is an infallible law imprinted not by this or that individual, the perishable work of a mortal, nor on parchment or slabs, a thing inanimate on materials inanimate, but by immortal nature, imperishable, on the immortal mind, which never perishes.

Mind *versus* Sense-Perception

Leg. 2.23–24: The soul is the power to grow, with the additional power of receiving impressions and being the subject of impulses. This is also shared by those who are without reason. Indeed, our mind has a part that is analogous to the soul of a creature without reason. Again, the power of the intellect is peculiar of the mind and also shares swiftness of the divine nature; but it is peculiar to the human among the mortal beings. This power is twofold: we are rational beings, being partakers of the mind, and we are capable of discourse. 24 Therefore, there is yet another power in the soul akin to these, a sister, sense-perception, and that is the subject of the passage here. For Moses is describing nothing other than the coming into being of sense-perception as an activity. And this is quite logical. For after the mind it was necessary that sense-perception be immediately fashioned as a helper and ally to the mind. After he has finished the creation of the mind, He molds the thing to be fashioned next both in order and in power, that is, sense-perception as an activity for the purpose of the completion of the whole soul and for the apprehension of external objects.

Leg. 2.36–37: Therefore, what is the idea that he wished to express? The word "perception" is used in two ways: first in that of a condition, in which sense is ours when we are asleep, and secondly in the sense of an activity. Thus, of perception in the former sense, as it is a state, there is no benefit, for it does not enable us to apprehend the objects about us. It is from the second kind of perception, as an activity, through which we are benefited from it; for our apprehension of the objects of sense-perception is made possible by this. 37 Thus, having brought into being the former sort of perception as a quiescent condition, at the time when He was bringing the mind with many faculties lying dormant, now He wishes to produce perception as an activity. Active perception is brought to pass when quiescent perception has been set in motion and extended to reach the flesh and perceptive organs. For just as growth is constituted by seeds being set in motion, so is activity by a condition of movement.

Leg. 2.49–52: "For this reason shall a man leave his father and his mother, and shall cleave unto his wife, and the two shall be one flesh" (Gen. 2:24). On account of sense-perception, the mind, whenever it becomes enslaved, leaves both the Father of the whole, God, and the Mother of all things, the virtue and Wisdom of God, and cleaves to and is united with sense-perception and becomes dissolved into sense-perception so that the two become one flesh and one passion. 50 Observe that it is not that the woman might join to the man, but conversely the man to the woman, the mind to sense-perception (*QG* 1.26, 94). For when that which is superior, the mind, might be united to the inferior sense-perception, it resolves itself into the worst, the family of the flesh, the sensible cause of passions. If the inferior sense-perception follows the superior mind, there will be no longer flesh, but both will be the mind. Such is the human of whom the prophet speaks (cf. Deut. 21:15–16), the one who prefers the love of his passion to the love of God. 51 But there is a different human, one who has been chosen as the opposite, Levi, who "said to his father and mother: 'I have not seen you,' and did not know his brothers, and knew his sons" (Deut. 33:9). This forsakes both father and mother, that is his mind and the material body, for the sake of having the one God as his portion, "for the Lord Himself is a portion to him" (Deut. 10:9). 52 The passion becomes a portion of the lover of passion, but the portion of Levi the lover of God is God. Do you not see again that he prescribes that on the tenth day of the seventh month they should bring two goats, "one portion for the Lord and one for the averter of evil"? (Lev. 16:8). For in fact, a portion of the lover of passion is a passion that needs an averter.

Mind and Sense-Perception

Leg. 3.188b–189: Therefore, what should be said? He went to talk about the woman and passed on to her offspring and beginning. But the mind is the origin of sense-perception, and mind is masculine, in speaking of which there is a need to use "he" and "his" and so forth (*QG* 4.119). Rightly, therefore, is it said to pleasure: "the mind, the chief and principal doctrine, will constantly watch you, and you yourself will watch it, the mind, which acts and rests upon those who do good." What is good is represented by the word "heels." 189 The words "shall watch" are known in two ways: one like "shall guard carefully and preserve"; the other equivalent to "shall guard carefully to destroy." The mind compels to be either bad or good. Thus, the senseless mind shall become the watcher and steward of pleasure; this senseless mind rejoices, but the good mind will prove its enemy, watching eagerly when the good mind will prevail and destroy the senseless mind. On the other hand, pleasure watches closely the senseless mind stepping on it and attempting to break up and destroy the way of life of the wise mind, believing that the wise mind is planning her destruction. Yet the senseless mind is devising the best means to preserve her.

Leg. 3.222b, 224: "To Adam God said, 'because you have listened to the voice of your wife and have eaten of the tree, of which I commanded you not to eat of it you have eaten, cursed is the ground in respect of your labor'" (Gen. 3:17). Most useless is that mind should listen to sense-perception, and not sense-perception to mind. For it is always right that the superior should rule, and the inferior be ruled, and mind is superior to sense-perception (*QG* 3.41). 223 . . . 224 Just as when the mind, the charioteer or helmsman of the soul, rules the whole living being just as a governor of a city, life holds a straight course; when the irrational sense gains the chief place, a terrible confusion gains possession of it, just as when slaves have risen against their masters. For then if it is necessary to say the truth, the mind is burned and set into fire, and that fire is kindled by the objects of sense, which sense-perception supplies.

Migr. 192–194: If in this way you learn to receive a deficiency of the mortal, you shall be educated about the doctrine of the Uncreated. You, surely, do not imagine your mind stripping off the body, sense-perception, and speech. You are able to see, apart from these, in their nakedness, the existing things; the mind of the whole, God, has not His abiding place outside all the material nature, containing, not being contained, or doubt that He has gone forth beyond its confines not in thought alone, just as a human being, but also in essential nature as befits God. 193 Our mind has not made the body, but it is the work of another. On this account, it is contained in the body as in a vessel (*QG* 1.50). But the mind of the whole has brought the universe into existence; and that which the Creator has made is mightier than what is created. So that it could not be included in its inferior, besides, nor would it be fitting that a father should be contained in a son.[15] 194 In this way, the mind, gradually passing from one point to another, will arrive at the Father of the piety and holiness (*QE* 2.83). The first distance is to relinquish astrology, which wins it over to accept that the universe is the primal God, but not the handiwork of the primal God, and that the motions and agitations of the stars are the cause to human beings of disaster, or, on the contrary, of good fortune.

THE MAKEUP OF THE HUMAN

The Tripartite of the Human Soul

Leg. 3.115: Our soul is tripartite: the first part is given to reasoning, the second to passion, and the third part to desire. Therefore, some philosophers have distinguished these parts from each another in regard to function only, some also in regard to their locations. They have distributed to the reasoning part the region of the head, saying that, where the king is, there too are the bodyguards, and the senses in the region of the head are the bodyguards of the mind, so that the king must be there, having obtained it, like a citadel in a city to dwell. To the passionate part they assigned the breasts, pointing out that nature has given that part firmness by means of a strong and solid array of continuous bones, as if arming a good soldier with shield and breastplate for defense against opponents. To the desiring part they assigned the region about the lower abdomen and the belly, for it is there that desire, irrational craving, has its abode (*QG* 2.7).

Her. 225: Therefore, the Craftsman, wishing that we should possess a copy of the archetypal celestial sphere with its seven lights, commanded this splendid work, the candlestick, to be wrought. We have shown also its resemblance to the soul. For the soul is tripartite, and each of its parts, as it has been shown,[16] is divided into two (see *Conf.* 21), making six parts in all, to which the holy and divine Logos, the All-server, makes a fitting seventh.

Memory

Leg. 3.92–93: But the inferior of this, recollection, is presented older than the superior memory: while recollection has many gaps of forgetfulness, memory is endless and eternal.¹⁷ For when we are introduced first into the arts, we are unable immediately to master their principles that bear upon it. So, finding ourselves liable to forgetfulness, at the outset, we subsequently recollect, until a repeated recurrence of forgetfulness and a repeated recurrence of recollection; an unfailing memory shall subsequently win the day. Accordingly, memory, being late-born, is formed as recollection's younger sister (*QG* 4.136). 93 Thus, it is said that Ephraim represents memory symbolically; for it is interpreted as "fruit bearing," for the soul of the one who is eager to learn has borne its own fruit, when it is able through memory to hold the secured principles of the art that is being learned. Manasseh represents recollection, for it is said to mean "out of forgetfulness" when translated, and he who escapes from forgetfulness necessarily recollects. Therefore, most rightly, Jacob, the overthrower of passions and the trained seeker of virtue, receives kindly the fruitful memory, Ephraim, and places Manasseh, who is recollection, worthy of the second place.

Post. 148–149: It is not sufficient that he should simply take in all the instructions given by the teacher. He also needs the reinforcement of memory. Therefore, Rebekah displays her generosity when she gives Abraham's servant all he can drink, and she helps him to draw water for his camels, which we say to be figures of memory. For the camel is a ruminating animal that chews food, and when the camel has knelt and receives a heavy load, it nimbly raises itself with much agility. 149 Thus, the soul of the keen learner, also, when it has been laden with the mass of speculations, does not become fainthearted but springs up rejoicing. And from the repetition, just as from rumination of the first deposit of mental food,¹⁸ gains memory of the things contemplated.

Agr. 132–133: For as the animal that chews the cud renders digestible the food taken in before it rises again to the surface, so the soul of the keen learner, when it has by hearing taken in this and that proposition, does not hand them over to forgetfulness, but in stillness all alone goes over them one by one quite quietly, and so succeeds in recalling them all to memory. 133 Though not all memory is a good thing, but that which is brought to bear upon good things only, for it would be the most pernicious that evil things should be unforgettable. That is why, if perfection is to be attained, it is necessary to divide the hoofs, in order that the faculty of memory being divided into two sections, the word that flows through the mouth, for which nature wrought lips as twin boundaries, may separate the beneficial and the injurious forms of memory.

Sobr. 27–29: It is in accord with these arrangements that the things regarding the sons of Joseph are consistent if we investigate them with much consideration. When the wise, who is inspired, having them both standing before him, does not lay his hand on their heads, directing them as the boys are straight before him and immediately, but crossing his hands, intending to touch with his left hand the boy who seemed to be older and the younger with his right hand (Gen. 48:13–14). 28 Now, the older boy is called Manasseh and the younger Ephraim, and when the names are translated into Greek language, they represent symbols of memory and recollection. For Manasseh translated means "from forgetfulness," and another name is "reminiscence," since anyone reminded of what he has forgotten is advancing out of a state of forgetfulness. Ephraim means "fruit-bearing," which is a very suitable title for memory; it is truly an unforgettable and unbroken memory, a most profitable fruit and a real food to souls. 29 Therefore, memories belong to those who have achieved settled adulthood, and therefore, having been brought forth late, are held younger. But forgetfulness and recollection coexist in succession in each of us almost from our earliest years. Therefore, theirs is the seniority in time and is placed on the left hand when the Sage marshals his rank. But memory will share the seniority of virtue, and the God-beloved will lay on them his right hand and adjust them worthy of the netter portion that is His to give.[19]

Body and Flesh

Gig. 29–30: The greatest cause of ignorance is the flesh and our affinity for it. Moses himself affirms this about the flesh: "because they are flesh" the divine Spirit is not able to abide (*QG* 2.22). Indeed, marriage too, and the rearing of children, the provision of necessities, the ill repute that comes in the wake of poverty, business both private and public, and a host of other things wither the flower of wisdom before it blooms. 30 Nothing, however, thwarts its growth so much as our fleshly nature, because this is the primary and main underlying foundation of ignorance and the diseased condition of an unknowing mind, on which each of the qualities named rises on it like a building.

Deus 141–143: Some will think that the speech is wrong, and we have here a mistake in diction, and that the correct phrase in grammatical sequence is as follows: "all flesh destroyed its way" (*QG* 1.99). For a masculine form like "his" cannot be properly used with reference to the feminine noun "flesh." 142 But perhaps the writer is not speaking merely about the flesh that defiled its own way, so giving reasonable grounds for the idea of a grammatical error, but of two things: the flesh, which is being corrupted, and another, whose way that flesh intends to maltreat and to defile. So, the passage must be explained thus: all flesh corrupts the perfect way of the Eternal and Incorruptible, the way that leads to God. 143 This way, you must know, is the way of wisdom. For this wisdom guides the mind straight through a high road existing in the beginning and reaches its goal, which is the recognition and knowledge of God. Each companion of the flesh hates and rejects this path and seeks to destroy it. For no two things are so utterly opposed as knowledge and pleasure of the flesh.

Her. 268: This is one subject to study, but another subject is that the things that are servile, ill-treatment, and a dire humiliation, as he himself declared, and that are connected with the soul according to the things of the earth, are not our own. For the passions of the body are truly bastards and strangers to the understanding, growths of the flesh in which they have their roots.[20]

Abr. 164–166: These and the like belong to philosophy. It is clear that wisdom and philosophy owe their origin to no other of our faculties but to the leader of the senses, sight (Plato, *Tim.* 47A). This alone of all the bodily regions did God preserve when He destroyed the other four senses, because they were enslaved to the flesh and the passions of the flesh. The sight has the strength to expand its necks upwards, and to look, and to find in the contemplation of the world and its contents pleasures far better than those of the body. 165 Thus, it was fitting that one of the five senses, which form a group of five cities, should receive a special privilege and continue to exist when the others were destroyed; because its range is not confined to moral things, as theirs is, but it deems worthy to find a new home amid incorruptible natures and rejoice in their contemplation. 166 Therefore, the most beautiful oracles clearly represent the city first as small and then not a small one (cf. Gen. 19:20), describing the sight. For sight is said to be small in that it is a little part of all we contain, but great in that great are its desires, because it is the whole world and the heavens which it yearns to survey.

The Soul

Cher. 101–104a: Therefore, in the invisible soul the invisible God has His earthly dwelling place. And that the house may have both strength and loveliness (*QG* 4.66). Put forward the foundations in natural excellence and instruction; let virtues and noble actions be erected on them, and let its finery be the acquisition of the preliminary learning of the schools. 102 For from natural excellence come quickness of mind, tenacity, and memory; from instruction, readiness to learn and diligence. They are like roots of a tree that is going to bring forth cultivated fruits, and without them the mind cannot be brought to its perfection. 103 From the virtues and accompanying good actions come the solidity and stability of a secure structure, and one who is determined to separate and banish the soul from the good is incapable of knowing steadfastness and strength. 104a From the study of the preliminary school learning come the things that serve as ornaments of the soul, which are attached to it as to a house.

Her. 55–56: The word "soul" is used in two ways: for the whole and for its dominant part, which properly speaking is the soul of the soul, just as the eye can mean either the whole sphere or the most important part by which we see. It seemed that for the Lawgiver the substance of the soul is twofold: blood being the essence of the soul as a whole, and a divine Spirit being the essence of the most dominant part of it. Thus, he says plainly, "the soul of every flesh is the blood" (Lev. 17:11). 56 He does well in assigning the blood with its flowing stream to the mass of the flesh, for each is akin to the other. On the other hand, he did not make the substance of the mind depend on anything created, but represented it as breathed into the human by God. For the Maker of all, he says, "blew into his face the Spirit of life, and the man became a living soul" (Gen. 2:7); just as we are also told that he was fashioned after the Image of the Maker (Gen. 1:27).

Congr. 58–60: Elsewhere, we have these texts engraved as on a stone: "when the Highest divided the nation when He dispersed the sons of Adam" (Deut. 32:8); that is when He drove away all the earthly ways of thinking, which have no real desire to look for any heaven-sent good, and he made them homeless beings without a city and rendering them truly wanderers on the face of the earth. For none of the wicked have preserved for them home, or city, and nothing else that tends to fellowship, but they are scattered without settlement, driven about on every side, always changing their place, and nowhere able to hold their ground. 59 Therefore, the wicked man begets vice by his legitimate wife and passion by his concubine (*QG* 4.169–174). For the soul as a whole is the legitimate life-mate of reason, and if it be a soul of guilt, it brings forth vices. The bodily nature is the concubine, and we see that through her passion is generated, for the body is the region of pleasure and desires. 60 This concubine is called Tamnah, whose name translated means "tossing faintness." For the soul faints and loses all power through passion when it receives from the body the flood of tossing surge caused by the storm wind that sweeps down in its fury, driven on by unbridled appetite.[21]

MAN AND WOMAN

Male

Leg. 3.28–31: Therefore, we have shown clearly the way the bad man is in exile and hiding himself from God. Now, let us see where he hides himself. It says, "in the midst of the wood of the garden" (Gen. 3:8), that is, in the center of the mind, which is also the center of what we may call the garden of the whole soul. For he, who runs away from God, flees for protection in himself. 29 There are two minds: that of the universe, which is God, and that of the individual mind. He, who flees from his own mind, takes protection with the mind of the whole. For he that abandons his own mind acknowledges that nothing is important and attributes all things to God. He, who flees from God, declares that He is not the cause of anything, but that he himself is the cause of all things that exist. 30 Indeed, many say that all the things in the world are borne along spontaneously, without any one to guide them, and that the human mind by itself established practices, arts, laws, customs, and the rules of conduct within the state, individual and communal, regarding both men and animals. 31 But you may see, O my soul, the difference between the two views. For the one abandons the particular, created, and mortal mind, and wholeheartedly puts itself under the patronage of the universal mind, uncreated and immortal. The other view, on the contrary, rejects God and by a grievous error calls as its ally the mind, which is insufficient even to help itself.

Ebr. 33: In the present discussion we must leave out the parents of the universe, and rather turn our attention to the disciples and pupils, who have obtained the care of and support of the souls. Now, we may consider that such souls are not unmanageable and without taste. Therefore, we say that the father is reason, masculine and perfect, and that the mother is the middle and encyclical course of study, and instruction, and learning. For us, these two stand in relation of parents to children, and it is good and profitable to obey them.

Her. 138–139: As He had divided the lifeless, He also did with those who participate in life; He separated the irrational from the rational according to species. Also taking each of them, He divided again the irrational into both the domesticated and the undomesticated, and the rational into both immortal and mortal. 139 Also He divided the mortal into two parts, one of which He bestowed the name of men and the other women. While following one principle, He split up the animal kingdom into male and female; and the division was also received by other necessary partitions, which distinguished the winged from the land animals, these from the aquatic animals, the last named being intermediate to both extremes.

Fug. 51–52: He called Bethuel Rebekah's father (Gen. 28:2). But how can the daughter of God, wisdom, be spoken of as a father? Is it because the name is wisdom, feminine, and the nature is masculine? Indeed, all the virtues have women's titles, but they possess the powers and activities of men. For that which comes after God, even if it were the highest of all other things, occupies a second place, and thus was called feminine in contrast to the Maker of the whole Who is masculine, and in accordance with its affinity to everything else. For the superior always pertains to the masculine, and the feminine always falls short and is inferior to the masculine (*QG* 4.18). 52 Let us, then, pay no attention to the distinction in the terms, and say that the daughter of God, wisdom, is both masculine and the father, inseminating and begetting in the souls a desire to learn discipline, knowledge, prudence, or sound sense, noble and laudable actions. It is from this household that Jacob the practicer seeks to win a bride. To what other place than the house of wisdom shall he go to find a partner, a faultless judgment, with whom to spend his days forever?

Virt. 18–21: There is so much anxiety and desire in the law to train and to exercise the soul in courage that legislates even concerning what sorts of clothes ought to be worn, strictly forbidding a man to wear a woman's dress, so that no trace or even mere shadow of the female might be attributed to him, resulting in the defilement of his masculinity. As it always conforms to nature, the law desires to establish rules that are suitable and consistent with each other down to the furthest details, even if, owing to their mundane character, they seem to be rather insignificant. 19 For since it is perceived, as if the figures of men and women were outlines on a flat surface, that the patterns of the corporeal are dissimilar, and that the life assigned to each of these forms is not the same: for to the woman is assigned the domestic life, and a civic life has been allotted to the man (*QG* 1.37; 4.8). In other matters, it judged it beneficial to appoint laws that, while not the works of nature itself, were always in conformity with nature and findings of good judgment. These were the laws concerning a way of life and a mode of dress and other things of that kind. 20 For it is considered that in such matters a true man should have to maintain his masculinity, especially in his clothes, which, since he always wears them both day and night, ought to have no suggestion of unmanliness. 21 In the same way, by training the woman in appropriate adornments, it forbade her to assume a man's dress, ultimately guarding against the manly woman as much as the womanly man. For it knew that, as in buildings, if one of the foundation stones is removed, the rest will not remain in the same place.[22]

Female

Opif. 153: While the man was still living a solitary life and the woman had not yet been built, it is told that a garden was planted by God (Gen. 2:8), which nothing resembles to those in our experience. For these have matter without soul, filled with all sorts of trees; some are always green and give continuous visual pleasure; others blossom and grow leaves in the spring season; others bear cultivated fruit for people, not only supplying the necessary nourishment, but also the unnecessary enjoyment of luxurious living, while others bear a different sort, which of necessity has been apportioned to the beasts (*QG* 2.27). But in the case of the divine garden all the plants in fact possess soul and reason, bearing fruits in the form of the virtues and besides the uncorrupt intelligence and shrewdness, by which the good things and bad things are recognized, as well as life without disease and incorruptibility, and everything that is of a similar nature.

Leg. 2.38b–39: Therefore, He adds the words, "He built it into a woman" (Gen. 2:22). With this He proves that the most proper and exact name for sense-perception is woman (*QG* 2.49). For just as the man is perceived in his "doing" or activity and the woman in her passivity, so the province of the mind has to do with activity, and that of the perceptive sense passivity, as in woman. 39 It is easy to learn this from what is before our eyes. Sight is in a passive relation to the objects of sight that set it moving, white, black, and the others. Hearing again is arranged by the sounds and the sense of taste by the savors, the sense of smell by odors, the sense of touch by things rough and smooth. The faculties of sense-perception are all dormant, until they may draw near to each of them from outside, that which is to set it in motion.

Her. 61–62: Right well, too, Moses introduces Damascus not from the father but from the mother, Masek, to teach us that the soul depending on blood, by means of which the irrational animals also live, has kingship with the maternal and female line, but has no share in the male descent (*QG* 4.188). 62 But not so was with virtue, that is Sarah. For she has none but a male offspring, being borne only of God, Who is the Father of all things, being that authority that has no mother. For "truly," it says, "she is my sister from the father, not from the mother" (Gen. 20:12).

Spec. 3.171–173: A woman should not be busy about the things outside her household but should seek to live in seclusion. She should not show herself off like a vagrant in the streets before the eyes of other men, except when she has to go to the Temple and pray. In this case, she should make sure to go not when the marketplace is full, but when most of the people have returned home; and so like a free-born citizen worthy of the name, with everything quiet around her, she makes her oblations and offers her prayers to avert evil things and gain good things. 172 Reviling under the pretext of assisting their husbands in the fight is reprehensible and shameless in a high degree. The law has considered that in wars and military services or in dangers that threaten the whole country, they should not have the right to scrutinize. In them there is accustomed the fitness of things that it was resolved to keep unshaken always and everywhere and was considered in itself to be more valuable than victory of any kind. 173 If indeed a woman, learning that her husband is outraged, gives way to his desires because of her love for him, she should constrain passion. She must not unsex herself by a boldness beyond what nature permits, but she must limit herself to the ways in which a woman can help. For it would be terrible if a woman, in her wish to rescue her husband from outrage, should outrage herself by befouling her own life with disgrace and being reproached for her incurable audacity.

Prob. 117: We think, then, while the women and the lads, the former endowed by nature with little sense, and the latter at an age so insecure, are imbued with so profound a love of liberty, that to save themselves from losing it, they seek death as eagerly as if it were immortality (*QE* 2.39). Can we suppose, I say, that those who have tasted of unalloyed wisdom are not at once thoroughly free, those who bear within them a wellspring of happiness, the virtue in themselves, which any malignant force has ever yet subdued because sovereignty and kingship are its everlasting heritage?[23]

Male *versus* Female

Det. 172–173a: Each of the seven faculties comes into existence as the male in one way, and as the female in another way. Since it is either in restraint or in motion; it is in restraint when at rest in sleep; and it is in motion when now awake and active, when regarded under the aspect of restraint and inaction, it is called female, owing to its having been reduced to passivity; when looked at under the aspect of movement and employment of force, being thought of as in action, it is named male. 173a Thus, in the wise, the seven faculties are manifested clean, but according to the law of contraries, in the wicked man, all are exposed to punishment.

Migr. 95–96: Also, I admire the all-virtuous Leah, because when she gave birth to Asher, a symbol of a sensible counterfeit wealth and visible, she cried out: "happy I am, for the women will call me happy" (Gen. 30:13). She was aiming at her gentle character, thinking not only from thoughts masculine and from men's attitude of mind to be truly praiseworthy by which the nature, undefiled and true integrity, is held in honor, but also from those who are more feminine, who are all at the mercy of appearances outside those who are able to understand contemplation. 96 It is characteristic of a perfect soul to aspire "to be" and also to be "thought," and to take pains, and not only to have a good reputation in the men's quarters, but also to receive the praises of the women's quarters as well.

Abr. 55: For the nature of the human is corruptible, but the nature of virtue is incorruptible. It is more reasonable that what is eternal should be conjoined with what is imperishable than with what is mortal, since imperishableness is akin to eternity, but death is at enmity with it.

Abr. 102: If anyone is willing to discard facts of the terms that tend to obscure them, and observe them in their nakedness in a clear light, he will understand that the virtue is male by nature, as it sets in motion and puts in order and suggests noble ideas of noble actions and words; but reason is female, as it is moved by another and is trained and helped and examined, and, in general, belongs to the passive category, in which passivity is its sole means of preservation.

Spec. 1.200–201: Although these contents of the ordinance are taken literally, they reveal another meaning, that of the mystical character that symbols convey. Words in their clear sense are symbols of the latent and obscure. Clearly, the victim of the burnt offering is masculine because the male is more perfect and superior and akin to active cause than the female. For the female is incomplete and in subjection and belongs to the category of the passive rather than the active. 201 There are two ingredients out of which our soul is combined: the rational and the irrational. The rational belongs to the mind and reason is of the masculine, but the irrational belongs to the sense-perception and is of the feminine. As the mind is superior to sense-perception, as man is to woman, mind belongs to the genus, wholly superior to sense-perception. The mind is unblemished and purged, as perfect virtue purges; it is itself the most religious of sacrifices and its whole being is highly pleasing to God (*QE* 2.108).

Gig. 4–5: The spiritual soul of the unjust is never male; instead, the offspring of men whose thoughts are unmanly, emasculate, and effeminate are female. Such effeminates plant no tree of virtue, whose fruit must be trueborn and excellent and noble, but trees of vice and passions, whose shoots are also effeminate. 5 This is why we are told that these men begat daughters, while none of the daughters is said to have begotten a son. For since the righteous Noah, who follows the perfect and right reason, begets masculine children (*QG* 1.88),[24] the injustice of the crowd appears exclusively to generate females. For it is impossible that the same things should be born of opposite parents; rather, they must necessarily have an opposite offspring.

Spec. 3.175: While all else might be tolerable, it is a grievous thing when a woman acts so defiantly as to catch hold of the genital parts of her opponent (Deut. 15:11–12). The fact that she does so with the clear intention of helping her husband must not absolve her. To restrain her overboldness, she must pay a penalty that will incapacitate her, if she wishes to repeat the offense, and frighten the more reckless women into proper behavior. The penalty shall be this: the hand that has touched what decency forbids to touch shall be cut off.

Contempl. 33–35: The wall between the two chambers is built up to the three or four cubits above the floor in the form of a breastwork, while the space above up to the roof is left open. This arrangement serves two purposes: that the modesty proper to women's nature is clearly to be maintained, and that the women seated within earshot with nothing to obstruct the voice of the speaker may obtain easy apprehension. 34 They lay down self-control as a sort of foundation of their soul to build up the other virtues. None of them may take bread or drink before sunset, since they judge philosophy to be worthy of the light, but the needs of the body are suitable to darkness, on which account they assign the day to the one and a brief portion of the night to the other.[25] 35 Some, in whom there is implanted a longing for knowledge, remember to take food even after only every third day. But others are so delighted and enjoy themselves in being banqueted by wisdom, which richly and free from envy, supplies her teachings, that they hold out double that time and scarcely after every sixth day partake of necessary sustenance.[26]

HUMAN SEXUALITY

Sex

Cher. 43–44: Thus, the right instruction must begin this way. Man and woman, the human male and female, in compliance with nature, join in sexual intimacy for the procreation of children (*QG* 4.15; *QE* 1.7–8). But virtues that are productive of innumerable perfections may not have mortal human for their lot; yet if they receive not the seed of generation from another they will never of themselves conceive. 44 Therefore, who is he who sows in them the good seed except He who is the Father of the universe, that is God the Uncreated and Begetter of all things together? He, thus, sows the offspring of His own. He, Who sows seed, bestows as a gift. For God engenders nothing for Himself, for He is in need of nothing, but all for him who begs to receive.

Sacr. 100–103: Therefore, who does not know that the two greatest blessings of human beings are a happy old age and a happy death, yet in neither has nature any share, for she knows neither old age nor death? What is incredible is that the Uncreated does not deign to use the good that belongs to the created, when even the created itself lays claim to virtues differing according to the different species into which it is divided? At any rate, men could not compete with women nor women with men, the functions that fitly belong only to the other sex. If women should imitate the practices of men, they would be looked upon as half of men, and if men attempt those of women, they would acquire ill-fame as men-women. 101 So, nature has discriminated some virtues, that not even long practice could make them common property. At any rate, to sow seed and beget belong to man and is his own excellence, and no woman can attain to it. Again, man's nature does not make him capable of a happy childbirth, which is a good thing belonging to women. Thus, even the phrase "as a man" cherished his son (Deut. 1:31) is not used of God in its literal sense, but it is a term used in a figurative sense, a word of help to our feeble apprehension. Separate then, my soul, all that is created, mortal, mutable, profane, from your conception of God, the Uncreated, the Unchangeable, the Immortal, the Holy, and solely Blessed. 102 And the words "of all that opened the womb, the males for the Lord" (Exod. 13:12) are indeed true to nature. For just as nature has given the womb to women as the most proper part for generation of living offspring, so she has set in the soul for the generation of things a power by which the understanding is pregnant and in travail it conceives many children. 103 Of the thoughts thus brought to the birth some are males, and some are females, just as in the case of living beings. Therefore, the female offspring of the soul is wickedness and passion, by which we are made feminine, which would affect us in each of our pursuits, while the male offspring is happiness and virtue, by which we are stimulated and strengthened. Of these the men's quarters must be dedicated wholly to God, and the women's quarters must be set to our own account, and therefore we have the command, "all that opened the womb, the males are for the Lord."

Spec. 3.176 The managers of gymnastic competitions also deserve praise for debarring women from the spectacle, so that they may not be present when men are stripping themselves naked, nor debase the approved coinage of modesty by disregarding the statutes of nature that she has laid down for each section of our race. Also, men cannot be present when women are taking off their clothes. Each sex should turn away from seeing the nakedness of the other and so comply with what nature has willed.

Aet. 69: We have now discussed adequately the nonsense things of those who fortify falsehood against the truth. We must know well that human beings spring from human beings; a man sows seed into the womb as into arable field, and the woman receives the seed safely; nature invisibly molds and shapes each part of the body and soul and bestows upon the race as a whole what individually we were not able to receive, that is, immortality. For the race remains forever, while particular specimens perish, in very truth an extraordinary and divine work. And if a man, a small portion of the All, is eternal, the world is surely uncreated as it is also indestructible.

Abr. 100–101a: Now marriage, where the union is brought about by pleasure, the partnership is between body and body, but in the marriage made by wisdom it is between thoughts that seek purification and perfect virtues. The two kinds of marriage are directly opposed to each other (*QG* 4.86). 101a According to the bodily marriage, the male sows the seed and the female receives the seed; but according to the mating within the souls, though the virtue seemingly ranks as wife, her natural function is to sow good counsels and excellent words and to inculcate tenets truly profitable to life, while thought, though held to take the place of the husband, receives the holy and divine sowings.[27]

EDUCATION AND PROPHECY

Education

Post. 140–141: Moses goes on to portray with great skill the method followed by the teacher who wants to do her pupils good: "she hastened," he says, "and let down the pitcher on to her arms." Through the "hastening" her keenness to do a kindness is revealed, a keenness that comes from a disposition from which envy has been utterly expelled. By the "letting down on to her arm" we are shown how the teacher comes down to the learner and attentively studies as one whom he is intimately concerned. 141 For teachers, who, when they set about giving their lessons, keep in view their own great superiority and not the capacity of their pupils, are simpletons, who are not aware how vast is the difference between a lesson and a display. For he, who is giving a display, employs to the full the rich yield of the mastery that he possesses, and without hindrance he brings forward into the open the results of hours spent in labor by himself at home. Such are the works of artists or sculptors. In all of this, he is trying to gain the praise of the public. The man, on the other hand, who is setting out to teach, is like a good doctor, who with his eyes fixed not on the vastness of his science, but on the strength of his patient, applies to all that he has ready for use from the resources of his knowledge; for this is endless but it is what the sick man needs, seeking to avoid both defect and excess.

Ebr. 34–36: Therefore, the prescription of the father, reason, follows the rules of nature and to pursue truth in her naked and undisguised form. But education, the mother, bids us to pay heed to the righteous laid down by human ordinances, rules that have been made in different cities and nations and countries by those who first embraced the apparent in preference to the true. 35 These parents have four classes of children: the obedient to both, the direct opposite, and gives heed to neither, while each of the other two is half perfect. One of them is heartily devoted to the father and gives ear to him but pays no regard to the mother and her injunctions. The other, on the contrary, seems to be a lover of its mother, and serves her in everything, but gives little attention to the things of its father. Of these four the first will carry off the prize of victory over all comers, and the second, its opposite, will receive defeat accompanied by destruction. Each of the others will claim a prize, one the second, the other the third; the second belongs to the class that obeys the father, and the third to the class that obeys the mother. 36 Thus, this last kind, which loves the mother, bows down to the opinions of the multitude, and undergoes all manner of transformations according to the ever-varying aspirations of life, like the Egyptian Proteus, whose true form remained a matter of uncertainty through his power to become everything in the universe, is most clearly typified by Jethro.[28]

Ebr. 80–81: Let us, then, speak next of those who are enemies of these last, but have given high honor to both education and right reason, among whom are the ones who attach themselves to one of the parents, being but half-hearted followers in virtue. These, therefore, are of the laws, which their father, right reason, laid down, and are bravest guardians and faithful housekeepers of the traditions, which their mother, instruction, has introduced. 81

Their father, right reason, has taught them to honor the Father of all; while the mother, instruction, has taught them not to make light of those principles that are laid down by convention and accepted everywhere.²⁹

Congr. 122–123: Therefore, the text continues as follows: "he came into Hagar" (Gen. 16:4), for it was suitable that the learner should resort to knowledge as his teacher to be instructed in the lessons suited to human nature (*QG* 4.156). In the present case, the learner is introduced to the teacher's school, but often knowledge rids herself of jealousy, runs out to meet the gifted disciples, and draws them into her company. 123 At any rate, Leah, the virtue, goes forth to meet and to see the man of practice (Jacob), when he was returning from the field; she says to him, "you shall come in unto me today" (Gen. 30:16). How does he, who is tending the seeds and the saplings of knowledge, come to virtue, the field of his husbandry?³⁰

Prophecy/Prophet

Deus 138–139: Every intelligent soul that is destined to become a widow and empty from evils says to the prophet "O man of God, you came in to remind me of my wrongdoings and of my sins" (1 Kgs. 17:18). For when he, the one who is inspired, entered the soul, and he, who is mastered of the celestial love and stirred to his very depth by the irresistible goads of god-sent frenzy, creates a memory of past wrong deeds and sins; not in order that the soul may return to them again, but that, with deep groaning and many tears for its former error, it may hate all that it has engendered, and reject them with aversion, and may follow instead the guidance of that reason which is the interpreter and prophet of God (*QG* 4.212, 245). 139 For the men of old days called the prophets sometimes "men of God," and sometimes "seers" (1 Sam. 9:9), affixing appropriate and suitable names to their inspiration and to the wide vision of reality, which they possessed.

Her. 69–73: Thus, if any yearning comes to you, my soul, to inherit the good things of God, leave not only your land, that is the body, and your kinsfolk, that is sense-perception, and your father's house (Gen. 12:1), that is speech; but also run away from yourself and drive out from yourself. Like persons possessed, be filled with inspired frenzy, even as a prophet who is inspired. 70 For it is the mind, which is under the divine afflatus, and no longer in its own keeping, but it is stirred excitedly in a heavenly love, and is led by the truly Existent One. It is pulled upward to Him, with truth to lead the way and remove all obstacles from its feet, so that it may advance on the path smoothly and easily. Such is the mind, which has this inheritance. 71 Therefore, to that mind I say, take courage and tell us the story about your departure from that first place. For to those who have been taught by hearing the things of the mind, you always say the tale: I migrated from the body when

I had ceased to regard the flesh; from sense-perception, when I understood all the things of sense-perception as nonexistent in reality, when I denounced its standards of judgment as spurious and corrupt and steeped in false opinion, and denounced also its judgments, as to entice and to deceive and ravish truth away from its place in the heart of nature; from the speech, when I sentenced its long speech, and indeed, its self-exaltation and self-pride. 72 For great indeed was its audacity, that it should attempt the impossible task, namely, to show me material through substances, and deeds through facts. Amid all its blunders, it chattered and gushed about, unable to present with clear expression those distinctions in things that baffled its vague and general vocabulary. 73 Thus, through experience, as a foolish and a silly child, I learned that it was better to depart from all these things and to ascribe the faculties of each to God, Who puts together the body with bodily forms, and provides the senses to perceive, and extends to speech the faculty of speaking.

Her. 259–260: Every clever man witnesses the gift of prophecy, which is the holy Word. A prophet does not speak his own opinion plainly, but all strange things correspond to someone else. The wicked does not become an interpreter of God's ordinances, so that no wretched person is Lord-inspired. This name only suits to the wise, since he alone is the vocal instrument of God, smitten and played by His invisible hand. 260 Thus, as many as all of those whom Moses describes as righteous are pictured as possessed and are leading in prophesying (*QG* 2.48). Noah was a righteous man. Was he not a direct prophet? Were not the curses that he called down on subsequent generations, the prayers that he made on their behalf, all of which the actual event confirmed, uttered by him under divine possession?

Mos. 1.174–175: "... Why are you quick to trust in the specious and plausible, and that only? When God gives help, there is no need to provide Him with anything. It is God's own property to find a way where there is no way. The things that are impossible to all created beings are possible to Him only, ready to His hand." 175 Further, he discoursed to them while standing still. But after a short time, he became possessed and being filled with the Spirit, which was accustomed to visit him, he prophesizes these words: "the army that you see armed to the teeth, you shall no longer see arrayed against you. For it shall all fall in utter ruin and disappear in depth, so that no remnant may be seen above the earth, and this shall be at not a distant time, but in the coming night."

Mos. 1. 277: He looked and said, "Oh king, you build seven altars to sacrifice a calf and a ram on each, and I will go aside and inquire of God, what I shall say." Advancing outside he becomes immediately possessed, and there fell upon him the truly prophetic Spirit (*QE* 2.27, 105), which banished utterly from his soul his prophetic art. For what was established as a custom for the magical Sophistry was not to live together with the inspiration of the Holiest. Then, turning back, he saw the sacrifices and the altars flaming.

Mos. 2. 69–70: This last thing he had disdained for many days, almost from the time when, possessed by the Spirit, he was the first to prophesize, since he held it fitting to hold himself always ready to receive the oracular message. And eating and drinking he paid no regard on the successive forty days, evidently because he had the better food of contemplation with which he was inspired from above from heaven, by which he grew in grace, first in mind, then in body, and through his soul, and in both (mind and body), he advanced in strength and well-being that those who saw him afterward were in disbelief. 70 For by God's command he ascended to an unapproachable and inaccessible mountain, the highest and holiest in the region. He remained in that place all that time, taking nothing that is needed to satisfy the requirements of bare sustenance. And after forty days, as he says, he descended with the appearance far more beautiful than when he ascended; so that those who saw him were filled with awe and amazement, and nothing could further hold their eyes against the bright splendor flashing after the approach.

Spec. 1.64–65: Since a desire to know the future has settled in all men and inquire this on the art of the diviner, they turn to other forms of prophecy, as if by these means they would find the clear truth in them. However, they are full of uncertainties and many of them always convict themselves of falsehood, while the prophet forbids them vehemently to vigorously follow such sources of knowledge, though he says that if they have true piety, they will not be denied the full knowledge of the future. 65 A prophet possessed by God will suddenly appear and give oracular prophecies. Nothing that he says will be his own. For he, who is controlled and is truly inspired, has no power of apprehension when he speaks, but he is a channel for the insistent words of another's prompting as if he is possessed by divine inspiration. For prophets are the interpreters of God, Who makes full use of their voices as instruments to manifest what He wills. Such things like these suggest an explanation about the conception of the One truly existing God. Next, he proceeds to indicate how the honors due to Him should be paid.

Spec. 1.315 If anyone assuming the name and appearance of a prophet, appearing to prophesize God's words, thinking to be possessed and inspired by the Spirit, lead us on to the religious worship of the gods recognized and honored in cities, we ought not to listen to him and be deceived by the name of prophet. For such a one is not a prophet, but a sorcerer; since he has fabricated his oracles and his pronouncements are falsehoods.[31]

NOTES

1. *Her.* 230–231; *Spec.* 1.80–81; 3.207.
2. See also *Conf.* 168–182; *Mut.* 27–32.
3. For a good study on this topic, see Sterling, "Different Traditions or Emphases: The Image of God in Philo's *De opificio mundi*," in Gary Anderson, Ruth Clements, and David Satran, eds., *New Approaches to the Study of Biblical Interpretation in Judaism of the Second Temple Period and in Early Christianity: Proceedings of the Eleventh International Symposium of the Orion Center for the Study of the Dead Sea Scrolls and Related Literature, June 2007* (Leiden: Brill, 2013), 41–56.
4. For further discussion on this important topic in Philo, see Tobin, *The Creation of Man*, 77–86, 102–134.
5. See also *Leg.* 1.31–32; cf. *QG* 1.4, 8a; 2.56. In Philo's interpretation of Gen. 2:7–8 and 2:15 the distinction is between "two minds" of the double creation of man: the human in Gen. 2:7–8 is the human created in Gen. 2:7 and the one in 2:15 is the human created in Gen. 1:26–27. The latter is "the pure mind" assimilated to the Logos, the archetype, the seal, a purer and clearer mind associated with virtue. The former is the molded mind, the earthly and perishable mind.
6. See *Opif.* 30, 53, 69; *Leg.* 2.6; *Fug.* 182; *Somn.* 2.207; *Abr.* 57; *Mos.* 2.82; *Spec.* 1.18; *Prob.* 146.
7. *Gig.* 60; *Deus* 46; *Plant.* 18.
8. *Her.* 152–153, 281–283; *Somn.* 1.33–34; *Spec.* 4.123; *QG* 2.59.
9. *Somn.* 1.34, 146; *Spec.* 3.207.
10. Paragraphs 53 and 55.
11. *Leg.* 2.4–5; *Mut.* 183–185; *Sacr.* 8–10.
12. *Sacr.* 71; *Post.* 156–157; *Praem.* 162–164.
13. *Gig.* 53–57; *Ios.* 143–147; *Mos.* 1.47–50, 244–249; 2.273–274; *Praem.* 4–5; *Aet.* 10–11; *Hypoth.* 11.16; *Legat.* 215–217.
14. This is the mind of the earthly human.
15. *Leg.* 3.49–50, 59–61, 182–185, 222–233; *Post.* 177–179; *Ebr.* 169; *Conf.* 73–74, 126–127; *Congr.* 11–12; *Somn.* 1.77–184, 118–119; *Legat.* 1–3.
16. Philo insists in the tripartite division of the soul found in various passages of his corpus, but the expression "as it has been shown" refers, particularly, to what has been said in para. 232, where he distinguishes one rational mind and one irrational, one true word and one false, and one sensorial apprehension corresponding to an objective reality and another that cannot grasp anything real. This division corresponds to the soul not in the broad sense composed of mind, an irascible part and desirable part, but in a restrictive sense of the cognitive soul, or "soul of the soul," as para. 55 says.
17. The part in parentheses is a hypothetical reconstruction to fill up the lacuna of the Greek text. The idea is that memory is the most recent because it supposes a fixation that commonly it is not given at the initial stage of the collecting memories.
18. The learned knowledge but not yet memorized.
19. *Det.* 65; *Deus* 41–44; *Sobr.* 27–29.
20. *Migr.* 14–15; *Abr.* 164–166.

21. *Opif.* 53; *Agr.* 25, 55–58; *Ebr.* 144–146; *Conf.* 176–177; *Somn.* 1.112–114; *Praem.* 10–14, 64–66; *Prob.* 158–160.

22. *Opif.* 165–169; *Leg.* 1.92–95; 2.73; *Agr.* 72–77; *Her.* 137–139, 274; *Fug.* 52–54; *Spec.* 178–180.

23. *Leg.* 2.19–23, 44, 50–51; 3.200–202; *Cher.* 40–42; *Migr.* 206; *Spec.* 2.135–139; *Virt.* 39–40; 22–225.

24. Shem, Ham, and Japheth (Gen. 10:1).

25. *Contempl.* 24–26, 65–67, 75–82, 88–90.

26. *Opif.* 152–153; *Leg.* 3.49–50, 56, 59–63, 189–191, 220–224; *Cher.* 40–41; *Ebr.* 69–71; *Migr.* 99–100; *Det.* 28; *Post.* 177–179; *Plant.* 105–106; *Congr.* 58–59; *Fug.* 51; *Abr.* 102; *Spec.* 3.2.1–3, 32–34, 60–61; *Virt.* 18–21.

27. *Ebr.* 220–222; *Aet.* 69–70; *Hypoth.* 11–14.

28. *Cher.* 72–73; *Her.* 48–49; *Congr.* 85–87; *Mut.* 261; *Sob.* 6–9; *Virt.* 208–210; *Aet.* 59–61.

29. *Ebr.* 30–33; *Mut.* 137–138; *Mos.* 2.207–208; *Spec.* 2.129–137, 226–229, 233–236; *Praem.* 134–135; *Aet.* 69–70; *Prov.* 2.2–6; *Hypoth.* 7.2–3, 14.

30. *Somn.* 2.68–69.

31. *Abr.* 111–113; *Mos.* 2.67, 76, 271–275.

BIBLIOGRAPHY

Baer, Richard A. *Philo's Use of the Categories Male and Female.* Arbeiten zur Literatur und Geschichte des Hellenistischen Judentums 3. Leiden: Brill, 1970.

Calabi, Francesca. *God's Acting, Man's Acting: Tradition and Philosophy in Philo of Alexandria.* Leiden: Brill, 2008.

Melnick, R. "On the Philonic Conception of the Whole Man." *Journal for the Study of Judaism* 11 (1980): 1–32.

Runia, David T. "God and Man in Philo of Alexandria." *The Journal of Theological Studies* 39 (1988): 48–75.

Runia, David T. "Philo of Alexandria on the Human Consequences of Divine Power. Pages 245–56 in *Pouvoir et Puissances chez Philon d'Alexandrie.* Edited by Francesca Calabi et al. Monothéismes et Philosophie 22. Brepols: Turnhout, 2016.

Sterling, Gregory E. "The Body as Metaphor: The Structure of a Human and the Meaning of Scripture." *Novum Testamentum* 61 (2019): 26–39.

Tobin, Thomas H. "Philo's *Legum Allegoriae*: The Thread of the Argument." *Biblical Research* 56 (2011): 9–22.

Winston, David. "The Psyche and Its Extra-Terrestrial Life in Philo's Anthropology." Pages 27–42 in *Logos and Mystical Theology in Philo of Alexandria.* Cincinnati: Hebrew Union College Press, 1985.

Chapter 4

Philo's Doctrine of Ethics

This chapter offers the reader a very good understanding of Philo's ethical understanding within the Greek philosophical understanding of virtue ethics. The Greek philosophical ethical systems of Plato, Stoics, Aristotle, and Middle Platonists are reflected in Philo's view of the various ethical topics and themes. His interpretation of virtues and vices is mainly dependent on the Platonic and Stoic traditions. His emphasis on the practice of virtues reflects his Hellenistic Jewish tradition and Greek influence, particularly the three elements of virtue: instruction (Abraham), practice (Jacob), and nature (Isaac). As Philo interprets the three Patriarchs' roles in the attainment of virtue, he interprets allegorically the four cardinal or generic virtues as the four rivers of Eden (Gen. 2:10–14), which is the wisdom of God. While Philo's interpretation of the middle path to virtue (that is perfection) is a clear reflection of the Aristotelian doctrine of the mean, his understanding of the virtue has been influenced by the understanding of the Socratic doctrine of "virtue is one." However, unlike Plato, the Stoics, Aristotle, and Middle Platonists, for Philo the virtue *par excellence* is piety, and not prudence. His connection between virtues and the knowledge of God clearly shows the tradition of Platonic and Middle Platonic interpretations. Also, his interpretation of the goal of human life (likeness to God or become like God) is certainly (Middle) Platonic; but it also is expressed in the Pythagorean (to follow God), Stoic (live according to nature), and the Aristotelian language of becoming godlike.

An important feature in Philo's ethical discourse is his centrality in God; his theocentric view, which is rooted in his Jewish tradition, goes intrinsically connected with the virtue of piety, the queen of all the other virtues. As in other Hellenistic Jewish texts, particularly *4 Maccabees*, Philo identifies piety as a cardinal or generic virtue and describes the practice of virtue (piety) as the way of the Jewish life. Likewise, he consistently connects Logos with virtue and the four cardinal virtues and treats goodness as a generic virtue. The ultimate prize of achieving the goal, happiness, is expressed in the language familiar to both the Jewish Hellenistic and Greek philosophical authors. In essence, Philo's writings are centered in ethics, and as the reader will know, his theology, cosmology, anthropology, and his understanding of the ethical commandments of the *Decalogue* in conjunction with the Jewish observances find a unity in his ethics.

VIRTUE-ETHICS

Virtues

Sacr. 26b–27: Suddenly, coming forward she appeared bringing forward all the marks of a free-born citizen; she walks standing firm; her person and her modesty alike without false coloring, her moral nature free from guile, also her conduct from stain, her will from craft, her speech from falsehood, reflecting faithfully the honesty of her sound thoughts. Her carriage was unaffected, her motion was not agitated, her clothing moderate, her adornment that of prudence and virtue. 27 And they bring to her piety, holiness, truth to laws and holy rights, fidelity to oaths, justice, equity, good arrangement, fellowship, self-mastery, temperance, orderliness, self-control, frugality, contentment, docility, modesty, love of quiet life, courage, nobility, good counsel, forethought, prudence, diligence, amendment, cheerfulness, kindness, gentleness, mildness, love of humanity, high-mindedness, blessedness, and goodness. The daylight will fail me if I were to say the names of the specific virtues.

Det. 60–61: Happiness also means the enjoyment of virtue, not only simply a possession. But I could not exercise it unless you send down the seeds from heaven to cause Sarah to be pregnant, and unless she gives birth to Isaac, happiness. I have made up my mind that happiness is the exercise of perfect virtue in a perfect life. Since He is also well pleased with the motive of his answer and consents to bring and pass in due season what he had requested. 61 To Abraham, therefore, the answer brought praise, acknowledging that even virtue by itself is insufficient without God's divine providence to assist. While to Cain, correspondingly, his answer brought blame; since he said that he did not know where his brother was. For he had treacherously slain him. He imagined that he would deceive God, to whom he gave the answer, as though He did not clearly see all things, and had not anticipated the deception to which he was going to resort.

Plant. 41–42: While man's possessions have wildest animals as guards and wild beasts as protectors to watch and guard them against being attacked and overrun, God's possessions are guarded by rational beings. For it says, "He placed there the human being whom He fashioned," that is to say, both the practices and exercises of the virtues belong to the rational beings only (*QE*

2.53). 42 This they received at the hands of God, as a preeminent privilege above the lives of the irrational creatures. And that is why it is stated in the most vivid manner that the true man in us, that is to say, the mind was set in the holiest offshoots and the plant growths of noble character; since among beings without understanding there is not one who is capable of tilling virtues, for they are by nature utterly incompetent to apprehend them.

Ebr. 133–135: Since the One Who is Creator made both the pattern and the copy in all that He has made, virtue was not an exception. He also wrought its archetypal seal and has stamped with this an impression that was its close counterpart. The archetypal seal, then, is an incorporeal idea, but the copy, which is made by the impression, is something else, a material something, naturally sense-perceptible, though not actually coming into relation with sense-perception. Just as we might say that a piece of wood buried in the deepest part of the Atlantic Ocean has a natural capacity for being burnt, though actually it will never be consumed by fire because the sea is around and above it. 134 Thus, we may consider the Tabernacle and the altar as "ideas": the first being a symbol of incorporeal virtue, the other a symbol of its sensible image. Now, the altar and what is upon it can easily be seen. For it is constructed outdoors and the fire that consumes the offering is never extinguished, and thus by night as well as by day it is in bright light. 135 But the Tabernacle and all the things placed on it are invisible, not only because they are placed in the innermost and the heart of the Sanctuary, but also because according to the ordinance of the law, anyone who touches them, or looks at them with a too curious eye, is punished with death, and against that sense there is no appeal. The only exception made is for one who should be free from all defects, not wasting himself with any passion great or small, but endowed with a nature sound and most perfect in all respect.

Her. 241–242: Some of our thoughts fly together with virtue leading upward to the divine and heavenly place, while others downward to the worse lot fall, for vice goes in front and pulls them by force toward the wrong direction. Also, the opposite character to which these two places belong is shown most clearly by their names. Virtue is so named not only because we choose it (*airesis*), but also because of its uplifting (*arsis*); for it is lifted and moved so high because of its continual yearnings for the celestial. Vice is so named because wickedness has gone down and because it compels those who have to do with it to fall down likewise. 242 At least, then, the hostile thoughts of the soul, hovering over and visiting them, again not only come down themselves, but also bring down the thoughts shamefully rushing upon the material things, not immaterial, to the things sensible not the intelligible, to the things imperfect not the perfect, to those that are corrupt not to those things that are likely to live. For they not only mix with bodies but also with parts of the bodies divided in two. And it is impossible that bodies divided in this way should ever admit of joining or unifying the spiritual strengths, which were the most congenital bonds broken in two.

Congr. 11–12: We must understand that great themes require great introductions, and the greatest of all the themes is virtue. For virtue deals with the greatest of materials, that is the entire life of human beings. Therefore, it is natural that virtue will employ no minor kind of introduction, but grammar, geometry, astronomy, rhetoric, music with all the other studies, which are symbolized by Hagar the handmaid of Sarah, as we shall show. 12 For Sarah, we are told, said to Abraham: "behold the Lord has shut me out from bearing. Go in unto my handmaid, so that you may beget children from her" (Gen. 16:1). We must exclude from the present discussion bodily unions or intercourse having pleasure as its goal. For the mind is a companion to virtue and desires to have children by her, and if it is not possible immediately, it is instructed to espouse virtue's handmaid, the intermediate education.

Mos. 2.180–181: The fruits were nuts, which in nature are the opposite of other fruits, for in most fruit, such as the grapes, the olive, the apple, there is a difference between the seed and the edible part, and this difference divides in their respective circumstances. For the edible part is outside, and the seed is shut up within. But in the case of the nut the seed and the edible part are the same, for the two of them merged into a single form, shielded and guarded on all sides by a double fence, composed partly from a very thick shell and partly of a substance equivalent to a wooden framework. 181 In this way, it signifies perfect virtue (*QG* 3.60; 4.214). For just as in a nut, beginning and end, are the same, beginning represented by the seed and the end by the fruit, so also it is the case with the virtues.[1] For there, too, it is the same that each is both a beginning and an end; a beginning because it springs from any other power but itself, and an end because it is the aspiration of the life that follows nature.[2]

THE ALLEGORICAL INTERPRETATION OF THE FOUR CARDINAL VIRTUES

Note

In the *Laws*, Plato asserts that there are four cardinal virtues,[3] and in their ethical system the Stoics followed Plato's four cardinal virtues.[4] In light of the traditions of Plato and the Stoics, Philo praises the four cardinal virtues, and allegorically, he treats them as the four rivers of Eden. Each of them takes the role of generic virtue from which all the virtues flow, and he identifies the virtue of prudence as the River Pheison and Eden as Goodness.

The Generic Virtues

Leg. 1.45–47: Therefore, God sows and plants earthly virtue for this mortal race as a copy and reflection of the heavenly virtue. For pitying our race and seeing that it was composed of plentiful and abundant evils, He caused earthly virtue to strike root, as an ally and defender against the diseases of the soul, a copy, as I said, of the heavenly and archetypal virtue, which Moses calls by many names. Virtue is figuratively called "garden," and a place, a home suited to the garden "Eden," which means "luxury." And peace and comfort and joy, in which living luxuriously truly consists, fit well with virtue. 46 Again, it mentions that the planting of the garden is "toward the east," for right reason does not set, nor is it quenched, but its nature is always to rise. And, I believe, just as the sun when it rises fills the gloom of the air with light, so too virtue, when it rises in the soul, illuminates its mist and scatters its deep darkness. 47 "And He placed there," it says, "the human being whom He molded." For God—since He is good and trains our race for virtue as the task most suited to it—places the mind amid virtue, so that as a good gardener it may clearly care for and honor nothing other than mind.

Leg. 1.77–79: It then says, "whose the gold is" (Gen. 2:11). It does not say only that the "gold is there," but that "there is he 'whose' it is." For prudence, which he has compared to gold, a genuine substance and pure and cleansed by fire and tested and precious in nature, is there in the Wisdom of God (*QG* 4.121; *QE* 2.3). But being there, it is not a possession of wisdom, but of him to whom wisdom itself also belongs, even God Who is the Maker and Owner of it. 78 "Now the gold of that land is beautiful" (Gen. 2:12a). Is there, then, other gold that is not beautiful? Yes, indeed, there is. For prudence is of two kinds: the one universal, and the other particular. The prudence that is in me, since it is particular, is not beautiful, for when I perish it perishes along with me. But the universal prudence, which dwells in the Wisdom of God and His dwelling place, is beautiful, for, being itself imperishable, it abides in an imperishable dwelling. 79 "And there is the ruby and the green stone" (Gen. 2:12b), these are two kinds, the one who is prudent, and the one who exercises prudence. The one is constituted in accord with prudence, and the person acting prudently is constituted by prudently acting. For it is for the sake of these that God sowed/planted in the earth-born human being prudence (in particular) and virtue (in general). For what would have been the use of it, if there had been no reasoning powers in existence to receive it, and to give impressions of its form? So that where prudence is, there is quite reasonably/suitably both the one who is prudent and the one who acts prudently, the stones (*QG* 2.23; 3.53; *QE* 2.17).

Fug. 176: Can you see the abundance of good things pouring upon them, great and ready for possession and enjoyment? The generic virtues are compared to cities because they have the greatest expanse; the special virtues to houses, for these are restricted to a narrower compass. And the souls endowed with good native ability are likened to cisterns, being ready to receive wisdom as these cisterns do water. Vineyards and olive-yards represent progress and growth and the production of fruits; the fruit of knowledge is the life of contemplation, winning for us unmixed gladness as from wine and intellectual light as from a flame, which oil feeds.

Somn. 2.241–244: Moses has provided to those who are able to see the clearest examples of both. For "a river," he says, "goes out from Eden to water the garden. From there, it separates into four heads" (Gen. 2:10). 242 He gives the name of Eden, which is interpreted "delight," to the Wisdom of the Existent One, because I suppose without a doubt, wisdom is a source of delight to God and God to wisdom; since in the Psalms the singer bids us to "delight in the Lord" (Ps. 37[36]:4). The Word of God comes down from the fountain of wisdom as a river to lave and water the heaven-sent celestial shoots and plants of virtue-loving souls who are as a garden. 243 This holy Word is separated into four heads and, I say, that it is split up into the four virtues, of which each is a queen. For separation into heads is not like separation into local regions but into kingdoms, and when he points to the virtues, he actually means to represent the wise, who possesses them as a king, a king appointed not by human beings but by nature, the infallible, the incorruptible, the only free elector. 244 For it was said to Abraham by those who perceived his cleverness, "you are a king from God with us" (Gen. 23:6). They laid down the doctrine for the students of philosophy, that the wise alone is a ruler and a king, and virtue a rule and kingship whose authority is final.

Mos. 2.185–186: But if it is necessary to say the truth that the holiest company of prudence, temperance, courage, and justice follow in the train of the practicers and many who devote themselves to a life of austerity and hardship, self-control, and patience, with simplicity and frugal contentment, through this the highest lord of all in us, reason, advances to sound health and well-being, diminishing the oppressive fort of the body, drunkenness and gluttony, and lewdness, and the other insatiable desires, the parents of that grossness of flesh that is the enemy of quickness of mind (*QG* 1.73). 186 Indeed, they also say that of all the trees that regularly bud in the spring the almond-tree is the first to flourish with a welcome promise of a plentiful crop of fruits, and the last to shed its leaves, extending the yearly old age of its verdure to the longest period. Each of these facts Moses takes as a symbol of the priestly tribe, intimating that it will be the first and the last of all the human race to blossom, in that day, whenever it shall be, when it shall please God to make our life as a springtime by destroying covetousness, that insidious foe and the source of our misery.

Mos. 2.215–216: It was customary on every day when opportunity offered, and primarily on the seventh day, as I have explained before, to practice philosophy with the ruler guiding and teaching what one must do and say, while they improved and advanced in goodness, moral character, and conduct. 216 Even now this practice is retained, and the Jews every seventh day occupy themselves with the philosophy of their fathers, dedicating that time to knowledge and contemplation of the truths of nature. For what are our places of prayer throughout the cities other than teaching places of prudence and courage and temperance and justice, both piety and holiness and of every virtue by which duties to God and human beings are discerned and rightly performed?[5]

Logos and Virtue

Sacr. 82–84: And this Logos should not be a confused language but should be divided into its proper parts. This is the meaning of "slicing" the offering. For order is better than disorder everywhere, but especially is it so in the nature of swiftly stream, Logos. Therefore, it must be divided into the main leading thoughts, the so-called "relevant topics," and each of these must be provided with its properly constructed development. In this way, we shall imitate the skilled archers, those who set up a mark before an object and send forth and pierce all the arrows at it. For the main thought is like the target, and the condition is like the arrows. 83 In this way, we weave together harmoniously the best of all garments, Logos. For the Lawgiver cuts the plates of gold into threads, to weave them properly and permanently (Exod. 36:10). Thus, Logos is dearer than gold, and constitutes a diversity of infinite forms brought to excellent perfection if it is cut into the utmost nicety of leading thoughts and points, and then through these the arguments and demonstrations that they need are passed like woof through the warp in harmony. 84 He gives, indeed, a command: "the burnt-offering flayed to distribute it into the limbs" (Lev. 1:6), in order in the first place that the soul may appear naked without the covering with which false and idle conjectures invest it, and then be divided as the limbs demand. For virtue, which is the whole and is seen also as a genus and is divided into its primary species prudence, temperance, courage, and justice, so that observing the differences between each of these, we may submit to a voluntary service of them both in their entirety and in particulars.

The Four Rivers of Eden

Leg. 1.63–65: "A river goes forth from Eden to water the garden; from there it separates into four heads (*QG* 1.12). The name of the one is Pheison; this is the one encircling all the land of Heuilat, there where the gold is; and the gold of that land is good; and there is also the ruby and the green stone. And the name of the second river is Geon; this encircles all the land of Ethiopia. And the third river is the Tigris; this is the river that flows opposite the Assyrians. And the fourth river is the Euphrates" (Gen. 2:10–14). By these rivers, Moses wants to indicate the particular virtues. They are four in number: prudence, temperance, courage, and justice. Certainly, the largest river, of which the four are streams, is generic virtue, which we have called goodness. The four streams are the virtues of the same number. 64 Therefore, generic virtue has its origin in Eden, the Wisdom of God, which rejoices, is joyful, and takes delight, glories, and boasts only in God its Father. But the specific virtues, four in number, are derived from generic virtue, which like a river waters the complete virtuous acts of each of them with an abundant flow of noble actions. 65 Now, let us look at the particular words: "a river," it says, "goes forth from Eden to water the garden." "River" is generic virtue, goodness. This goes forth from Eden, the Wisdom of God. And this is the Logos of God; for in accord with it generic virtue has been brought into being. And generic virtue waters the garden; that is, it waters the particular virtues. "Heads" he takes not in terms of locality but of sovereignty; for each of the virtues is truly a sovereign and a queen. The phrase "it separates" is equivalent to "has boundaries to define it." Prudence establishes boundaries for them concerning things to be done; courage for things to be endured; temperance for things to be chosen; and justice for things to be assigned/distributed.

Cher. 12–13: Of the first sense, that of hostility, we find an example in what is said of Cain that "he went out from the face of God and dwelt in a land of Nod over against Eden" (Gen. 4:16). And "Nod" is translated as "tossing" and "Eden" means "delight," the former is the symbol of the vice creating tumult in the soul, and the latter of the virtue wining for the soul happiness and delight, not the weak through irrational passion and pleasure, but that sense of profound content and joy, which knows not toil and trouble. 13 When mind goes forth from the vision of God, it was good and profitable for it to be anchored, then immediately, like a ship at the sea is battling with violent winds; it is tossed in every direction, having disturbances as it were for its country and its home, a thing that is the very opposite of the constancy of the soul, which is the gift of joy that has the same name, Eden.

Post. 127b–129: Thus, in this way the Logos of God waters the virtues; for this is the source and spring of good actions. 128 The Lawgiver makes it clear saying: "and a river goes out of Eden to water the garden. From there it is divided into four sources or heads" (Gen. 2:10). For there are four universal virtues, prudence, courage, temperance, and justice. And each of these is a sovereign and queen; and the one who has acquired them is, by the mere fact of acquisition, a ruler and king, even if he has no abundance of any material treasure. 129 For what "is divided into four heads" does not mean a division among them, but power and sovereignty belong to virtues. These have sprung from the divine Logos as from one root, which is likened to a river by the unbroken flow of the constant stream of words and doctrines ever sweet and fresh, by which it brings along and nourishes the souls that love God.

THE VIRTUE *PAR EXCELLENCE* AND KEY VIRTUES

Note

Philo gives piety (*eusebeia*) a special place in his ethics within the understanding of the Greek cardinal or generic virtues: prudence (*phronēsis*), justice (*dikaiosunē*), temperance (*sōphrosunē*), and courage (*andreia*). Often Philo classifies piety as a cardinal virtue.[6] Rather than listing piety simply as a part of, or subordinated to, the generic virtue of justice, Philo catalogs piety among the four cardinal virtues, and as the virtue *par excellence*, sharing the same special attributes with the chief virtue, prudence.[7] In several texts Philo highlights the centrality of piety in his ethics, and he does so in different ways: piety is the "beginning," "origin," or "source" of all the virtues (*Decal.* 52), the "power" of every kind of virtue (*Det.* 72), the "most splendid of possessions" (*Mut.* 76), the "chief" or "greatest" of all the virtues (*Abr.* 60; *Spec.* 4.97), the "highest" and "most profitable" of lessons (*Mos.* 1.146), the "queen" of the virtues (*Spec.* 4.147; *Decal.* 119; *Spec.* 4.135; *Virt.* 95; *QE* 2.38a), the "highest" of virtues (*Abr.* 60), the "queen of the dance" (*Praem.* 53), the "best" of the virtues (*QG* 1.10; *Decal.* 100), the "most godlike of qualities" (*Somn.* 2.186), "pure," "undefiled" (*Abr.* 129; *Spec.* 1.30), and "divine" (*QE* 2.15b).

Piety is not the only virtue to which Philo gives such a high prominence. He calls faith the "most perfect virtue" (*Her.* 91), the "most sure and certain" of the virtues (*Virt.* 216), and like piety, "queen" of the virtues (*Abr.* 270). Similarly, Philo identifies godliness as the "greatest of the virtues" (*Opif.* 154), and names the Platonic chief virtue, prudence, the "most approved" virtue (*Leg.* 1.66). Philo privileges the place of both piety and holiness; he does it by listing the two virtues as separate virtues, not as "one" virtue, as in *Spec.* 4.135. Philo uses both virtues frequently in parallel constructions, and sometimes the two virtues seem to be used interchangeably.[8] For Philo, these are special virtues equated with the four cardinal virtues. He calls piety and holiness "great virtues" (*Plant.* 35), "powers" (*Ebr.* 92), and "queens" among the virtues (*Decal.* 119); in three occasions, Philo labels the virtue of holiness alone as "worthy holiness" (*QE* 1.7; 2.83; *QE* 1.12). Despite the special titles of these virtues, piety prevails as the virtue *par excellence*. It is the only

Greek virtue holding the highest position in Philo's list of ethical virtues that even goes beyond the special place given to the four generic virtues in Greek catalog of virtues.

Piety

Det. 72–73: The Sophists are bound to find the powers within them at strife, words running counter to arguments and wishes counter to words in absolute and utter discord. At any rate, they make our ears tedious with their demonstrations of the social character of justice, the beneficial nature of moderation, the nobility of self-control, the most benefits conferred by piety, the power of every kind of virtue to bring wholesomeness and safety (*QG* 4.12, 200; *QE* 2.38). And again, they dwell at great length on the unsociability of injustice, on unhealthy intemperance, unlawful impiety, and every other form of evil that seriously harms. 73 And nevertheless, they entertain all the time sentiments quite at variance with the things that they say. At the very moment when they are singing the praise of prudence, temperance, justice, and piety, then, they are found to be more than ever practicing foolishness, licentiousness, injustice, and impiety, confounding and overturning all divine and human ordinances.

Migr. 132b: What thus is the cementing substance? What? Piety, surely also faith. For these virtues adapt and unite the intention to the incorruptible nature. Of Abraham it is said, precisely, that when he believed he "came near to God" (Gen. 18:23).

Spec. 1.67–68: It is necessary not to restrain the impulses of human beings to pay their tribute to piety and desire by means of sacrifices either to express gratitude for the blessings that befall them, or to ask for forgiveness and intercession for their sins (*QG* 4.67–68). But Moses ordered that neither in other places nor in this place shall be built a temple; he judged that since God is One, also there should be only One Temple. 68 Moreover, he does not allow to perform rites in their houses to those who wish, but he urged to raise up from the ends of the earth to come to this Temple. In this way, he also applies the necessary test to their dispositions. For one who is not going to sacrifice in a religious spirit would never bring himself to leave his country and friends and kinsfolk and sojourn in a strange land, but clearly, it must be the stronger attraction of piety that leads him to endure a separation from his most familiar and dearest friends, who forms as it were a single whole with himself.

Spec. 2.237–239: But one may give positively a proof of filial piety not only in the ways above mentioned, but also by courtesy shown to those who share the seniority of the parents. For he, who respects an old man or old woman who does not belong to his race, may be regarded as having remembrance of his father and mother. He looks upon them as prototypes and are placed as the images of his parents. 238 Therefore, in the holy scriptures the young people are commanded to abandon not only the front seat for the old persons, but also to make room for them as they pass (cf. Lev. 19:32), in respect to their gray hairs, that mark the age to which they may hope to attain those who judge it worthy of precedence. 239 The most admirable to me is that it seems to prescribe other ordinances, for he says: "let each fear his father and mother" (Lev. 19:3). He places fear before honor, not as better than on every occasion, but as more serviceable and profitable for the occasion that he has before him. First of all, parents, who educate and admonish the foolish, come together; and folly is not the remedy of fear (*QG* 2.70). Second, it would not be suitable to include in the enactments of the Lawgiver an instruction on the duty of filial affection; for nature has implanted this as an imperative instinct from the very cradle in the souls of those who are thus united by kinship.

Spec. 4.145–148: This is an example of what I say (cf. *Mut.* 163). Courage, the virtue whose field of action is what causes trouble, is the knowledge of what ought to be endured, and is known to all who are not completely devoid of learning and culture, even if they attribute it to a small education (*QE* 2.103). 146 But if anyone, indulging the ignorance, who comes through arrogance and believing himself to be a superior person capable of correcting what stands in no such need, ventures to add to courage; he changes its likeness altogether and stamps upon it a form in which ugliness replaces beauty. By adding he will make rashness, and by taking away he will make cowardice, not leaving even the name of courage, which is highly profitable to life. 147 In the same way too, if one adds anything small or great to the queen of virtues, piety, or on the contrary takes something from it, in either case, he will change and transform its form. For addition will beget superstition, and subtraction will beget impiety, leading astray piety, a sun rising and shining, indeed, a blessing that every person should well pray for, because it is the source of the greatest of blessings, since it gives the knowledge of the service of God, which we must hold as lordlier than any lordship, more royal than any sovereignty. 148 Much the same can be said of the other virtues, but as it is my habit to avoid lengthy discussions by abridgement, I will content myself with the foresaid examples, which will sufficiently indicate what is left unsaid.

Praem. 53: Now all the virtues are virgins, but the most beautiful among them all, the acknowledged queen of the dance, is piety, which Moses who teaches especially about God has appointed, and through it gained a multitude of other gifts, which have been described in the treatises dealing with his life, four special rewards: the offices of king, legislator, prophet, and high priest.[9]

Holiness

Sacr. 37–39: Choose any good thing whatsoever, and you will find that it results from and is established through toil. Piety and holiness are good (*QG* 4.53), but we cannot attain them without the service of God, and the service is closely united with the ambitions in toil. Prudence, courage, justice, all these are noble and excellent and perfectly good things; but these are not attained with easiness. It is much indeed if by constant care and practice to arise a kindliness between us and them. Service pleasing to God and to virtue is like an intense and severe harmony, and in no soul is there an instrument capable of sustaining it, without such frequent relaxation and unstringing of the chords that it descends from the higher forms of the arts to the lower forms. 38 But even in all the lower forms is the same; it demands much toil. Observe all those who practice the encyclical branches of the so-called elementary education. See those who labor on the soil and all those who get their life by some trade or profession. These cast their cares aside neither by day nor by night. But always and everywhere they cease not to bear affliction, as the saying goes, in hand, in foot, and in every faculty, so that they often choose death in its situation. 39 But just as those who desire to have their soul attuned and favorable must need to cultivate the virtues of the soul, even those who propose to gain the same qualities for their body must cultivate health and the powers that accompany health; indeed, all who take thought for the faculties within them, which are compounded to make them what they are, do so cultivate them with constant and unremitting toil.

Ebr. 91–92: Therefore, it shall show the same thing happening in the power residing in the Sage. For under the name of piety and holiness and the things about heaven it deals with the attributes of the really Existent; under the name of natural study, with all that concerns the heavens and the heavenly bodies (*QG* 1.55); under the name of meteorology, with the air and the consequences that result through its changes and variations both at the main seasons of the year and those particular ones that follow cycles of months and days; and under the name of ethics, with what tends to the improvement of the human conduct, and this last takes various forms: politics dealing with the city, economics dealing with the management of a house, convivial dealing with banquets and festivities, and further we have the kingly faculty dealing with the control of men, and the legislative dealing with the commands and prohibitions. 92 All these, piety and holiness, natural study, meteorology, ethics, politics, economics, royal power, legislative power, and many other powers, find their home in him who is in the truest sense many-voiced and many-named, even the Sage, and in all he will be seen to have one and the same form.

Abr. 198–199: Here we have the most affectionate of fathers; he himself did begin the sacrificial rites as priest with the very best of sons for victim. Perhaps with the law of burnt offerings he would also have dismembered his son (cf. Lev. 1:6) and offered him limb by limb. Thus, he did not incline some partly to the boy, and partly to piety, but devoted his whole soul through and through to holiness disregarding the claims of their common blood. 199 Which of all the points mentioned is shared by others? Which does not stand by itself and defy description? Thus, everyone who is malignant, and a friend of an evil person, must be overwhelmed with admiration for his extraordinary piety; he needs not to take into consideration at once all the points that I have said, for any one of them would be sufficient. For to picture in the mind one of these, however small the form that the picture takes, though no work of the Wise is small, is enough to show the greatness and loftiness of Abraham's soul.

Mos. 1.307: "The contest before you is not to win dominion, not to appropriate the possessions of others, which is the only principal object of the other wars, but to defend piety and holiness, from which our ancestors and friends have been perverted by the enemies, who indirectly caused their victims to perish miserably.

Mos. 2.136–138: Outside the outer vestibule, at the entrance, there was a brazen laver, the artificer having not taken any unworked material as is usually done but having employed on its formation vessels that had been already fashioned with great care for other purposes. These the women brought, filled with fervent ambition, competing with the men in piety, having resolved to win a noble prize and eager to use every power that they had, so that they might not be outstripped by them in holiness. 137 For with spontaneous eagerness at no other bidding than their own, they arranged the mirrors, which they used in adorning their comely persons, a suitable first-fruit offering of their temperance and chastity in marriage, and of their beauty of soul. 138 These, the artificer thought good to take, and, after melting them down, construct therewith the laver and nothing else, to serve for lustration to priests, who intend to enter the Temple to perform the appointed services, particularly the washing of the hands and feet—a symbol of a blameless life, of years of cleanliness employed in laudable actions and in straight traveling, not on the rough road or more properly pathless waste of vice, but on the smooth high road through virtue's land.

Spec. 4.134–135: The Ten Commandments, which are the virtues of universal value, for each of the ten pronouncements separately, and all of them in common, incite and exhort us to prudence, justice, godliness, and the other company of virtues, with good thoughts combining wholesome words with good intentions and deeds of true worth with words, so that the soul with every part of its being attuned may be an instrument making harmonious music, so that life becomes a melody and a consent in which there is no faulty note. 135 Thus, of the queen of the virtues, piety and holiness, we have spoken earlier and also of prudence and temperance. Our theme must now be justice, whose ways are close akin to them.[10]

Wisdom and Knowledge

Ebr. 158–161: Also knowledge, the opposite of ignorance, may be the eyes and the ears of the soul. For you pay heed to those who say that the mind may contemplate the things created and admit neither to neglect nor to disobey anyone; but the soul surveys and observes everything that is worthy to be heard and seen. If it is necessary to travel and take a ship, it makes its way to the ends of the earth or ocean, to see something more or to hear something new. 159 For nothing is so active as love for knowledge; it hates sleep and loves watchfulness. Thus, it always arouses and excites and sharpens the intellect, and compelling it to range in every direction makes it greedy to hear and instills an everlasting thirst for learning. 160 Surely, then, knowledge keeps safe to perceive and to hear, by means of which they owe each case of right conduct. For he, who sees and hears, knows what is suitable for him, and by choosing this and rejecting its opposite, finds himself benefited. But ignorance entails a more grievous mutilation of the soul than the mutilation of the body; it is the cause of all sins; since it cannot take any assistance from outside itself through the warnings, seeing and hearing might give it. Thus, standing utterly alone, and left unguarded and unprotected, it is exposed to the haphazard hostility of men and circumstances alike. 161 Let us, then, never drink so deep of strong liquor as to reduce our senses to inactivity, nor become so estranged from knowledge as to spread the vast and profound darkness of ignorance over our soul (*QG* 4.100–101, 108).

Migr. 37–40a: This tree does not only offer nourishment but also immortality. For it is said that the tree of life was planted in the middle of Eden (Gen. 2:9), even goodness with the particular virtues and the deeds that accord with them to be its bodyguard. Virtue has obtained a place in the soul, the central and the most honorable place. 38 He who sees it is the wise. For the fools are blind or dim-sighted. Because of this, in former times human beings were called the prophets, the seers (1 Sam. 9:9); and the practicer was eager to exchange ears for eyes, and to see before he heard, and going beyond the inheritance that has hearing as its source, he obtains that of which sight is the ruling principle. 39 For the current coin of learning and teaching is reminting into the seeing Israel, after which Jacob was named. Hereby, it comes the vision of the divine light, identical with knowledge, that opens wide the soul's eye and leads it to apprehensions distinct and brilliant beyond those gained by the ears. For as the principle of music is apprehended through the science of music, and the practice of each science through that science, even so, through wisdom comes discernment of what is wise (*QG* 4.6). 40a But wisdom is not only, after the manner of a light, an instrument of sight but sees also its own self. Wisdom is the archetypal luminary of God, and the sun is a copy of the image.

Congr. 79–80: And indeed, just as the encyclical branches of education contribute to the acquisition of philosophy, so does philosophy to the attaining of wisdom (*QG* 3.32). For philosophy is the cultivation of wisdom and wisdom is the knowledge of God and the science of things divine and human and their causes. Therefore, just as the encyclical education is the servant of philosophy, so is philosophy the maid of wisdom. 80 Now, philosophy teaches us self-control of the belly, self-control of the parts below the belly, and also self-control of the tongue. It is said that these are desirable things in themselves, but they will assume a grander and loftier place if pursued for the sake of honoring God and pleasing Him. Thus, we must keep the sovereign lady in mind when we are about to court her handmaids, and we must count to be their husbands, but let her be our wife in actuality, and not merely in name.

Legat. 69: Concerning Macro they said: "his pride extended beyond reasonable limits, he did not read well the Delphic motto, 'know yourself.' It is said that knowledge is the source of happiness. What reason had he for reversing his part and transferring the subject to the rank of ruler, and Gaius, the emperor, to the place of a subject? It is part of a ruler to command, and that is what he did; but it is the duty of a subject to obey, and that was what he believed that Gaius was to submit to."[11]

Faith

Mut. 181–184: But it may be said: "why therefore did he, because he has believed, is receiving a trace or shadow or breeze of unbelief whatsoever?" It seems to me that this question amounts to a wish to make out the created to be uncreated, the mortal immortal, the perishable imperishable, and if it is a custom to say that the human being is a god. 182 For it is faith, which human being possesses, should be so strong as to differ not at all from the faith that belongs to the Existent One, a perfect faith and complete in every way. For Moses says in the Great Song: "God is faithful, and there is no injustice in Him" (Deut. 32:4; cf. Exod. 15). 183 It is a great ignorance to believe that the human soul can contain the unwavering, absolutely steadfast virtues of God. Enough for a human being is to be able to acquire the image of these, images in the scale of number and magnitude far below, the archetypes. 184 And it was never expected, because by forces the virtues of God are unmixed, since God is not compounded but of a single nature; but the virtues in human beings are mixed, since we are also created mixed, composed of divine and mortal blended in us and formed into a harmony in the proportions of perfect music, and a compound of more than one ingredient is subject to natural counterforces drawing it to each of these ingredients.

Mos. 1.224–225: There are three things that we desire to know: the size and strength of the population, whether the cities are favorably situated and strongly built, or on the contrary, if the country is productive and wealthy, well adapted to produce every kind of fruit from cornfields and orchards, or on the other hand is thin and poor. Thus, we may fortify the strength and number of the inhabitants with equal forces, and the strength of their position with machines and siege engines. Knowledge of the fertility or infertility of the land is also indispensable, for if it is poor it would be folly to court danger to win it. 225 Our arms and engines and all our power rest entirely in faith in only God. Equipped with this, we will defy every terror; for faith, which is able to overpower and more than overpower, forces the most unconquerable strength, in good health, courage, experience, and number, and by it we are supplied in the depths of the desert with all that the rich resources of cities can give.[12]

THE PRACTICE OF VIRTUES

The Perfect Human (Gradual Progress)

Plant. 96–98: Accordingly, it is unable to plant fruit-trees before migrating into the country given by God. In fact, God says: "when you shall come into the land, you shall plant every tree yielding food." So, while staying outside, we shall not be able to cultivate these trees. And that is, I understand, in no time suitable. 97 For so long as the mind has not come to the road of wisdom but has turned in another direction and wanders away far off, its attention is given to trees of wild growth, which are either barren and yield nothing, or, though they are productive, bear no edible fruit. 98 But when the mind has stepped on the road of good sense and in the company of prudence comes into and runs along that way, it will begin to cultivate the useful trees, which are capable of bearing edible fruits: instead of passions freedom from them, knowledge in place of ignorance, good things in place of evil things.

Sacr. 86–87: Then, after the "slicing" must come the "pounding," that is after division we must continually dwell and linger over the thoughts presented to our minds. For constant practice causes a solid knowledge, as its absence causes ignorance. At least, then, the multitude of those who contest with laziness have released the strength of their nature. They do not imitate those who fed their soul with divine nourishment, which is called manna.

They grind and crush it and made of it buried cakes (Num. 11:8), judging it right to crush and grind virtue's heaven-sent discourse, that its impress on their understanding might be firmer. 87 Therefore, when "new" is the highest point and the "roast" is set on fire, an invincible reason, and the "sliced" is the division and distinction of the reality, and "pounded" is the persistent practice and exercise in what the mind has grasped, you will bring an offering of the first-fruits, even the first and best offspring of the soul. And yet even if we are slow, He Himself is not slow to take to Himself those who are fit for His service. For "I will take you," He says, "to be my people and I will be your God" (Exod. 6:7), "and you shall be to Me a people. I am the Lord" (Lev. 26:12).

Agr. 160–161: If our friends do come into this conflict, professionals engaging in a struggle against trained and seasoned fighters, they will undoubtedly be seized; and the one who is only beginning, because he lacks experience, and the one who is progressing, because he is incomplete, the one who has reached perfection, because he is not yet thoroughly practiced in virtue. It is necessary that the plaster should become firm and fixed and acquire stability; so too the souls of those that have been perfected should become more firmly settled, strengthened by constant practice and continual exercise. 161 Those who do not reach these advantages have indeed the name among the philosophers of wise men, but it is without their own wisdom. For those who have advanced as far as the edge of wisdom and have just come for the first time into contact with its borders should be conscious of their own perfection. For both things cannot come about at the same time, the arrival at the goal and the apprehension of the arrival; but ignorance is at the limit between the two; not that ignorance, that it is not far removed from knowledge, but that it is near to it, and close to its doors.

Praem. 36–37: After the self-taught, the one enriched by the many natural gifts, the third who reached perfection is the man of practice who received a special reward, the vision of God. For reaching every side of the human life and being acquainted with everything human and having shrunk from no toil or danger, if thereby he might descry the truth, a quest well worthy of such love, he has found mortal life set in the deep darkness spread over earth and water and the lower air and ether too. For ether and the whole heaven have presented to him the semblance of night, since the whole sense-perceptible realm is by nature limitless. The indefinite is a brother, even akin to darkness. 37 The eyes of his soul have been closed, now by the continuous striving, he began to slowly open them and to separate and to throw off the mist that had overshadowed him. For a beam purer than ether and incorporeal suddenly shone upon him and revealed the conceptual world ruled by its charioteer.[13]

ATHLETIC LANGUAGE IN THE PRACTICE OF VIRTUES

Prize

Agr. 120–121: Therefore, these athletes excel over their opponents, but they are also competing among themselves for the first place. For they do not all win the victory in the same way, but all are worthy of honor for overthrowing and bringing down the strongest and most hostile opponents. 121 Most worthy of admiration is the one who prevails among these, and no one must envy him as he receives the first prizes. No one must cast down those who have been held worthy of the second or third prize. For these are prizes offered with a view to the acquisition of virtue, and to those who cannot reach the topmost virtues are gainers by the acquisition of the less lofty ones. They say that theirs is also the most steadfast gain, since it escapes the envy that ever attaches itself to preeminence.

Migr. 27–29: For this reason, it was declared: "turn away to the land of your father and of your kindred and I will be with you" (Gen. 31:3) as much as to say, you have become a perfect athlete and been worthy of prizes and crowns with virtue deciding and holding forth to you prizes of victory. But now it is time for you to have done with strife, so that you may never toil, and have power to enjoy the fruits of those who are also working hard. 28 This you will never find while dwelling with the objects of sense-perception and spending your days with the bodily qualities whose head and chief is Laban, bearing a name that means "variety of quality." It is necessary to become a migrant in the father's land, the land of the Word that is holy and in some sense father of those who submit to training. That land is wisdom, the best possible dwelling for virtue-loving souls. 29 In this country, there is the self-taught for you, its own teacher, that needs not to be fed on milky nourishment of childhood, and that has been prevented by divine oracle to go down into Egypt (Gen. 26:2) and to meet with the enticing pleasures of the flesh. That nature is, namely, Isaac.

Her. 253: For all the elements of practice were rendered eatable: inquiry, examination, reading, listening to instruction, concentration, perseverance, self-control, and indifference for things indifferent. Of all these things the tester naturally eats samples only, not the whole. For it is necessary that the practicer must have his proper food left for him, like prizes for his efforts.

Fug. 39–40: Patient guides to the man of practice, but the actual words need careful treatment. "Behold," he says, "Esau your brother is threatening you." But is it not the case that the character, which is hard and wooden, whose ignorance makes it disobedient, the character named Esau, who has a grudge and offers the baits of the mortal life to destroy you, money, glory, pleasures, and the like to seek to kill you? But you, my child, flee from the present contest; for your strength has not yet reached its full development, but like in any boy, the sinews of your soul lack firmness. 40 This is why she addressed him as "child," a name that at the same time is an expression of affection and of a proper tender age. For we regard the character of the practicer both as young compared with the fully developed, and as lovable. Such a one is adequate to win the prizes given to children, but he is not yet able to win the prizes given to men; and the best prize that men can obtain is the service of the only God.[14]

The Three Elements to Acquire Virtue

Conf. 79–81: So, then, naturally Abraham, raising up from the life of death and vanity, will say to the guardians of the dead and the housekeepers of mortality: "I am a stranger and sojourner with you" (Gen. 23:4). "You" means children of the stock, or of the land, who honor the dust and clay of the soul, and have deemed worthy a precedence to the man named Ephron, who is interpreted as "clay." 80 Naturally, the words of the practicer, Jacob, when he laments his sojourn in the body, says, "the days of the years of my life, the days which I sojourn, have been few and evil, they have not reached to the days of my Fathers who sojourned" (Gen. 47:9). 81 Also, Isaac, the self-taught, proclaimed an oracle to him saying: "go not down into Egypt," that is passion, "but dwell in the land which I would say to you," that is in the invisible and incorporeal prudence, "and sojourn in this land" (Gen. 26:2, 3), that is in the form of existence, which may be shown and is perceived by the senses. The purpose of this is to show him that the wise man does sojourn in this body, which our senses know, as in a strange land, but dwells in and has for his fatherland the virtues known through the mind, which God utters, and which thus are identical with divine words.

Migr. 125–126: The most palpable example is Noah the righteous one, who, when so many parts of the soul were swallowed up by the great flood, steadfastly floating upon the waves and swimming over, stood firmly high above every peril, and when coming safe through all, put forth from himself fair and great roots, out of which there grew up like a plant, wisdom's breed and kind. And attaining goodly fertility bore those threefold fruits of the seeing one, Israel, that mark the threefold divisions of eternity: Abraham, Isaac, and Jacob. 126 For it is, will be, and has been in each virtue, which overshadowed by unfitness of proper time among men but again uncovered in proper time that follows God. In that also Sarah, who is prudence, begets children, blooming not according to the changes of the year measured by lapse of time, but according to the fullness of season that time does not determine. For it is said: "I will certainly return unto you according to this season when the time comes round, and Sarah who is your wife will have a son" (Gen. 18:10).

Congr. 34–38: Now these men, Abraham and Jacob, as the holy ones reveal in Scriptures, came into being and became also husbands of many women and concubines as well as legitimate wives. But Isaac had neither many wives nor concubines at all but only his lawful wife. She is the one who shares his home throughout. 35 Why is this? Because the virtue that comes through teaching, which Abraham pursues, needs the fruits of several studies: those born of wedlock that deal with prudence, and the base-born, those of preliminary instruction of the schools. Through practice virtue is perfected, which Jacob appears to have made his aim. For many and different are the truths in which practice finds its exercising ground, truths that lead and follow, hasten to meet it and wait behind, and bringing sometimes greater, and other times lighter labor. 36 But the self-learned kind, of which Isaac is a member, is the best of good emotions, and has a share with simple, unmixed, and pure nature. Joy binds neither practice nor teaching, which entails the need of concubines and the legitimate forms of knowledge. When God rains down from heaven, the good of which the self is a teacher and learner, it is impossible to live with the slavish arts and concubines, yearning for bastard opinions as his children. 37 He who has obtained this privilege is registered as the husband of the mistress and queen virtue. In Greek it is called "endurance" and in Hebrew "Rebekah." For he who has gained wisdom without toil and patience, because his nature is happily gifted and his soul is fruitfully good, does not seek for any means of further improvement. 38 For he has ready beside him in their fullness the gifts of God, conveyed by breathing upon the most honored graces of God, but he wishes and also prays that these things would remain with him. Therefore, I think, it seems that his Benefactor, willing that His graces once received should stay forever with him, gives him steadfastness for his wife.

Mut. 81–86: It has come to terms that to change Jacob's name to Israel is not from a purport. Why so? Because Jacob is the supplanter, and Israel is called the one who sees God. Therefore, it is the work of the supplanter, who practices virtues to set in motion and to shake and to upset the supports on which passion rests, and on which there is in them firmness and stability. But these are not treated affectionately, to be made without effort apart from struggle in the arena, but whenever someone is training the contest of prudence to the end and drilled in the gymnastics of the soul wrestles with the thoughts that oppose and hold it fast in their grip. The work of the one who sees God does not go way from the holy arena uncrowned, but it carries off the prizes of victory. 82 And what garland more fitting for its purpose could be woven for the victorious soul than the power that will enable him to see the Existent One with clear vision? A beautiful prize it is set forth to the athlete-soul that it should be endowed with eyes to apprehend Him in bright light,

He, Who alone is worthy of our contemplation. 83 It is worthy to inquire why Abraham after a change of his name is no longer called by his old name, but always receives the same title as his right, whereas Jacob, after he is addressed as Israel, is in spite of this called Jacob many times. Thus, it is said that these are also distinctive marks, to which the virtue acquired by teaching differs from the virtue acquired by practice. 84 For he who is improved by teaching is endowed with a happy nature, which, with the cooperation of memory, ensures his retentiveness, gets a tight grip, and with a firm arm-hold of what he has learned, and thus remains constant. And whenever the practicer exercises intensely, he breathes between times and again relaxes a little, bringing together and regaining himself the power broken into pieces by his labor, such as they also anoint their bodies. For these men are also weary with exercise; they pour oil upon their limbs in order to prevent their forces from being utterly shattered by the intensity and severity of the contest. 85 Then, the man, who is improved by teaching, having an immortal monitor, receives from him a harmonious and imperishable advantage, without suffering any change. But the practicer has only his own will, and he exercises and drills, so that he may overthrow the passion, which is natural to a created being; and even if he may reach perfection, through weariness he still returns to his old kind of toil. 86 He is more patient to endure toil, but the other is more blessed by fortune. For this last has another teacher, while the toiler, self-helped only, is busied seeking and inquiring and zealously exploring the secrets of nature, engaged in labor ceaseless and unremitting.

Somn. 1.168–171: For Abraham, the earliest of them, had teaching as his guide to the path toward the good and beautiful, as we shall show to the best of our ability in other treatises. Isaac, who is the second, the self-acquired and self-learned by nature, and Jacob who is the third and relied on exercises and practices and preparations for the strenuous toil of the arena (*QG* 4.175). 169 Therefore, there are three methods by which wisdom is superior; it is the first and third that are most intimately joined together. For what comes by practice is the offspring and product of that which comes by learning, and what comes by nature is, to be sure, kin with them, being like a root at the bottom of all three, but the prerogative allotted to it is obtained uncontested and effortless. 170 Thus, it is natural to say that Abraham, who owes his improvement to teaching, was the father of Jacob, who was shaped and drilled by exercises, not meaning that Abraham was the father of Jacob, as the faculty of hearing ready to learn begets and produces the faculty of exercise and practice so serviceable in contest. 171 If, however, the practicer exerts himself and runs to the goal and comes to see clearly what he formerly saw dimly as in a dream and receives the impress of a nobler character and the name of Israel, he who sees God, in place of Jacob, the supplanter, he then no longer claims as his father Abraham, the man who learned, but Isaac, the one who was born good by nature.

Abr. 52–54: Therefore, these words do seem to appear to be said of these holy men, but they are also statements about an order of things that is not so perceived naturally. For the holy word seems to be searching into types of souls, all of them of high worth, one that pursues the good through teaching, one through nature, and one through practice. The first called Abraham, the second Isaac, and the third Jacob, are a symbol of teaching, virtue, and practice. 53 But we must not fail to note that each possesses the three qualities but gets his name from that which chiefly predominates in him. For teaching cannot be consummated without nature or practice, nor is nature capable of reaching its zenith without teaching and practice, nor is practice without first laying the foundation of nature and teaching. 54 Therefore, Moses properly joined these three together, nominally men, but really, as I have said, virtues, teaching, nature, and practice. Another name is given to them by men, who call them the graces, also equal in number. They are freely given to our kind by God for perfecting its life; they have given themselves to the reasonable soul as a perfect and most excellent gift, so that the eternal name manifested in his words is meant to indicate the three said values, not the actual men.

Mos. 1.75–76: God replied, "And first He says to them that I am He Who Is, so that they may expect to learn the difference between what is and what is not, so that no name at all can properly be used of Me, to Whom alone existence belongs. 76 And if in their natural weakness, they seek a name, make clear to them not only this, that I am God, but that I am also the God of these three men, who have derived their names from virtue; each of them has gained the exemplar of wisdom: Abraham by teaching, Isaac by nature, and Jacob by practice. And if they still disbelieve, three symbols, which no person has ever before seen or heard of, will be sufficient lesson to convert them.[15]

THE GOAL OF HUMAN LIFE

Note

Philo's ethics show his strong philosophical background, which is clearly reflected in his direct connection of the goal of human life with philosophical ideals of the human life. In their ethical systems, Greek philosophers were known as *eudaimonists,* for they viewed "happiness" (*eudaimonia*) as the goal of human life. In Philo the practice of the ethical commandments enshrined in the *Decalogue* and its particular laws seek perfect virtue and happiness.[16] To achieve a life of happiness meant "to become like God" (*hōmoiōsis theō*), to live a life in harmony according to nature (living *kata phusin*).[17] The Platonic term *hōmoiōsis theō*, found for example in *Theaet.* 176A–177A,[18] is equated with the Stoic goal of "life according to nature."[19] Philo also follows the Pythagorean goal of life "to follow God" (*epesthai theō*),[20] and the Aristotelian notion of becoming God-like.[21] He more than any other Hellenistic Jewish writer is deeply affected by Platonism, especially in terms of the development of Middle Platonism. Like most Middle Platonists, especially Eudorus of Alexandria, Philo grounds his ethics in the notion that a virtue-loving soul must strive to move from this world to the immaterial realm of the Existent One. Strategically, Philo develops this philosophical ideal and further presents piety as the divine virtue that possesses a "god-like" quality and functions as the foundational virtue to lead virtue-loving souls to God.[22]

Happiness

Leg. 3.86–87: What is it then that has made this one also to be praised before his birth? Some good things assist us when they have reached us and are present, such as health, keen perception, wealth perhaps, glory—for even these may be loosely called good things. Some not only when they have come, but when their coming has been prophesied, like joy—this is happiness of the soul—for it delights not only when it is present actively in action, but also when hopes and cheers. For here again is a peculiar advantage that it possesses. But the other good things operate in their own goodness only, and joy is a particular and a general goodness (*QG* 4.19). See how it comes to add to and enrich the whole; for we also rejoice over health and over freedom and over honor and over the other good things, so that we properly say that nothing is good unless joy is attached to it. 87 But we rejoice over the other good things not only when they have already come about beforehand and present, but also when they are looked for in the future, as when we hope to grow rich or shall obtain office, or shall win praise, or shall discover a way of getting rid of disease, or shall obtain our share of health and strength, or shall no longer be ignorant, but men of knowledge. We are glad in no small measure. Seeing then, that joy, not only when present but also when hoped for, pours and delights over the soul, God naturally held Isaac, even before he was begotten, worthy of his great name and therein of a vast endowment: for Isaac means laughter of the soul and joy and gladness.

Agr. 157: Thus, the letter of the law perhaps suggests all these questions and more than these. But that no one of ingenious arguments is confident, speaking allegorically, we may say that the law intends to bind, first, not only about some acquisitions of good things to be trained, but also about the enjoyment of what he has acquired, and that happiness results from the practice of perfect virtue, seeing that such excellence secures a life sound and complete in every way (*QG* 4.43). Second, what the law means is that a person's main consideration is not a house or a vineyard or the agreement of a wife already betrothed; how he is, thus, to marry her as an accepted suitor; how the planter of the vineyard is to pluck off and crush its fruit, and then drink large draughts of the intoxicating beverage and his heart be glad; or how the one who has built the house is to occupy it; but that the faculties of a man's soul, through which he has come to terms and made a beginning, take both progress and perfection, and be praised in practice.

Her. 284–285: The phrase "nourishes with peace" is not an addition from the aim, but it means that the greatest part of the human race is nourished for war and out of war for all its attendant evils. Now, war arises from things outside us, which brings forward ill-repute, deficiency, meanness, and the things alike. Another kind arises from the intestines in the body: diseases, mutilations, blindness, complete disablements of the senses, and other multiple calamities piled on each other; in the soul: passions, diseases, disorders, fierce, painful infirmities, oppressive insurrections, the inexpugnable despotism of folly, and injustice and their fellow tyrants. 285 Therefore, "nourished with peace" means that he acquires a calm and peaceful life, as a happy truly blessed life (*QG* 4.191). Thus, when will this come to terms? When we may have a passage to abundance and glory outside us, and a passage in the body to both health and strength, and a passage in the soul to the enjoyment of virtues.[23]

Praem. 31–32: After faith is set forth, he gains a prize, virtue, through nature and without effort. That prize is joy. The Greeks called his name laughter, but the Hebrews called the name Isaac. Laughter is the visible and bodily symbol of the unseen joy in the mind. 32 Joy is indeed the best and noblest of the higher emotions. By it the soul is filled through and through, rejoicing in God, the Father and Maker of all, and also rejoicing in all His doings in which evil has no place, even though they do not conduce to its own pleasure, rejoicing because they are created beautifully and in the permanence of the whole.[24]

Becoming Like God

Leg. 1.48–49: Now one might ask, "why, since to imitate God's works is holy, am I forbidden to plant a grove by the altar, but God plants the garden? For it says, "you shall not plant for yourself a grove; you shall not make for yourself any tree alongside the altar of sacrifice of the Lord your God" (Deut. 16:21). What, then, does this mean? That it is fitting for God to plant and to build up virtues in the soul. 49 But the mind, when it supposes itself equal to God, shows itself to be a lover of self and godless; and while supposing itself to be acting, it is found under scrutiny to be acted upon. Since it is God Who sows and plants noble qualities in the soul, the mind that says "I plant" acts impiously. Thus, you shall not plant whenever God is cultivating His plants. But if you also do put plants in the soul, O understanding, plant all plants that bear fruit. But do not plant a grove, for in a grove there are trees both of a wild and of a cultivated sort. And to plant in the soul wickedness, which is infertile, along with cultivated and fruit-bearing virtue, is a leprosy, similar to its twofold and confused nature.

Fug. 62b–64a: But evil remains here, removed as far as possible from the divine company, making our mortal life its haut and unable of quitting the human race by dying. 63 This truth found noble utterance in the *Theaetetus*, where a man highly esteemed, one of those admired for their wisdom, says: "but neither evil things are able to pass away—for there must always remain something which is antagonistic to good—nor to set up among the gods in heaven, and to go about the mortal nature and this place. Wherefore, we ought to fly away from earth to heaven as quickly as we can; and to fly away is to become like God. For to become like Him is to become just and holy with prudence." 64a Therefore, Cain shall not die, the symbol of wickedness, which must of necessity always live among men in the mortal race.

Somn. 1.73–74: And marvel not if the sun, in accordance with the rules of allegory, is likened to the Father and Ruler of the universe. For nothing is truly like God; there have been accounted so in human opinion two things only, one invisible and one visible; the soul is invisible, and the sun is visible. 74 Thus, the soul's likeness to God Moses has shown in another saying: "God made man, after the Image of God He made him" (Gen. 1:17), and also in the law enacted against murderers: "he who sheds man's blood, in requital for his blood shall there be bloodshed, because in the Image of God made I man" (Gen. 9:6); while the sun's likeness to God he has indicated by figures (*QG* 4.25, 188).[25]

Spec. 4.73: For what someone of the men of old aptly said it is true, that in no other action does man so much resemble God as in showing kindness, and what greater good can there be than that they should imitate God, they the created Him the Eternal?[26]

God-Like

Post. 91–93: Probably, Moses then calls right reason the father of our soul, and of elders to the associates and friends of right reason. These were the first that fix the boundaries of virtue. To the school of these it is advisable to go, and to learn by their teaching the essential matters. The essential matters are these: when God distributed and divided the nations of the soul, causing division and separating those of one common tongue from those of another tongue, He sowed seed and rejected from Himself the children of the earth, whom Moses calls "sons of Adam"; then, he fixed the boundaries of the offspring of virtue corresponding to the number of angels (*QE* 2.15). For so much are the words of God, so much are also both nations and forms of virtues. 92 But what are the portions of His angels and what is the allotted part of the Lord of all and the Ruler? The particular virtues in kind belong to the servants, and the chosen race of Israel to the Ruler. For he who sees God by surpassing beauty has been allotted as His portion to Him Whom he sees. 93 How then should Jobel escape rebuke, whose name when translated into Greek is "altering" the natures of things or making them other than what they are? For he changed the forms of prudence, of endurance, of justice, and of the other virtues; all of them are forms of God-like beauty, substituting contrary to the shapes of intemperance, and unwholesomeness, injustice, and all wickedness, obliterating the shapes that had been impressed before (*QG* 4.87, 153).

Somn. 2.223–224: Indeed, so vast in its excess is the stability of the divine, since he imparts to chosen natures a share of His steadfastness as their richest possession. Further, let us say of His covenant filled with His own graces—and the law is also the most honored of the existing things—that this God-like image shall be firmly planted with the just soul as its pedestal. He declares when he says to Noah, "I will establish my covenant with you" (Gen. 9:11). 224 These words also emphasize two meanings: first, that justice and the covenant of God are the same, and second, that while gifts bestowed by others are not the same as the recipients, God gives not only these gifts, but in them He gives the recipients to themselves. For He has given myself to me and each that is to itself, for "I shall establish my covenant with you" is the same as "I shall give yourself to you."[27]

Imitation of God

Spec. 4.187–188: For this is to follow God [see Chapter 2]. . . . 188 These things good rulers must imitate if they have any aspiration to be assimilated to God.

Virt. 167–168: But it is incumbent upon the one who is prudent, as far as possible, to make his neighbors shrewd, and the one who is moderate to make them temperate, and the one who is valiant to make them noble, and the one who is just to make them just, and, in all, for the good person to make them good. For these, I think, are powers, which the one who is good will embrace as most suitable for himself. But incapacity and weakness, their opposites, are alien to an excellent character. 168 Elsewhere, he teaches the rational nature the most proper knowledge to imitate God as much as possible, neglecting none of the things contributing to such assimilation. "Therefore," he says, "since you have received strength from the most Powerful, you must give a share of your strength to others, do to them as has been done to you, so that you might imitate God by giving gifts of the same kind. . . . "[28]

To Follow God

Migr. 131: Therefore, to follow God is, according to the most holy Moses, our main object, as he also says elsewhere, "you shall go back again into the steps of the Lord your God" (Deut. 13:4). He is not speaking of movement by the use of the legs, for earth carries humans, and I do not know whether even the whole universe carries God, but it is evidently employing figurative language to bring out how the soul should comply with those divine ordinances, the guiding principle of which is the honoring of Him to Whom all things owe their being.

Migr. 145–147: Hence, the law names virtue the accurate name Leah, which when translated is "growing weary" (Cher. 41). For virtue has, as it is fitting, made up her mind that the life of the wicked, being burdensome and heavy by nature, is wearisome, and she refuses so much as to look at it, turning away from those whose eyes are fixed only on the beautiful (morally speaking). 146 But let the mind be bent not only to follow God, ceaselessly and energetically, but also to keep the straight course. Let it be on the straight path inclining to neither side, neither to what is on the right nor to what is on the left, on which the earth Edom has his lurking holes, now being the victim of the excesses and extravagances, now of the shortcomings and deficiencies. For better is to walk on the middle path, the path that is truly the King's (Num. 20:17), seeing that God, the Great and only King, laid out a broad and goodly way for virtue-loving souls to keep virtue. 147 Hence, it is that some of those who followed the mild and social form of philosophy have said that the virtues are means, fixing them in a borderland, feeling that the overweening boastfulness of a braggart is bad, and that to adopt a humble and obscure position is to expose yourself to attack and oppression, whereas a fair and reasonable mixture of the two is beneficial.

Abr. 60–61: And we must next speak of the superior merits shown in each separately, beginning with the first. Abraham, then, filled with zeal for piety, the highest and greatest of virtues, was eager to follow God and to be obedient to his commands; understanding by commands not only those conveyed in speech and writing but also those made manifest by nature with clearer signs, and apprehended by the senses the most truthful of all and superior hearing, on which no certain reliance can be placed. 61 For anyone who contemplates the order in nature and the constitution enjoyed by the world, whose excellence no words can describe, needs no speaker to teach him to practice a well-ordered and peaceful life and aim at the beauties assimilating himself to them. But the clearest demonstrations of his piety are those that the holy Scripture contain.

THE PRACTICE OF VICES

Note

Philo skillfully combines important elements from the Greek tradition according to his own experiences and purposes to speak of the acquisition of virtues and the avoidance of vices. In Philo's ethics the greatest of evils is impiety. As the source of all the other vices, passions, and desires, it not only stands above all the other vices; it is the cause of the greatest punishment and eternal death.[29]

Vices

Agr. 17–18: These, therefore, are the promises held out by soul-husbandry in its inaugural proclamation. The trees of folly and licentiousness, of injustice and of cowardice, I will wholly cut down; I will also extirpate the plants of pleasures and desire, of anger and wrath, and of passions, even though they have grown up to heaven (*QG* 2.18); I will burn up their roots, letting go the rush of fire to the depths of the earth. So that no part, or footstep, or shadow of them be absolutely left behind. 18 Then, these I will destroy, but I will plant for souls in their childhood suckers whose fruit shall nurse them. These suckers are the learning to write easily and read fluently; the diligent search of wise poets have written: geometry and the practice of rhetorical composition, and the whole of the education embraced in school-learning (*QG* 3.21; *QE* 1.5). For in those souls at the stage of youths and of those now growing into men, I will implant the better and more perfect things suited to their age: the plant of sound sense, that of courage, that of temperance, that of justice, that of all virtue.

Sobr. 42–43: Conversely, there are thousands of hostile things to see corresponding with those who are unmanly, licentious, foolish, unjust, and impious at heart, but are incapable of displaying the ugliness of each vice, because of the inconvenience of their opportunity to sin (*QG* 2.35). But whenever there is an opportunity, suddenly it descends upon them with all its impetuous force, and fills up the earth and sea to their utmost bounds with an untold host of evil deeds. They leave nothing, great or small, without exception, and they overturn and destroy everything in one force. 43 For just as the power of fire is dormant or kindled into activity as fuel is absent or present, so the powers of the soul, which have vice and virtue in view, are quenched by inconvenience of opportunities and burst into flame when chance throws facilities in their way.

Her. 243–245: Moses introduces a very true thought when he teaches us that the soul loves justice and every virtue, but that the body loves injustice and every vice; what is friendly to the one is altogether hostile to the other, a teaching given now as at another time. He speaks in riddles of the soul's enemies as birds desiring to be entangled and to be rooted themselves in bodies and to inflict themselves with the flesh. It is to restrain the onsets and inroads of which it is said the clever man wishes to sit down in their company (Gen. 11:15), whomever they may be, like a chairman or president of a council. 244 Since the houses are also divided by civil faction and the hostile bands are at variance, such a one would bring a council of all concerned and investigate the points of difference, in order that using the power of persuasion, he may be able destroy the external war or put an end to the civil commotion. In the one case, he would scatter abroad the foe who rushed in irreconcilable hatred like a storm cloud, and in the other case, he would restore the old feeling of friendly kinship. 245 Therefore, the implacable and irreconcilable enemies of the soul are written on the list of follies; their acts of licentiousness, cowardice, injustice, and all the other irrational desires are so constantly born of overabundant appetite (cf. *Conf.* 90; *QG* 4.198), which prance and struggle against the yoke and hinder the understanding from preceding its straight course, and often rend and overthrow its whole frame.[30]

Impiety

Leg. 1.43: "And God planted a garden in Eden toward the east and placed there the human being whom he had molded" (Gen. 2:8). By using many words for it Moses has shown that the sublime and heavenly wisdom is called by many names. For he has called it "beginning" and "Image," and "vision of God." And now, He establishes through the planting of the garden that earthly wisdom is a copy of this wisdom as of an archetype. For let no such great impicty seize human reasoning so as to suppose that God tills the soil and plants gardens, since we should immediately be at a loss about what His motive could be. Let no such mythmaking ever enter our mind.

Ebr. 16–18: It has been acknowledged clearly and evidently that to obey virtue is good and profitable, and on the contrary, to disobey virtue is disgraceful and highly unfavorable. But if contentiousness is added to disobedience, it involves a vast increase of evil. For the disobedient is an evil knave, fond of quarrels; since he merely disregards the commands he receives and nothing more, while the other takes active pains to carry out what is opposed to these commands. 17 Let us consider how this shows itself. The law, for instance, commands us to honor our parents; he then who does not honor them is disobedient; and he who dishonors them is fond of strife. Again, it is a righteous action to preserve one's country. He who avoids this particular duty is to be classed as disobedient; he who actually purposes to betray it as a man of strife and contention. 18 He who does not practice kindness toward his neighbor, in opposition to another who thinks that it is necessary to give help, is disobedient. But one who, besides withholding his kindness, works all the harm he can, is moved by the spirit of strife to deadly error. Again, he who fails to make use of the holy rites and all else that relates to piety is disobedient to the commandments that the law and custom regularly prescribe in these matters, but rebellious or strife-stirrer is the name for him who turns aside to their direct opposite, impiety, and becomes a leader in godlessness.

Conf. 152–155: The words, "and they began to do this" (Gen. 11:6), express no moderation or indignation. They mean that the unscrupulous is not a sufficiently righteous thing to destroy the only race, but they also dared to attack the rights of heaven by sowing injustice and reaping impiety (*QE* 2.45). 153 With the wretched there is no advantage, for they accomplished much of what they wished, and their works confirmed what their senseless deliberations have taken into account, yet the case is not the same with those who are impious. For the things divine are unharmed and unhurt, and when these reprobates turn their transgression against them, they attain the beginning only, and never arrive at the end. 154 Therefore, we also have these words, "they have begun to do." For when satiate to transgress the law, the insatiable ones have taken their fill of sins against all that is of earth and sea and air, whose obtained nature is subject to corruption, and they intended to change the divine natures in heaven, that is to slander those who are outside, a custom that does not intend at all to put order. Indeed, he brings some penalty to slander not those who abuse, but those who accuse irreparable misfortune. 155 Yet that they only began and were unable to come to the end of their impiety, because there is no reason why they should not be denounced as they would have, they carried out all their intentions. Thus, he speaks of their having completed the tower, though they had not done so. "The Lord came down to see the city and the tower," not that they are going to build, but that they had already built.

Hypoth. 7.2: So, too, if you commit an outrage on the body of a slave or a free person; if you confine him in bonds or kidnap and sell him; so too with larceny of things profane and sacred; so too with impiety not only of acts but even of a casual word, and not only against God Himself (may He forgive the very thought of such a thing that should not even be mentioned), but also against a father or mother or benefactor of your own, the penalty is the same, death, and not the common, ordinary death: the offender in words only must be stoned to death. His guilt is as great as if he were the perpetrator of impious actions.[31]

Ignorance

Sacr. 45–49: After hearing these things, the mind turns away from pleasure and clings to virtue, apprehending her most revered beauty, her most natural state, and most noble character. Then, also, the mind becomes a shepherd of the sheep, who guides the chariot and the helmsman against the soul of the irrational faculty, who does not suffer them to divide into two parts, disorder and discord, without a master or a leader, lest their unbridled instincts come to perdition. They lack the protection and control of a father's hand, and help is far away. 46 At least, then, taking up with the most proper virtue, the practicer submits "to shepherd the sheep of Laban" (Gen. 30:36), of him, that is, whose thoughts are fixed on colors and shapes and lifeless bodies of every kind, he felt that it was a task most congenial to virtue. He does not tend all the sheep, "but the ones that were left" (Gen. 30:36). What does it mean? The irrationality or unreasonableness is by nature twofold: one is the unreasonableness that defies convincing reason, as when men call the foolish man unreasonable. The other one is the state from which reason is eliminated, as with the unreasoning animals. 47 Therefore, by the irrational movements of the mind, I mean the activities that defy convincing reason, are the charge of the sons of Laban, who were "three days journeying away" (Gen. 30:36), a parable that tells us that they were severed for all time from a good life. For time is tripartite: compounded of past, present, and future. But the forces that are unreasonable in the other sense, not those that defy right reason but merely lack reason—and in these the irrational animals have a share—the practicer will demand attention. He feels that error has befallen them not so much through sinful wickedness, as through untutored ignorance. 48 Thus ignorance is an involuntary state, a light matter, and its treatment through teaching is not unworkable (*QG* 4.156). But wickedness, being a willful sickness of the soul, admits of no remedy but such as if difficult, and almost impossible. Then, Jacob's sons, trained by the all-wise father, may go down into Egypt, the passion-loving body, and meet with the Pharaoh, the disperser of the good (*QG* 4.177); he is the king, who deems himself the sovereign of the animal and the composite; yet they will not be struck down by his abundance and splendor, but they will confess that "they are shepherds of sheep, and not only they, but their fathers too" (Gen. 47:3). 49 And further, no one could in power and sovereignty find so lofty a cause for boasting as these can in their office as shepherds. To be sure, to those who can reason, it is a prouder task than kingship to have the strength to rule, as a king in a city or country, over the body, the senses, the belly, the pleasures whose seat is below the belly, the other passions, the tongue, and in general all our compound being, vigorous and exceedingly strong, suitable to lead the way. For like the charioteer he must sometimes give the rein to his team, sometimes pull them in and draw them back, when they rush too wildly, resisting the haste of the steeds toward the world of external things.

Ebr. 162–163: And there are two kinds of ignorance: one is simple, total insensibility, and the other is twofold, when a person afflicted not only by a lack of knowledge, but also, led on by a false notion of his own wisdom, thinks he knows what he does not know at all. 163 Thus, the first evil is a lesser one, for it is the cause of minor and perhaps involuntary sins; the second is the greater, for it engenders great wrongs, not only those that are involuntary, but also those already premeditated.

Prob. 158–159: Therefore, let us do away with the vain glory, to which the great multitude of human beings feebly cling, and fixing the holiest of possessions, truth, we may dedicate neither to citizenship nor to slavery or slaves, whether homebred or bought with silver, but dismissing questions of race and certificates of ownership and bodily matters in general, study the nature of the soul. 159 For if the soul is driven toward desire or enticed by pleasure or turned away by fear, or shrunken by grief or overpowered by anger, it enslaves itself, and makes his soul a slave to a host of masters. But if it vanquishes ignorance with prudence, incontinence with temperance, and cowardice with courage, and covetousness with justice, it gains not only freedom from slavery but the gift of ruling as well.[32]

THE MIDDLE PATH BETWEEN TWO EXTREMES

Note

In light of Aristotle's doctrine of the mean in his ethical system,[33] Philo treats the virtues as "means." Philo understands the concept of virtue as a *mean* between two extremes.[34] He considers the *mean,* like Aristotle, a characteristic of perfection, and the extremes (deficiency and excess) characteristics of vices of the soul. Metaphorically, virtue as "middle path" embraces a perfect state halfway between the two extremes. According to Aristotle, the mean is where the acme of virtue is; in other words, it is "what is intermediate."[35] He explains, "in everything that continues and is visible" there is an excess, a *mean*, and a deficiency, and both the excess and the deficiency are characteristic of vice.[36]

The Mean

Post. 100–102: And about Jubal, Moses says, he is the brother of Jobel (Gen. 4:21), and Jubal is interpreted as "shifting to the other side" through a symbol, which is after the uttered word. For this word in its nature is brother to understanding. It is a suitable name for the utterance of a mind that violently alters the things that have been done, for it comes to assist in a manner to play a double game, swaying up and down as a pair of scales or like a ship at sea being struck by huge waves and rolling toward each side of the ship. For the foolish man has never learned to say anything sure or well grounded. 101 But Moses thinks that one should incline neither to the right nor to the left nor to any part of earthly Edom at all, but to pass by along the middle road, which he most properly calls the royal road (Num. 20:17). Since God is the First and sole King of the universe, the road leading to Him, seeing that it is the King's road, is properly called royal. Take this road as philosophy, which in the present time is not pursued by a crowd of Sophists, who, having practiced the arts of speech in opposition to the truth, called their sophistry wisdom, assigning a divine title to their miserable work. It is, rather, the philosophy that the ancient band of devotees achieved with great effort, turning aside from the bland charms of pleasure, elegantly and rigorously engaged in the study of virtue. 102 Certainly, this royal road, then, which we declared to be true and legitimate philosophy, is called by the law, the utterance, and Word of God. For it is written, "you shall not turn aside from the word, which I command you today to the right hand nor to the left hand" (Deut. 28:14). Thus, it is clearly demonstrated that the Word of God is identical with the royal road, if, namely, He exhorts us to turn away neither from the Word of God nor the royal way, as being synonymous, but with upright mind to advance on the straightforward path, the middle roadway.

Deus 162–165: And let them not turn aside to the right or to the left of the king's way, but advance forward to the middle path. For deviations in either side, whether of excess or of deficiency, whether they tend to strain or to relaxation, are in fault. In this way the right side is no less blameworthy than the left side. 163 Alongside those who live recklessly, the boldness is the right and cowardice the left. To those who are churlish in money matters, parsimony is the right and extravagance the left. All those who are oversharp and calculating in business count the knave's qualities worthy of their choice, but the simpleton's qualities of their avoidance. And others pursue superstition as the right side, but they flee from impiety as a thing to be shunned. 164 But, that we may not, through turning aside from the right road, be compelled to yield to the vices that war against us, let us wish and pray that we may walk straight along the middle path (*QE* 1.15–16). And courage is the middle between rashness and cowardice, and temperance between careless extravagance and illiberal parsimony, prudence between knavery and folly, and piety between superstition and impiety. 165 These lie in the middle between the deviations to either side, and all of the high roads meet for the traveler's use, wherein we are bound in duty to walk continually, not with the mechanism of the body, but with the motions of the soul, which seeks the best.

Abr. 24: This is why Moses said that the transferred "was not found," being hard to find and hard to seek. Thus, he passes across from ignorance to instruction, from folly to sound sense, from cowardice to courage, from impiety to piety, again from voluptuousness to self-control, and from vaingloriousness to simplicity (*QG* 4.186). What wealth is equal in worth to these, or what possession of royalty or dominion more profitable?

Praem. 27: Therefore, the leader of the one adopting the godly doctrine, who first passed over from vanity to truth, came to perfection by virtue gained in teaching, and he received a prize, that is faith in God (cf. *Abr.* 262–263). To him, who happily acquired the virtue naturally, self-acquired and self-taught, the reward that is given is joy.[37] The man of practice, who by unwearied and unswerving labor has made the excellent his own, his own has for his crown the vision of God.[38] Belief in God, lifelong joy, the eternal vision of the Existent One, what can anyone conceive more profitable or more august than these?[39]

PASSIONS AND THE STOIC FOUR PASSIONS

Passions

Leg. 3.113–114: It is cursed also beyond all the beasts. Certainly, I mean the passions of the soul, for by these the mind is hurt and destroyed. Why then is it accounted to be worse than the other passions? Because it is at the bottom of them all, like a staring-point and foundation. For desire comes into play through love of pleasure; grief arises as pleasure is withdrawn; fear again is engendered owing to a dread of being without pleasure. It is clear then that all the passions depend on pleasure, and these would have never taken shape at all, if first there had not been deposited that which is productive of them, that is pleasure. 114 "On your breast and the belly you shall walk" (Gen. 3:14). For passion works in these parts: the breast and the belly. When pleasure has the materials, it needs to produce it, and then, it haunts the belly and the parts below it. But when it is at a loss for these materials, it occupies the breast where wrath is. For the lovers of pleasure when deprived from the pleasure grow bitter and angry.

Congr. 81–82: Sarah gives Hagar to Abraham not immediately at his arrival in the land of the Canaanites (*QG* 2.65), but after he has stayed there for ten years. And why is this? This should require careful consideration. In the first stage at the beginning of our creation the soul is furnished with natural passions only, griefs, pains, excitements, desires, pleasures, which come to it through sense-perception; reason is not yet able to see good and evil and to form an accurate judgment of the difference between them, but it is still slumbering, its eyes closed as if in deep sleep. 82 But as time goes on, when we leave the age of boyhood and are adolescent, there springs from the single root the twofold stalk: virtue and vice. We form an apprehension of both, but necessarily choose one or the other, the better natured choosing virtue, the opposite kind vice.

Spec. 4.113b–114: Reptiles with four legs and many feet represent the miserable slaves of not just one passion, desire, but all passions, which generically are four in number, each having many species. The tyranny of one passion is cruel, the tyranny of many passions cannot but be the most harsh and intolerable. 114 Creeping things, which have legs above their feet, so that they can leap from the ground, he designates these as clean (cf. Lev. 11:21). These are, for instance, the different kinds of grasshoppers and the snake-fighter, as it is called; here again, by symbols he searches into the character and ways of the reasonable soul. For the natural gravity of the body pulls down with it those of little mind, strangling and overwhelming them with the multitude of the fleshy elements (*QG* 4.152).[40]

The Four Passions: Pleasure, Desire, Grief, Fear

Det. 119–120: To the godless Cain, on the other hand, the earth attributes nothing to endurance, in spite of his being laborious with nothing beyond the concerns of earth. Therefore, it is a natural consequence of this that he is found "groaning and trembling upon the earth" (Gen. 4:12), that is to say, proclaiming in fear and grief. Such as this is the life of the wretched man, to whom the painful four passions have been allotted: fear, grief, the one identical with groaning, the other with trembling. For such a life some evil thing must either be present or on its way. Therefore, the expectation of that which is on its way begets fear, the experience of that which is present begets grief. 120 But the one who pursues virtue is counted among those who are in harmony with happiness. For he has either won the prize or is on the way to win it; thus, to have it renders joy, the fairest of possessions; and to be expecting that you will reach it produces that food of souls that love virtue, hope, through which makes us cast away hesitation, and essay with hearty alacrity all noble deeds.

Her. 269–272: And the slavery is for four hundred years, and he shows the powers of the four passions (*QG* 4.16). When pleasure leads the way, the temper is lifted and is puffed up, being raised with empty levity. When desire rules, a desire for what is not arises and suspends the soul on an unaccomplished hope as on a noose. For the soul is always in thirst but unable to drink, patiently enduring the torment of Tantalus. 270 Under the tyranny of grief, it is pinched and shrinks, like trees that shed their leaves and wither. When fear has a tyrannical disposition, no one thinks it worthy to stand his ground, but abandons himself to flight and escapes, expecting that in this alone will safety be found. For while desire has an attractive power and forces us to the pursuit of the desired object, fear causes a sense of estrangement, producing alienation and separating us far apart from what gives light. 271 The sovereignties of the passions here named entail a grievous slavery on their subjects, until God the arbitrator and judge makes a separation between the ill-treater and the ill-treated, brings forth the one to full liberty, and renders to the other the recompense for his misdeeds. 272 For it is written, "the nation whom they shall serve I will judge, and after this they shall come out hither with much stock" (Gen. 15:14). It must be a need that the mortal man shall be oppressed by the nation of the passions and receive the calamities, which are proper to created beings; but it is the will of God to lighten the evil things, which are inherent in our race.

Abr. 236–239: Thus, this is what we find in the scriptures when read literally; but those who can contemplate such incorporeal things stripped of the body and in naked reality, those who live with the soul rather than with the body, will say that of these nine kings; four are the power exercised within us by the four passions, pleasure, desire, fear, and grief, and that the five are the five senses, sight, hearing, taste, smell, and touch (*QG* 2.21; 3.4). 237 For these nine are in a sense our kings and rulers, but not all in the same way. The five are subjects of the four and are forced to pay them the tolls and tributes determined by nature. 238 For griefs, pleasures, fears, and desires arise out of what we see or hear or smell or taste or touch, and none of the passions would have any strength of itself if it were not furnished with what the senses supply. 239 These are forces of the passions, in colors and shapes, or sounds spoken or heard, or in flavors or scents or the qualities in tangible things, in soft and hard or rough and smooth or warm and cold. For all of which are provided through the senses to each of the passions.

Praem. 158–160: Then, like a loving mother she will pity her sons and daughters whom she has lost them, who in death and when alive, they were grief to their parents. Young once more she will be fruitful and will bear a blameless generation, a correction of the one that went before. For she who is a barren, says the prophet, will be blessed with many and kind children, a saying which also conveys an allegory of the soul. 159 For when the soul is many, full of passions and of evil things, as gathering around with her children, pleasures, desires, folly, intemperance, injustice, she is feeble and sick and perishable to death (cf. *Mut.* 10, 143). But when she has become barren and ceases to produce these children or indeed has cast them out bodily, she is transformed into a pure virgin. 160 When receiving the divine seed, she forms and gives life of precious qualities and wonderful beauties: prudence, courage, temperance, justice (*QG* 4.206), holiness, piety, and the other virtues and good emotions. Not only is it well the source of these goodly children to be brought to birth, but good also is the expectation of this birth cheering the weakness with hope.[41]

THE ALLEGORICAL INTERPRETATION OF "THE FALL"

Note

Philo interprets Gen. 2–3, particularly Gen. 2:7 (the second account of the creation of man) and Gen. 2:21–3:1a (the creation of woman), in the *Legum Allegoriae* 2 and carries them through the rest of the *Legum Allegoriae* 3. In *Leg.* 2.53–3.253, Philo's interpretation of Gen. 3:1–19, is where the issues of ethical significance are most apparent and most acute. Philo interprets the text in Gen. 2:1–24 allegorically in such a way as to establish the basic makeup of each human being: allegorically the man is the mind (or intellect), the woman is allegorically sense-perception, and the serpent (Gen. 3:1a) is symbolically pleasure. Especially with the entry of the serpent, the drama of the human soul reaches a new stage, a stage in which Philo is more interested. Philo not only adds the moral component in his allegory of the soul, but he interprets the texts in such a way that his allegorical interpretation describes how the human soul can live properly according with nature and become like God.

Man

Leg. 3.49–50: "And the Lord God called Adam and said to him, 'Where are you?'" (Gen. 3:9). Why is Adam alone called, his wife having hid herself with him? One must speak first that the mind is called even there where he was, when it receives reproof and a check is given to its defection. But not only is the mind itself called, but also all his faculties, for without its faculties the mind by itself is found naked and not existent; and one of the faculties is also sense-perception, which is woman. 50 Therefore, he has called both Adam, the mind, and the woman, sense-perception. But He does not call her with a special call; why? Because being irrational, she is not able to receive reproof from herself. For neither sight nor hearing nor any of the other senses is susceptible to instruction, so it is unable to perform the act of apprehending objects. For He who made sense-perception, woman, made it capable of distinguishing between material things only. But the mind, man, is the one who receives instruction, and that is why He summons mind but not sense-perception.

Agr. 66: Accordingly, when the mind, the ruler of the flock, taking the flock of the soul in hand with the Law of Nature's instruction vigorously leads the way, the mind turns it out complete, worthy of praise and approval;

but when the soul is a disparager, it behaves transgressing the law slackly and carelessly. Similarly, the one will take on him the name of king and be hailed "shepherd," but the other that of a sort of a cook or baker and be entitled "a cattle-keeper," serving up rich fare as a feast for beasts who make a habit of gluttony.

Agr. 30–31: Nature has engendered flocks and herds akin to us. The soul puts forth, as it were, from one root two shoots, one of which has been left whole and undivided and is called mind; and the one part divided by six parts is made into seven kinds: five outward senses and two other organs, that of utterance and production. 31 All this herd, being irrational, is compared to flocks and herds, but by nature's law a herd cannot do without an experience in ruling. Whenever, therefore, a man, who is ignorant of how to rule and is wealthy, rises up and appoints himself governor, he becomes the author of a multitude of evils to his charges.

Woman

Leg. 3.220: "And to your husband," he says, "shall be your resort" (Gen. 3:16). Sense-perception has two husbands: one who is lawful, and the other who is seducer (*QG* 1.27). For after the fashion of a seducing husband the thing seen acts on the sight, the sound acts on the hearing, the flavor acts on the palate, and so with the rest of the senses one by one. And these turn away and invite to themselves the irrational sense and get the mastery of it and govern it. For beauty enslaves the senses corresponding to them.

Agr. 107–109: Therefore, Eve's serpent is introduced as thirsting for man's blood—for Moses says in the curses pronounced on it, "he shall watch for your head, and you shall watch for his heel" (Gen. 3:15); and Dan's serpent of which we are now speaking, is introduced as biting, not a man's, but a horse's heel. 108 For Eve's serpent being, as was shown before, a symbol of pleasure, attacks a man against the reasoning faculty in each of us; for the delightful experience of abounding pleasure is the destruction of understanding; 109 whereas the serpent of Dan, being a figure of endurance, a most sturdy virtue, will be found biting a horse, the symbol of passion and wickedness, as temperance makes the overthrow and destruction of these its aim.[42]

Snake

Opif. 157–158: Now, there are two mythical fictions, such as poets and Sophists delight in, but modes of making ideas visible, bidding us resort to allegorical interpretation guided in our renderings by what lies beneath the surface. Following a probable conjecture one would say, first, that the snake spoken of is a symbol of pleasure; second, because he takes clods of earth as food; third, because he carries poison in his teeth with which it is his nature to destroy those whom he has bitten. 158 The lover of pleasure is exempt from none of these traits, for it is with difficulty that he can lift up his head, being weighted and dragged down, he is thrown down and tripped up by intemperance: he feeds not on heavenly nourishment, which wisdom by discourses and doctrines offers to lovers of contemplation, but on that which comes up out of the earth with the revolving seasons, and which produces drunkenness, voraciousness, and greediness. These, causing the carvings of the belly to burst out and fanning them into flame, make the man a glutton, while they also stimulate and stir up the stings of his sexual lusts. . . . Hence, we see that, no less than the snake, he carries his poison in his teeth.

Opif. 165: Pleasure does not venture to bring its wiles and deceptions to bear on the man, but on the woman, and by her means on him. This is a telling and well-made point: for in us mind corresponds to man, the sense to woman; and pleasure encounters and associates itself with the senses first, and then by their means cajoles also the sovereign mind: for after each sense has been subjugated to its sorceries, delighting in what it offers: the sense of sight in variegated colors and shapes, the sense of hearing in harmonious sounds, the sense of taste in delicate savors, and the sense of scent in the fragrance of perfumes that it inhales, these all receive the gifts and offer them like handmaids to the reason as to a master, bringing them persuasion to plead that it reject nothing whatever. Reason is immediately ensnared and becomes a subject instead of a ruler, a slave instead of a master, an alien instead of a citizen, and a mortal instead of an immortal.

Leg. 2.71–75a: "And the snake was the most subtle of all the beasts upon the earth, which the Lord God made" (Gen. 3:1; *QG* 1.31, 47). Two things: mind and sense, having already come into being, and these being in nakedness in the manner that has already been set forth, it was necessary that there should be a third subsistence, pleasure, to bring both of them together to the apprehension of the objects of mental and of sense-perception. For neither the mind is able to apprehend an animal from sense-perception nor a plant or a stone or a log or any bodily shape whatever; nor could the sense-perception apart from the mind be able to maintain the act of perceiving. 72 Since, then, it was necessary that both of these should come together for the apprehension of the objects about them, what was it that brought them together but a third, a bond of love and desire, under the rule and dominion of pleasure to which the prophet gave the symbolic name of a snake? 73 God the Creator fashioned the order exceeding well. First, the mind, that is the man, for it is the most venerable in a human being; then, it is sense-perception, that is the woman; then, after them, on the third place, it is pleasure. But it is only potentially, that is, as objects of thought, that they differ in age; for in actual time, they are equal in age. For the soul brings all things together with herself, but some parts it brings in their actual existence, and other parts in virtue of the potentiality to arrive, even if they have not yet reached the goal. 74 The reason why pleasure is likened to a snake is this: the movement of pleasure is just like that of the snake; it is intricate and manifold. First, it takes its gliding course in five ways, because pleasures are occasioned by sight and by hearing and by taste and by smell and by touch. But the most vehement and intense are those that are concerned with the excessive sexual intercourse with women, and this is the method ordained by nature for the purpose of production. 75a And yet, the fact that pleasure insinuates itself about all the organs of the irrational position of the soul is not the only reason for our calling her variable; for it is also complex about each part. For instance, it is concerned with complex pleasures through sight: all those produced by each scriptural, artistic creation, and by all other artistic works that charm the eyes; so also, by the differences of plants as they shoot up, bloom, and bear fruit; by the beauty of animals seen in many forms.[43]

NOTES

1. Cf. Gal. 5:22–23.
2. *Cher.* 95–97, 101–105; *Agr.* 78–79; *Ebr.* 119–123; *Migr.* 36–37, 86–90; *Her.* 307–311; *Abr.* 22–25; *Mos.* 1.154–156; 2.8–11; *Virt.* 84; *Praem.* 119–125, 157–161; *Aet.* 1–2.
3. Plato, *Leg.* 631C-D; 688A–B; 963A–965E.
4. Plutarch, *Stoic. rep.* 1034C-E; *Virt. mor.* 440E–441B.
5. *Sobr.* 37–41; *Mut.* 145–156; *Abr.* 217–224; *Spec.* 2.60–62; 4.145–148; *Prob.* 69–72.
6. *Cher.* 96; *Spec.* 4.135.
7. Naveros Córdova, *Philo of Alexandria's Ethical Discourse*, 85–102.
8. Walter T. Wilson, *Philo of Alexandria, On Virtues: Introduction, Translation, and Commentary* (Philo of Alexandria Commentary Series 3; Leiden: Brill, 2011), 137.
9. *Ebr.* 17–18, 75–79, 107–110; *Conf.* 128–132; *Somn.* 2.64–67; *Abr.* 114–116; *Mos.* 1.300–304; *Decal.* 52–63; *Spec.* 1.313–314; *Contempl.* 24–26; *Legat.* 239–245.
10. *Mos.* 1.196–202; *Spec.* 1.53–55.
11. *Cher.* 120–123; *Sacr.* 49–51, 64–65, 85–86; *Det.* 115–118; *Post.* 78–82; *Her.* 18–21, 100–108; *Deus* 140–144; *Conf.* 145–147; *Fug.* 82–83; *Congr.* 113–115, 154–157; *Praem.* 79–81.
12. *Conf.* 30–32; *Migr.* 43–46; *Mut.* 201–203; *Abr.* 262.
13. *Sacr.* 85b–86; *Congr.* 111–113; *Somn.* 1.118–119, 150–152; *Abr.* 23–26.
14. *Agr.* 110–114; *Plant.* 144–145; *Migr.* 134–135, 166–167, 199–201; *Mut.* 47–51.
15. *Mut.* 11–15; *Somn.* 1.167–174, 193–196; *Mos.* 1.75–76.
16. *Cher.* 106.
17. *Abr.* 4–6, 60–61; Plato, *Laws* 716A; Aristotle, *Eth. nic.* 2–10; 6.13.1145a6; Stobaeus 2.75.11–76.8; Stobaeus's *Anthology*, 2.73; Alcinous, *Didaskalikos*, 1.152.2–3;

16.172.6–10; Diogenes Laertius 7.107. Cf. Long & Sedley, *The Hellenistic Philosophers* (2 vols.; Cambridge: Cambridge University Press, 2012), 58C–D, 1:354–55; 63A, 1:394.

18. See also *Meno* 88C; *Resp.* 465D, 613B.

19. E.g., Cleanthes, fragment 552.

20. Plato, *Phaed.* 252D-E; see also the Stoic Epictetus, *Diss.* 1.30.4.

21. Aristotle, *Eth. nic.* 1.9.1099b15–17; 4.3.1123b35; 10.7.1177b1–4; Diogenes Laertius 7.119; Cleanthes, *Hymn to Zeus,* vol. 4 (*SVF* 1.537); cf. *Let. Arist.* 210, 261.

22. Naveros Córdova, *Philo of Alexandria's Ethical Discourse,* 157–65.

23. *Cher.* 49–50; *Mut.* 51–53; *Virt.* 117–118; *Prov.* 2.42.

24. *Migr.* 157; *Mut.* 167–171; *Spec.* 2.46–55, 184–185, 214; *Praem.* 159–161.

25. *Spec.* 2.225.

26. *Spec.* 4.188–189.

27. *Mos.* 1.157–159; *Prob.* 150–151; *Contempl.* 66–67.

28. *Spec.* 4.72–73.

29. *Post.* 39 and *QE* 1.10.

30. *Sacr.* 14–18; 21–22; *Conf.* 84–95; *Mut.* 49–51; *Mos.* 1.295. List of virtues: *Conf.* 117–118; *Post.* 52–62; *Ios.* 80–84; *Spec.* 1.295; *Virt.* 182; *Praem.* 52–56; *Contempl.* 2; *Prov.* 2.8, 39.

31. *Deus* 111–113; *Ebr.* 77–79; *Conf.* 111–114; *Spec.* 3.124–128; *Praem.* 127–129; *Flacc.* 128–132; *Prov.* 2.24–25.

32. *Sacr.* 85–86; *Det.* 175–176; *Agr.* 161–164; *Migr.* 17–18; *Fug.* 82; *Mut.* 16–19; *Legat.* 1–2, 69–70.

33. See Aristotelian, *Eth. nic.* 2.6.1107a6–8; 2.6.1106b33–34; *Ethic. eud.* 2.3–3.7.1234b12; 2.31220b21–24.

34. *Migr.* 147–148; *Det.* 18, 24.

35. *Eth. nic.* 2.5.6.1106a–1107a1–25.

36. Naveros Córdova, *Philo of Alexandria's Ethical Discourse*, 107–119.

37. *Plant.* 169–170; *Congr.* 35–36.

38. *Migr.* 199; *Agr.* 42.

39. *Spec.* 4.168–177.

40. *Deus* 71–73; *Ebr.* 105–106; *Conf.* 26–28; *Congr.* 81–82, 172; *Prob.* 45–46; *Legat.* 237–238.

41. *Ebr.* 111–113; *Congr.* 91–94.

42. *Leg.* 2.64–67; 3.59–64.

43. *Opif.* 163–164; *Leg.* 2.53–56, 87–93, 105–108.

BIBLIOGRAPHY

Jastram, Daniel N. "Philo's Generic Virtue." *Society of Biblical Literature Seminar Papers* 30 (1991): 323–47.

Lévy, Carlos. "Philo's Ethics." Pages 146–71 in *The Cambridge Companion to Philo*. Edited by Adam Kamesar. Cambridge: Cambridge University Press, 2009.

McPherran, Mark L. "Piety, Justice, and the Unity of Virtue." *Journal of the History of Philosophy* 38 (2000): 299–328.

Naveros Córdova, Nélida. *Philo of Alexandria's Ethical Discourse: Living in the Power of Piety.* Lanham, MD: Lexington Books/Fortress Academic, 2018.

Williamson, Ronald. "The Ethical Teaching of Philo." Pages 201–305 in *Jewish in the Hellenistic World: Philo*. Cambridge: Cambridge University Press, 1989.

Chapter 5

Biblical Characters

In this chapter the reader encounters the most important biblical characters mentioned by Philo in his exegesis. I do not intend to present all the biblical characters that Philo mentions but provide Philo's way of describing metaphorically the biblical names in the Pentateuch. As it is characteristic of this chapter, the translations are mostly short statements regarding the major biblical characters that have strong ethical significance only. So, the reader gets a sense of not only Philo's representation generally in an allegorical fashion, but also his high level of philosophical thinking, in particular his consistent association of the biblical names with virtue and vices.

Philo's creativity in describing the biblical characters reflects a combination of Jewish understanding of these biblical figures and his sophisticated interpretation in the context of virtues and vices. Philo draws on narratives in the Pentateuch, but not exclusively from Genesis. He also draws on a collection of legal texts from Deuteronomy, in such a way that the biblical characters in the narratives become part of his overall allegory of the soul. They are interpreted as symbols of parts of the human soul or as various virtues and vices. Several significant names, such as Cain, Abel, Moses, Joseph, Noah, Laban, Hagar, the three Patriarchs, and the Matriarchs, are already interpreted in the previous chapters, and their names also appear in the next two chapters. However, most of these names Philo interprets as specific places, virtues, vices, words, and phrases to add compelling ethical reflections to his biblical exegesis. Philo internalizes the biblical narratives so that the characters represent parts of the soul in its struggle to become virtuous and to overcome vice. In this sense, most of the biblical figures in the narratives serve to support or exemplify the overall allegorical interpretation of the three books as a whole (*Legum Allegoriae* 1–3). For example, the names of the Matriarchs (e.g., Sarah, Rebekah, and Leah) are consistently associated with virtue, and the names of the "good" men with mind and virtues. These metaphorically represent humans of noble character. This is not the case for the figures like Cain and Laban, who are often connected with vices, sense-perception, passions, and the pleasures of the body. What is also interesting in this selection of biblical names is that they are related in one way or another to God the Existent One, the created world, and the obedience to the ethical commandments of the Mosaic Law.

I included the two Jewish groups of Essenes and Therapeutes for two reasons: first, Philo's testimonial offer new insights about these groups; indeed, Philo is the only source to date that provides valuable information about the Therapeutes; second, they are an addition to Philo's contribution to first century Judaism and Christianity.

JEWISH NAMES

Adam

Leg. 1.92: Quite appropriately, therefore, Adam, that is to say the mind, although he names and comprehends other things, assigns no name to himself, because he is ignorant of himself and his own nature (*QG* 1.53; 2.17). And it is this one, and the one that came into being after His Image and after the idea, that God commands. For the latter, even without urging, possesses virtue by being self-taught; but Adam, without instruction, could have no part in prudence.

Leg. 3.1: "And Adam and his wife hid themselves from the face of the Lord God in the midst of the garden" (Gen. 3:8). Moses introduces a doctrine that teaches that the bad man is a fugitive. For if virtue is a city belonging to the wise men, he who has no power to partake of virtue has been driven away from the city, in which the bad man is incapable of taking part. Immediately, the exile from virtue has been hiding from God. For if the wise men, as being His friends, are in God's sight, it is evident that all bad men have been disappearing and have been hiding from God, as is to be expected in men who cherished hatred and are hostile to right reason.[1]

Cain and Abel

Cher. 52b: Why, then, oh soul, biding to live a virgin life in the house of God and to embrace knowledge, you should stand separated from these virtues and receive with joy sense-perception, which makes you effeminate and also defiles you? Therefore, you shall give birth to the offspring, the one of confusion and destructive breeding, the fratricide and the accursed Cain, the possession that is not possession. For Cain means "possession" (*QG* 1.59).

Sacr. 2–3: Well then, it has come to terms that there are two opposite and contending views: one that ascribes all things to the mind as a master, whether we are using our reason or our senses, in motion, or in quietness, and the other that follows God as it believes itself to be a handicraft.[2] The first image is Cain, who is called "possession" because he believes to possess all things, and the other is Abel, for he is interpreted as "one who brings forth all things to God." 3 Thus, both of these views lie in the womb of the single soul. But when they are brought to birth, they need to be separated. For it is impossible for enemies to live together forever. Until then the soul brought forth the God-loving doctrine, Abel, the self-loving, Cain, was dwelling in her. But when she engendered the recognition of the Cause, she abandoned the recognition of the mind.

Sacr. 11–12: "And Abel became a shepherd of sheep, but Cain was working the earth" (Gen. 4:2). Why is it that while he showed us Cain as older than Abel, he has now changed the order and mentions the younger first after their choice of occupation? For the probability seemed to be that the elder preceded to his cultivation first, and the younger at the later time to his care of the sheep. 12 For Moses embraces no value on probable and plausible things, but he pursues the pure truth. When he comes alone on his own to God, he says with boldness that he has no desire for eloquence or persuasiveness, and this, he says, has been his condition from a few days ago when God first began to talk with him as His servant (Exod. 4:10).

Det. 96: On Cain, who rejects repentance (*QG* 2.13, 43), He proceeds, owing to the enormity of his guilt to set the most appropriate curses to the murderer of a brother. At first, He said to him: "now also accursed you are from the land" (Gen. 4:11), making clear that it is not now the first time, when he has perpetrated the treacherous deed, that he is abominable and accursed, but also that he was so before, when he deliberated on the murder, since the purpose is as important as the completed act.

Agr. 21–22: For he says, "Cain was working the earth" (Gen. 4:2), and a little later, at the time when he was discovered to have incurred the pollution of fratricide, it is said, "accursed are you from the earth, which opened her mouth to receive the blood of your brother from your hand, with which you shall work the earth, and it shall not add its strength to give it to you" (Gen. 4:12f.). 22 How, therefore, could anyone be able to show more clearly than in this manner that the Lawgiver considers the bad man the worker of the soil and not a husbandman? One must not, thus, suppose that what is spoken of is either about a person able to work with hands and feet and the other powers of the body, or that it is soil on the hill or plain. But it is about the faculties of each one of us. For the soul of the bad man has no other interest than in his earthly body and all the body's pleasures (*QG* 1.69).

Conf. 124–125: Therefore, Cain also tilled the ground, of which he was keeping the firstlings to himself to offer in turn only the fruits to God. Indeed, it is said, he had near him a sound example. For his brother Abel offered in sacrifice the first-born younglings, not the after-born of his flock, thus confessing that the eldest causes, which come higher in the chain of causation, owe their existence to the cause that is highest and first of all. 125 The impious man thinks the opposite, that the mind is the absolute ruler of what is planned, and the sense-perception is also the absolute ruler of what is perceived. He holds that the latter judges corporeal things and the former judges all things, and that both are free from fault or error.

Det. 32: . . . For Abel, referring all things to God, is a God-loving doctrine, but Cain, referring all things to himself—for his name means "acquisition"—is a self-loving doctrine. And the self-lovers, having stripped and prepared for conflict with those who honor virtue, keep up the boxing and wrestling until they have either forced their opponents to give in or have completely destroyed them.

Det. 45–48: Thus, it was suitable for Abel to use caution and save virtue and to stay at home, paying no regard to the challenging, contentious, and wrangling struggle. He should have imitated Rebekah, who is "patience." When Esau, who represents wickedness, threatens to kill Jacob the practicer of virtue, she charges him against whom the plot was being hatched to go away, until Esau's cruel madness against him be allayed. 46 Expecting an intolerable threat, he holds over him, when he says, "let the days of my father's mourning draw near, so that I shall kill my brother" (Gen. 27:41). For he prays that Isaac, the only example without passion beneath the sun, who receives the divine warning "not to go down into Egypt" (Gen. 26:2), may fall upon irrational passion, desiring him, so that I think, to be wounded by the tortures of pleasure or grief or some other passion. So, he makes clear that he who falls short of perfection and knows only toilsome progress shall be liable not to be wounded only, but he shall receive complete destruction. God, indeed, in His lovingkindness will neither cause a being of an invulnerable kind to be the victim of a passion, nor will He hand over the practice of virtue to a mad murderer for ruin. 47 Therefore, the words that come next, "Cain rose up against his brother Abel and killed him" (Gen. 4:8), suggest, so far as superficial fantasy, that Abel has been done away with, but when examined more carefully, it is that Cain has been done away with by himself. One must understand that "Cain rose up and killed himself," not someone else. And he fairly suffered for this. 48 For the soul that has eliminated from itself the principles of love of virtue and the love of God, has died to the life of virtue. Therefore, Abel, unexpectedly, has been put to death and also lives. He is destroyed out of the mind of the foolish, but he is alive with the happy life in God.[3]

Seth

Post. 125–127: Seth is interpreted as "watering" (*QG* 1.78). Therefore, as the earth's seeds and plant trees after being watered grow and sprout and are prolific in producing fruits, but being deprived of irrigation, wither away, so likewise the soul, as is evident, when fostered with drinkable streams of wisdom, shoots forth and improves. Watering is either the act of one watering, or the experience of one being watered. . . . 127 It is in this way that the Logos of God waters the virtues, for this Logos is the source and spring of noble conduct.

Post. 172–173: When he says that Seth has sprung up as another seed, he does not make clear that he is "another." Is it in respect of the murdered Abel or of Cain, who slew him? Perhaps the new offspring is different from each of them; from Cain as one hostile to him—for thirst of virtue is a thing utterly at war with wickedness, which plays the part of a deserter—and from Abel, the one who is friendly and akin to him. For it does not say "alien from him," but "different," as that which is but beginning differs from that which is full-grown, and that which is in communion with the uncreated. 173 For this reason, Abel, relinquishing and removing the mortal, has gone to the better existence, and Seth, since he is sprung from human virtue, shall never relinquish the race of human beings but shall obtain enlargement.

Enoch

Post. 35: Thus, what is the impious man's opinion? The human mind is the measure of all things. It was an opinion held, they tell us, by an ancient Sophist named Protagoras, an offspring of Cain's madness. I recognize, hence, that by "wife" this opinion is meant from the fact that when Cain knew her she bore Enoch (*QG* 1.83, 85). And Enoch means "your gift." For if human is the measure of all things, all things are present and the gift of the mind.[4]

Noah

Leg. 3.77: Exactly, then, as God hates pleasure and the body without accusations, so also does He promote goodly natures apart from any manifest cause, acknowledging no action of theirs acceptable before bestowing his commendations upon them. For if anyone should question why Moses says that Noah found grace in the presence of the Lord God (Gen. 6:8) without doing fair deed, we shall give a suitable answer to be of an excellent nature from his birth, for Noah means "rest" or "righteous" (cf. Gen. 5:29; *QG* 1.87). But it is a necessity that he who rests from unrighteousness and sinfulness rests upon justice and what is good.

Deus 117–118: For he says, "These are the generation of Noah. Noah was a righteous man, being perfect in his generation. Noah was well pleasing to God" (Gen. 6:9; *QG* 1.97). The offspring of creatures compounded of body and soul must also themselves be compounded. For horses necessarily beget horses, lions beget lions, bulls beget bulls, and so similarly with human beings. 118 And not such are the offspring proper to the good mind, but they are virtues mentioned before in the text, the fact that he was a man, that he was just, that he was perfect, that he was well pleasing to God. And since the very man was the most perfect man and the definition of the highest happiness, he is put at the end of them all.[5]

The Three Patriarchs

Cher. 40–41a: Those whose virtue the Lawgiver has testified, such as Abraham, Isaac, Jacob, Moses, and others of the same zeal, are not introduced as knowing women (*QE* 2.114). 41a For since we hold that woman is sense-perception figuratively, and that knowledge comes into being through separation from sense and body, it will follow that those who are lovers of wisdom reject sense-perception rather than choose it.

Sacr. 5–6: Thus, when God added the good conviction Abel to the soul, he took away the harmful intention, Cain. So, too, when Abraham left the mortal life, "he is added to the people of God" (Gen. 25:8), in that he enjoyed immortality and became equal to angels. For angels are hosts of God, incorporeal and blessed souls. In the same manner, the practicer Jacob, it is said, is added to what is good (Gen. 49:33) when he leaves the wicked thing. 6 Isaac, to whom was granted the higher gift of self-learned knowledge, abandoned all such corporeal elements that have been interwoven with the soul, and is added and allotted to another company.

Post. 62: The soul that is wedded to goodness has obtained inhabitants excelling in the virtues, whom the double cave (Gen. 23:9) has received in pairs, Abraham and Sarah, Isaac and Rebekah, Leah and Jacob, these being virtues and their possessors.[6]

Note

In his treatise *On Abraham*, Philo offers a discussion of the second triad, Abraham, Isaac, and Jacob (*Abr.* 48–52). Unlike the first triad, Enos, Enoch, and Noah (*Abr.* 7–47), who represent progress toward virtue, the three Patriarchs are represented as living examples of perfection, not only because their lives embodied the Unwritten Laws before the Written Laws. Philo appoints the three Patriarchs as representatives or symbols of the three elements required to acquire virtue. He associates Abraham with "instruction" or "teaching" because he attained perfection (virtue) through instruction or teaching; as such, he is often referred to as "wise" or "the wise man." Philo connects Jacob with "practice" because Jacob attained perfect virtue by way of practice and training; thus, he is usually spoken of as "the practicer." Unlike Abraham and Jacob, Isaac was a soul who was naturally virtuous without any human effort; by nature, he possessed virtue and perfection (*Abr.* 1–4). He had no need of laws, neither "practice" nor "instruction," because his nature was in a state of virtue. Isaac is called "self-learned." The depiction of the three Patriarchs as exemplars of virtue through nature, instruction, and practice resembles the Greek models of education.[7]

Abraham: Instruction

Cher. 45: I will provide security as a warrant for my words that none can dispute, Moses the holiest of men. For he shows Sarah conceiving at the time when God visited her in her solitude (Gen. 21:1), but when she brings forth her son, it is no longer to the author of her visitation, but to him who seeks to win wisdom, whose name is Abraham (*QG* 3.3; 4.46).

Gig. 62–64: Certainly, Abraham, while he was journeying in the land of the Chaldean, that is to say, in opinion, before he received a new name, and while he was still called Abram, was a man of heaven. He was raised from the ground and was in nature of the lofty and ethereal region, investigating the events occurring there and their causes and the like, on which account he received a name suitable to the studies he pursued. For "Abram" interpreted means "a lofty father," the name of the father-mind that examines the things lifted from the ground and celestial, for it is the father of our compound being, which reaches out to the ether and even further. 63 But when he is made more excellent, he is destined to be called by another name; he becomes a man of God in accordance with the oracle that was proclaimed to him: "I am your God: walk before me, and become blameless" (Gen. 17:1). 64 Now, if the God of the world, the only God, is also, through a singular grace, his God in a special way, he must himself necessarily be a man of God. For he is called "Abraham," which interpreted signifies "the elect father of sound," that is, "the good man's reasoning"; for he is chosen and purified, and a father of the voice through which we produce concordant sound. Such reasoning is attached to the One and only God, it becomes an attendant directing the path of its whole life to the royal road, which is the way of the sole and Almighty King, turning aside neither to the right nor to the left.[8]

Jacob: Practice

Leg. 3.190–192: Despite her thinking to throw and deceive the clever mind, she herself will be thrown by Jacob, who in practice is wrestling, not wrestling the body but that which the soul wrestles against—her adversary—and fights against passions and vices. And Jacob shall not let go the heel of his adversary, passion, until it has given in and has acknowledged that it has been thrown and conquered twice, both in birthright and the blessing. 191 For "rightly," says Esau, "his name was called Jacob, for he had already supplanted me twice; then he has taken my birthright, and now he has taken my blessing" (Gen. 27:36). The careless person regards bodily things in higher esteem; the clever person regards the things of the soul. These are truth in a higher esteem, not in age but in power and dignity, and really first, as is the ruler in a city; and it is the soul that is sovereign over the composite being. 192 Therefore, he who is first in virtue has received the first things, which indeed belong to him; for he has also received the blessing with perfect prayers. But vainly deeming himself wise is the one who says, "my blessings and my birthright he has taken": for what he took, O man, was not yours, but was rather the opposite to what was yours; for the things that are yours have accounted for slavery, but his have accounted for lordship.

Ebr. 82–83: In the case of Jacob, the practicer, now in the last fight of his exercises in virtue, who was about to exchange hearing for eyesight, words for deeds, and progress for perfection, since God in His bountiful wishes to plant eyes in his understanding, so that he might see clearly what before he had grasped by hearing, for sight is more trustworthy than the ears. The oracles resounded the proclamation, "your name shall not be called Jacob, because you have been strong with God and with the power of men" (Gen. 32:28). Now, Jacob is the name for learning and progress, gifts that depend upon hearing; Israel is the name of perfection, because the name reveals the vision of God (*QG* 4.88). 83 And what among the virtues can be more perfect than the sight of the Existent One? He who has the sight of this blessing has his fair fame acknowledged in the eyes of both parents, for he has gained the strength that is in God, and the power that avails among men.

Congr. 70: It is said that when Jacob was sent to marry into his mother's family, "Jacob heard his father and mother and went to Mesopotamia" (Gen. 28:7). "Heard them," it says, not their voices or words, for the practicer must be the imitator of a life, not the hearer of words. Since the latter is the characteristic mark of the recipient of teaching and the former of the strenuous self-exerciser, here we may comprehend, then, the difference between the practicer and the learner, how the course of one is determined by what a person says, and the other by the person himself.

Sacr. 118–120: And we have it on the authority of Moses that the Levites, who instead of the first-born were appointed to serve Him who alone is worthy of service, are a ransom for all the others. For "and I," he says, "behold I have taken from the Levites from the midst of the sons of Israel, in the place of every first-born that opens the mother's womb from among the sons of Israel. They shall be their ransom, and the Levites shall be mine, and every first-born is mine. On the day I smote every first-born in the land of Egypt, I hallowed to myself every first-born in Israel" (Num. 3:12, 13). 119 It is reason, who has fled to seek refuge with God and become His supplicant, that is named Levite. God took reason from the most mindful and sovereign part of the soul; that is, He took it and allotted it to Himself, and appropriated to it a portion of the eldest son. Hence, it is clear that Ruben is the first-born of Jacob, and Levi is the first-born of Israel; the former carries seniority in years, and the latter in honor and power (*QG* 4.123). 120 For hard labor and progress, of which Jacob is the symbol, have their source in natural ability, which gives Ruben his name, but Levi is the symbol of service. Therefore, just as Jacob appears as inheritor of the birthright of Esau, when labor striving for the good was victorious over the craving that pursues evil, so too Ruben, the man of natural gifts, must yield the rights of the elder to Levi, whose life is one of perfect virtue. The pattern of perfection is shown clearly in that he makes God his refuge and forsakes all dealing with the world of created things.[9]

Post. 63: Since He calls Israel, being younger in age, His first-born son in high status (Exod. 4:22), bringing it forward that he who sees God (*QG* 4.233), Who is the most ancient Source, has been honored as the earliest offspring of the Uncreated One, conceived by virtue the object of the hatred of mortals and as he to whom there is a law that a double portion, the right of the first-born, should be given as being the eldest (Deut. 21:17).

Isaac: Nature

Sacr. 110: There are powers that are pure of evil in the whole and through the whole, and these we must mutilate by separating into their parts. These are like undivided sacrifices, the whole burnt-offerings of which Isaac is a visible example, whom God commanded to be offered as sacrificial victim, because he had no part in any passion that breeds destruction.

Det. 124–125: For God is the Creator of good laughter and joy, so that Isaac's source is not molded but a work to be accounted as uncreated (*QG* 3.38). For if Isaac is interpreted as laughter, and God is the Maker of laughter, according to Sarah's unerring witness, God may with perfect truth be said to be the true Father of Isaac (*QG* 4.90, 92). But he gives to Abraham, the wise man, a share in His own title, and by cutting grief away from him, He has bestowed upon him the offspring of wisdom to rejoice with Him. If someone is, therefore, sufficient to hear God's poetry, he is of necessity glad himself, and he too rejoices with those who had heard it already. 125 You will find no form of myth but poetry of God, and truth's inexorable rules all observed as though graven on stone. In turn, you will find no measures of tone and rhythms, and loud sounds charming their ears through music, but the most perfect works of nature, works that possess a harmony all their own. And even as the mind is fond when hearing the poems of God, so the speech rejoices, being in harmony with the thoughts of the understanding, and in a manner that it is aware of it.

Migr. 101: Therefore, the self-taught Isaac also prays to the lover of wisdom to receive the good things of both the intelligible and the sensible realms; he says, "may God give to you of the dew of heaven and of the fatness of the earth" (Gen. 27:28), which is equivalent to saying in the first place: "may He pour down on you perpetually the heavenly rain apprehended by the mind alone, not violently so as to deluge you, but in gentle stillness like dew so as to do good to you." Secondly, may He grant you the earthly, the outward and visible wealth; may that wealth abound in marrow and fatness and may its opposite, the poverty of the soul and its parts, be withered and dried up by His grace.

Joseph

Leg. 3.237: So Joseph, too, the self-controlling character, when pleasure says to him "sleep with me" (Gen. 39:7), and being a person, a passionate human being, who enjoys the delights of passions that come in life's course, refuses to comply with her, saying: "I shall be sinning against God, who is the lover of virtue, if I become a lover of pleasure; for this is a wicked action."

Agr. 56–57a: Joseph, who was always studying that knowledge, which is conversant about the body and vain opinions, does not know how to govern and direct irrational natures. To offices such as these it is customary for older men to be appointed; but he is always a young man, even if he has attained the old age that comes by mere lapse of time. Being accustomed to feed and fatten irrational natures instead of ruling them, he imagines that he will be able to win the lovers of virtue and also change over to his side in order that, devoting themselves to irrational and soulless creatures, they may no longer be able to find time for the pursuits of a rational soul. 57a For he says, "if that mind, whose realm is the body, inquires what your work is, tell him in reply, we are the keepers of cattle" (Gen. 46:33–34).

Sobr. 12b–13a: It is in accordance with this that Joseph is always called the young and youngest. When he is keeping the flock with his bastard brothers, he is addressed as a young man (Gen. 37:2). And when his father prays for him, he says, "my youngest son, having grown up, return to me" (Gen. 49:22). 13a Now Joseph is the champion of bodily ability of every kind, and the staunch and sincere henchman of abundance in external things, but the treasure, which ranks in value and seniority above these, the seniority of the soul, he has not yet gained in its fullness.

Ios. 28: After the literal interpretation it is also fitting to explain the underlying meaning, for roughly all or most of the lawbook is an allegory. Therefore, the kind of character here under discussion is called in Hebrew "Joseph," but in Greek is "addition of a Lord," a most accurate title and quite appropriate for the thing being indicated. For polity as found among the various peoples is an addition to nature, which possesses a universal lordship.

Ios. 143–144a: Thus, life being full of much confusion, disorder, as well as uncertainty, the statesman comes forward and like a wise interpreter of dreams interprets the daytime visions and appearances of those who think themselves awake, and with suggestions commended by reason and probability shows them the truth about each of these visions: that this is beautiful, that is ugly, this is good, that is bad, this is just, that is unjust; and so on in the same way with respect to the prudent, courageous, pious, holy, beneficial, profitable, and conversely unprofitable, unreasonable, ignoble, impious, unholy, deleterious, harmful, and selfish. 144a And still Joseph will give other lessons, such as, "this is another's, do not covet it."[10]

Sarah

Leg. 2.82: Do you not see that Sarah, who is the leader in wisdom, says, "for whoever shall hear of it shall rejoice with me" (Gen. 21:6). For instance, someone has succeeded in hearing that virtue has given birth to happiness, Isaac, and immediately, he will sing a congratulatory song of praise. As, then, he who has heard is joy, so is he who has purely seen temperance and God, Who does not die.

Leg. 3.217–219: On the contrary, you will find full virtue with exceeding joy at her pregnancy, and the good man begetting with laughter and a glad heart, and the offspring of both parents is laughter itself. As, then, the wise man begets with joy and not sorrow, the divine Word shall witness to us in these words, "God said to Abraham, Sarai your wife shall not be called Sarai but Sarah shall be her name. I will bless her and give to you a son from her" (Gen. 17:15–16). He says further, "and Abraham fell on his face and laughed and said, shall he that is a hundred years old have a son, and shall Sarah who is ninety years old bear?" (Gen. 17:17). 218 Abraham surely rejoices and laughs, because he is to beget Isaac, who is happiness, and Sarah, who is virtue, laughs too. The same book shall witness to us this when it says, "it ceased to be with Sarah after the manner of women, and she laughed in her mind and said, not yet has happiness befallen me till now but my Lord, the Divine Word, is greater (Gen. 18:11–12). . . . "

Ebr. 59–61: For the customs of women still prevail among us, and we are not yet able to cleanse ourselves from them or flee to the dwelling place where the men have their chambers, since we are told that it was mind that loved virtue, named Sarah. 60 For Sarah is introduced through the oracles, "having left all the things of women" (Gen. 18:11), when her travail was at hand and she was about to bring forth the self-taught nature, named Isaac (*QG* 3.59). 61 She is declared to be without a mother, and to have inherited her kingship from her father's side, not from her mother's, and thus having no part in female parentage. For someone has said somewhere, "Indeed, she is my sister, the daughter of my father but not of my mother" (Gen. 20:12). She is not born of that material substance perceived by the senses, always in a state of formation and dissolution, the material that is called mother or foster-mother or nurse of created things by those in whom first the young plant of wisdom grew. She is born of the Father and Cause of all things.[11]

Hagar

Cher. 3: Since we may see that Hagar or the middle education, whose sphere is the encyclical system, while she departs twice from virtue in the person of Sarah, does once retrace her steps. On this occasion, hers was a voluntary flight, not a banishment, and when she met the angels or divine Logos, she returned to her master's house (Gen. 21:14).

Post. 130–131: The quality of these souls Moses teaches very fully, using the guidance of the natural arts as the means of instruction. For he shows Hagar filling the water-skin and giving the child drink. Hagar represents imperfect training, being the handmaid of Sarah, who represents perfect virtue and is perfectly true to principles. Therefore, whenever she comes to the depths of knowledge, which is called a "well," she draws water from it into the soul, just as into a pitcher, both the doctrines and speculations, which are in quest, and thinks to feed her child (Gen. 21:19) with that on which she herself has been fed. 131 And "child" is the name he gives to the soul until it reaches instruction, and now becomes to some extent engaged in learning. It is in accordance with this that when the child grows to manhood he becomes a Sophist, for which Moses's name is "archer." For whatever topic he determines as an object, at this he discharges proofs as arrows with sure aim.

Congr. 20: The main characteristics of the middle education are expressed by two symbols, race and name. In race it is Egypt, but its name is Hagar, which is interpreted as "sojourning." The votary of the encyclical education, the friend of wide learning, must necessarily be associated with the earthly and Egyptian body (*QG* 3.19); since he needs eyes to see and ears to hear, and the other senses to unveil the several objects of sense.

Rebekah

Post. 132–133: Rebekah is found watering no longer with progress but with perfection. How so the law itself shall give directions, for the virgin, it says, was exceedingly beautiful in appearance. She was a virgin; a man did not know her. And going down to the spring, she filled up the pitcher and came up. And the servant ran toward her and said to her, give me to drink now a little water out of your pitcher. And she said, drink, sir. . . . 133 . . . Moses said that Rebekah was a virgin and a very beautiful virgin, because virtue is naturally pure and unadulterated and undefiled, and the only thing in all creation that is both beautiful and good. Indeed, it was from virtues that the Stoic doctrine grew that the only beautiful is good.

Post. 146: Thus, Rebekah must be praised for following the commands of the Father, taking down from a higher place the vessel of wisdom on her arm, and for holding out to the learner the teaching, which he is able to receive from her.[12]

Leah

Plant. 134–135: And a clearest example of what has been said is found in the sons of Leah, who is virtue; not in all of them, but in the fourth and fifth. For after recording the birth of the fourth son, Moses says that "she ceased from bearing" (Gen. 29:35), and he is called Judah, which means "confession to the Lord." And the fifth son she calls "Issachar," a name that interpreted means "reward." . . . 135 It follows that Judah, the mind that blesses God and is ceaselessly engaged in pouring forth hymns of thanksgiving to Him, was himself the fruit that is really "holy and for praise to God," fruit born not by earth's trees but by those of a rational and virtuous nature.

Hannah

Deus 5: He finds a disciple and successor, Hannah, who is the gift of the Wisdom of God. For the name Hannah is interpreted as "her grace." For when she conceived, she became pregnant by receiving the seed from God, and when she reached the consummation of her travail and had brought forth the type of character that has its appointed place in God's order, which she named Samuel, a name that being interpreted means "appointed to God," she took him and rendered him in due payment to the Giver, judging that no good thing was her own particular property, nothing that was not a grace and bounty from God.

Ebr. 144–146a: Perhaps there existed a man called Samuel; but he is conceived not as a living compound of soul and body, but as mind that rejoices in the service and worship of God only. For his name by interpretation means "ordered to God," because he thinks that all actions that are based on idle opinions are grievous disorder. 145 His mother is Hannah, whose name means in our language "grace." For without divine grace it is impossible either to leave the ranks of mortality or to remain forever among the immortal. 146a When grace fills a soul, that soul immediately rejoices and smiles and dances. For it is possessed and inspired, so that to many of the unenlightened it may seem to be intoxicated and crazy and beside itself.

Tamar

Leg. 3.74: Thus, when O soul shall you in full measure assume yourself to bear a dead body? Shall it not be when you are perfected and accounted worthy of prizes and crowns? For, then, you shall be a lover of God, and not of the body (*QG* 1.60). And you shall win the rewards because your wife shall be Tamar, the bride of Judah, and Tamar, being interpreted, means "a palm tree," a symbol of victory. Now, the proof of it is this. When Er has married her, he is immediately found wicked and slain. For it says, "and Judah took for Er his first-born a wife whose name was Tamar" (Gen. 38:6), and right afterward, it continues, "and Er was wicked before the Lord, and God slew him" (Gen. 38:7). For when the mind of virtue has carried off the rewards of victory, it condemns the dead body to death.

Deus 136–137: This is also represented in the Book of Kings, the widow discoursing with the prophet (1 Kgs. 17:10). She is a widow, not in our sense of the word, when she has lost her husband, but because she is widowed of passions, which corrupt and maltreat the intelligence, just as Tamar in the Books of Moses. 137 For it was commanded to Tamar to remain a widow in the house of her father, her one and only savior (Gen. 38:11), on whose account she has left forever the intercourse and society of mortals; she remains desolate of intercourse and widowed of human pleasures. She receives, thus, the divine seed, and being filled with the seeds of virtue, she is pregnant and in travail with noble actions. When she has brought them forth, she wins the prizes over her adversaries, and is enrolled as victor with the palm as a symbol of her victory. For Tamar is by interpretation a "palm."

Moses

Leg. 3.100–101a: There is a mind more perfect and more thoroughly purified, which has been initiated into the great mysteries, a mind that gains knowledge of the Cause not from what has been created, as one may learn of the abiding object from its shadow, but transcends beyond creation and obtains a clear vision of the Uncreated One, so as from Him to apprehend both Himself and His shadow; 101a that is, the Logos and this world. This mind, which I speak of, is Moses, who says, "manifest yourself to me, let me see you clearly" (Exod. 33:13).

Agr. 79–80: There is a divine army in wintertime, the virtues, champions of the lovers of God, whom it becomes, when they see the adversary defeated, to sing a most beautiful and befitting hymn to God, the Giver of victory, and the glorious triumph. . . . 80 The choir of the men will declare Moses its leader, who is mind in perfection. And that of the women shall be led by Miriam, sense-perception, who was made pure and clean (Exod. 15:1, 20). For it is right with both mind and sense-perception to render hymns and sing blessings to the Godhead without delay, and tunefully to strike each of our instruments, that of mind and that of sense-perception, in thanksgiving and honor paid to the only Savior.[13]

Phineas

Conf. 57: Therefore, Moses tells how peace was given as a prize to the most warlike reason, which is called Phineas (Num. 25:12). Because of his taking zeal for virtue and taking away a war against evil, he ripped open the whole of generation; how in turn that prize is given to those who, after diligent and careful scrutiny following the more certain testimony of sight rather than hearing, have the will to accept the faith that mortality is full of infidelity and clings only to opinion.

Methuselah

Post. 73–74: What issue awaits him who does not live according to the will of God, save death of the soul? And to this it is given the name Methuselah, which was interpreted as "an apostleship of death." Wherefore, he is the son of Mahujael (Gen. 4:18), of the one who abandons his own life, to whom death is sent, that is to say the death of the soul, which is nothing other than a conversion of it by the impetus of irrational passion. Indeed, when the soul is pregnant with this passion, it brings forth with sore travail-pangs, incurable sicknesses, and debilities. . . . 74 Therefore, to all this the name Lamech has been given; for it has been interpreted as "humiliation," so that Lamech may prove reasonably to be son of Methuselah (Gen. 4:18), being the passion of the soul's death, humble, yielding, a sore debility, which is the child of irrational impulse.

Essenes

Hypoth. 11.1–2: Multitudes of well-known men the Lawgiver trained on fellowship; they are called Essenes, deemed worthy of their designation, and I think, for their holiness. They live in many cities and villages of Judea and are grouped in big and crowded societies.[14] 2 Their focus of life is not family or race, for race is not written characters with voluntary associations, but on their zeal for virtue and yearning for love of humanity.

Hypoth. 11.14: Furthermore, they reject the very man who accordingly intends to dissolve marriage quickly, seeing marriage altogether at odds with the maintenance of the communal life. Especially, they practice self-control; no Essene takes a wife, because the woman is selfish and jealous, and lacks moderation. She is apt to entrap the character of a man and to seduce him in a continuous and deceitful attraction.[15]

Therapeutae

Contempl. 2–3a: And the way of life of these philosophers is at once disclosed through their name. For they are called, according to the true meaning of the words, *Therapeutae* and *Therapeutrides*, a name derived from *therapeuō,* which literally means "healing." They claim that their healing is better than that practiced in the cities. For the city cures only the body, while theirs heals also the souls mastered by grievous and incurable diseases, inflicted by pleasures and desires, and griefs and fears, by covetousness and folly, and injustice and other never-ending passions and vices, or else they are so called because they have been taught by nature and the holy laws to worship the Self-Existent, Who is better than the good, purer than the one, and more primal than the monad. 3a Who among those who profess piety deserve to be compared with these?

Contempl. 11–12: But the *Therapeutae*, a sect, taught always in advance to exercise their sight, may aim at the vision of the Existent One and soar above the sense-perceptible sun and never leave their place, which leads them to perfect happiness. 12 And those who come to this service, neither through force nor by custom, nor by the advice and admonition of others, but because they have been carried away by a heavenly passion, give way to enthusiasm, being possessed like Bacchants and Corybants until they see the object for which they have been earnestly longing.

NOTES

1. *Leg.* 3.49–50; *Cher.* 57–64; *Post.* 91–93; *Plant.* 32–35.
2. The Greek words here are corrupt, especially the ending, and it is difficult to complete the sentence.
3. *Cher.* 124–125; *Sacr.* 136; *Det.* 77–78, 119; *Post.* 40–43; *Agr.* 127–130; *Fug.* 64–66.
4. Enos: *Det.* 138–140; *Abr.* 7–14.
5. *Det.* 120–121; *Gig.* 5; *Deus* 104–108, 122–126; *Abr.* 31–35.
6. *Leg.* 2.55–60; *Cher.* 45–47.
7. In Plato's dialogues, especially in the *Protagoras* and the *Euthydemus,* the virtue of prudence (*phronēsis*) and its acquisition through instruction require good teachers of virtue (*Prot.* 318A–B; *Euthyd.* 273D; 274E–275A). Seneca suggests that the person who needs moral progress needs helpers, who demonstrate virtues in their deeds (*Ep.* 52.1–9).
8. *Sacr.* 42–44.
9. *Sacr.* 64–68; *Congr.* 61–62; *Fug.* 4–10; *Mut.* 209–214; *Somn.* 1.150–152, 166–172, 249–255.
10. *Leg.* 3.90–93; *Deus* 120–121; *Conf.* 71–72; *Ios.* 32–36, 55–57, 85–87, 157–162.
11. *Cher.* 4–6, 48–50; *Det.* 28–29, 59–60; *Congr.* 6–10.
12. *Det.* 30–31, 45–46; *Post.* 136–139.
13. *Leg.* 3.11–14, 94, 204–208; *Plant.* 46–49, 61–63.
14. See also Josephus, *Jewish War,* 2.119, 158, 160; *Antiquity of the Jews,* 13.171–172.
15. *Prob.* 76–80.

BIBLIOGRAPHY

Birnbaum, Ellen. "What in the Name of God Led Philo to Interpret Abraham, Isaac, and Jacob as Learning, Nature, and Practice?" *The Studia Philonica Annual* 28 (2016): 273–96.

Niehoff, M. R. "A Roman Portrait of Abraham in Paul's and Philo's Later Exegesis." *Novum Testamentum* 63, no. 4 (2021): 452–76.

Niehoff, Maren R. "Jewish Identity and Jewish Mothers: Who Was a Jew According to Philo?" *Studia Philonica* 11 (1999): 31–54.

Sterling, Gregory E. "Platonizing Moses: Philo and Middle Platonism." *The Studia Philonica Annual* 5 (1993): 96–111.

Van Veldhuizen, Milo Dean. "Moses: A Model of Hellenistic Philanthropia." *Reformed Review* 38 (1985): 215–24.

Wegner, J. Romney. "Philo's Portrayal of Women: Hebraic or Hellenic?" Pages 41–66 in *"Women Like This": New Perspectives on Jewish Women in the Greco-Roman World.* Edited by A. J. Levine. Early Judaism and Its Literature 1. Atlanta: Scholars Press, 1991.

Chapter 6

Jewish Law and the *Decalogue*

This chapter contains major themes within the topics concerning Philo's exposition of the Jewish Law and the *Decalogue*. The reader gets a clear sense of the significance of the ethical character of the Jewish Law. The central topics that this chapter presents are in connection to Philo's Ten Heads or *Decalogue*, where the numbers seven and ten are honored (*QG* 3.17), as well as the particular or specific laws. Philo deals expansively with the *Decalogue* and the particular laws in the *Special Laws* 1, 2, 3, and 4, found in volumes VII and VIII of the LCL. Useful texts are translated so that the reader shall learn the way Philo presents his exposition of the *Decalogue*, called the Ten Heads, and the particular or special laws.

For Philo, the Jewish Law is superior to other laws and is desirable and precious in the eyes of non-Jews. Within the philosophical tradition, Philo describes the Mosaic Law not only as written Laws but also as Unwritten Laws. While other ancient laws were given by intermediaries, the Mosaic Law was given directly by God Himself to Moses. The Jewish Law is the perfect law in harmony with the whole universe (*Opif.* 3).[1] It is the ideal, superior, and divinely inspired law.[2] Philo also describes the Jewish Law as the written expression of the eternal Unwritten Law, which was dearly sought and esteemed by ancient philosophers.[3] Interestingly, he identifies the Patriarchs as living expressions of the Unwritten Law or Law of Nature before the written law. He shows that the Mosaic Law offers a superior ethics, not only in teaching but also in practice, in ways that other religions and philosophies did not do. What is distinctive in Philo's biblical interpretation is that the ethical commandments improve human character and control desires, passions, and vices (*Spec.* 1.257; *Contempl.* 2; *Post.* 52; *Spec.* 2.163) to a higher degree than those who are governed by other laws (*Spec.* 4.55, 314).

In Philo's exposition of the Ten Words (Heads), there are two sets of five commandments, and each set is under two generic virtues: the first set of five commandments (five Heads) is under the virtues of piety and holiness and the second set (five Heads) under the virtues of justice and love of humanity.

Something that the reader must notice is Philo's allegorical and/or metaphorical description of each of the ethical commandments and the particular laws. The sharp contrast between virtue and vices represents Philo's ethical expressions of piety and impiety (*QE* 2.26). Furthermore, the reader will notice that throughout his exposition Philo emphasizes consistently the negativity of passions, desire, pleasures, and wickedness; these are consistently connected with the belly and the vice of gluttony or insatiability of the belly. He also shows virtues in radical opposition to these vices by emphasizing the virtues of temperance and self-control.

Moreover, what is unique about Philo's fifth commandment, the honoring of parents, is his understanding of the role of parents and their place in creation. God as the Creator of the universe has given parents a privileged place on the list of the *Decalogue* (Ten Heads). Not only their superiority and human mind are highlighted, but also their role as begetters, or "creators" of other human beings. Metaphorically speaking, he explains the place of the fifth heading as the borderline between the human and the divine; that is, this commandment is, for Philo, the link between the first set of five commandments related to God (piety and holiness) and the second set of five commandments related to human beings (justice and love of humanity).

THE *DECALOGUE*

Note

For Philo, the *Decalogue* or Ten Commandments is the heart of his ethics. The ethical commandments of the *Decalogue* gain a universal significance when Philo makes the written Law equal to or the very same Law as the Law of Nature, which, according to him, is also the Unwritten Law.[4] Philo associates the *Decalogue* with virtue itself (*Leg.* 3.245; *Post.* 89).[5] He describes the Law as "perfect virtue" (*Agr.* 157; *Decal.* 132; *Spec.* 4.131), "natural virtue" (*Cher.* 101), "beauty," and "loving wisdom" (*QG* 2.12). In order to attain virtue, one is to live ethically because it is from ethics that virtues spring (*Virt.* 8). Therefore, the *Decalogue* as virtue itself promotes the enhancement of human character (*Ebr.* 91). Philo views the laws of their fathers as the "trainers" (*Prob.* 80) under which the human soul must be trained to live virtuously (*Virt.* 18; *Praem.* 5), and according to nature (*Mos.* 2.48). A life guided by the ethical commandments promotes virtues, noble actions (*Cher.* 101; *Det.* 18), and happiness (*Cher.* 106; *Agr.* 157). For Philo, the practice of the law is to be shown in the conduct of life (*Praem.* 79; 82), so that the whole of one's life is to be an exhibition of virtue (*Prob.* 74).

The practice of the ethical commandments enshrined in the *Decalogue* and its particular laws seeks perfect virtue (*Agr.* 157). One who lives according to nature has the law engraved in his or her soul (*Spec.* 4.160) through reason.[6] One who lives governed by reason, according to Philo, is called a "virtue-loving soul";[7] and one who is a virtue-loving soul obeys the divine laws (*Spec.* 2.163; *Praem.* 119). In conversation with Greek culture, Philo describes the *Decalogue* not only as the principle of ethical conduct, but also as the supreme catalog of virtues. The *Decalogue* and its particular laws are the best course to attain Greek virtues.[8] They inculcate both Greek intellectual virtues, such as piety, godliness, holiness, and faith, and Greek cardinal virtues or moral virtues, such as prudence, temperance (or self-control), courage, and justice.

The Ten Heads

Decal. 32: These points, therefore, have been discussed enough. Now, it is necessary to weave together what follows next. The Ten Words or Oracles, in truth laws or ordinances, were delivered by the Father of the universe (*QG* 4.92; *QE* 2.41), when men and women of my nation were assembled all together.

Decal. 154: Enough on this subject. But it is necessary not to forget that the Ten Words are Heads of the special laws, which are recorded in the Holy Books and run through the whole of the legislation.

Spec. 4.132: . . . For if it is right to describe the main Heads delivered by the voice of God as generic laws, and all particular laws of which Moses was the Spokesperson as dependent species, for accurate apprehension free from confusion scientific study was needed, with the aid of which I have assigned and attached to each of the Heads what was appropriate to them throughout the whole legislation.[9]

The Two Headings of the Two Sets of Five Commandments

Her. 167–168: Again, are not the stones of the Ten general laws, which Moses calls tablets, two equals in number to the parts of the soul (*QG* 1.75), the rational and irrational, which must be trained and chastened? These tablets also were cut by the divine Legislator and by Him only. For "the tablets were the work of God and the writing on them was the writing of God, carved on the tablets" (Exod. 32:16). 168 So, the Ten Words on them are laws of the Lord that have been divided equally into two sets of five, the former comprising duties to God and the latter duties to human beings.

Decal. 19–20: Therefore, it happens that those which He gave through His own person and by His own "mouth" alone include both laws and Heads summarizing the particular laws. But those in which He spoke through the prophet Moses all belong to the particular laws. 20 I will speak about both to the best of my ability, taking those that are rather of the nature of Heads first. Here the admiration is at once aroused by their number, which is neither more nor less than is the supremely perfect Ten.

Decal. 50–51: . . . Now we must turn to the Words themselves and investigate all the different matters. He divided the Ten into two sets of five, which He engraved on two tablets: the first set of five obtained the first place, and the other set of five was deemed worthy of the second place. Both are good and useful for life: a wide road, leading at the end to a single goal, roads along which the soul always desires the best to travel without stumbling. 51 Thus, the superior set of five deals with the following matters: the monarchical principle by which the world is governed; idols of wood or stone and images in general made by human hands;[10] taking the name of God in vain; the holy seventh as befits its holiness; the honoring of parents, both separately to each, and to both in common. Thus, one set of enactments begins with God and Father, and Maker of all, and ends with parents, who copy His nature by begetting particular persons. The other set of five contains all the prohibitions, namely, adultery, murder, theft, false witness, and desire.

Spec. 2.63: . . . It is said literally that among the vast number of particular truths and principles and ordinances there are two higher Heads: one is the duty to God shown by piety and holiness and the other is the duty to human beings shown by love of humanity and justice, each of them splitting up into multiform branches, all laudable.

Praem. 1–2: The Words that have come through the prophet Moses are in three kinds: the first is creation of the world, the second is history, and the third is the legislation. The creation of the world has been revealed in the universe beautifully and divinely, beginning with the origin of heaven and ending up with the framing of man. For heaven is the most perfect of incorruptible things as man is of mortal things, weaving together immortal and mortal as the original components out of which the Maker made the world; the one created, then and there, to take command, the other subject, as it were, to be also created in the future. 2 The historical part is a record of good and bad lives and of the sentences passed in each generation, the rewards and punishments set apart for each class in each generation. The legislative part has two divisions, one in which the subject matter laid down is more general, and the other consisting of the commandments of the particular or specific laws. There are Ten Heads or summaries, the very thing which it is said were not delivered through an interpreter but were fashioned high above in the air and were articulated in the form of a speech. The specific ordinances of the oracles were given through the prophet.

THE NATURE OF THE MOSAIC LAW

The Mosaic Law

Mos. 2.43–44: The laws are shown as worthy of imitation and fought for in the eyes of all, in both uncultivated persons and rulers, and this too at the time when our nation has not prospered for a long time. It is but natural that when people are not flourishing their affairs to some degree are under a cloud. 44 . . . I believe that each nation would abandon its peculiar ways, and throwing overboard their ancestral customs, turn to honoring our laws alone (*QE* 2.49).

Mos. 2.48: For he did not, like any historian, make it his business to leave behind for posterity records of ancient actions for the pleasant but unprofitable favor that they give; but in relating the history of early times, and going for its beginning to the creation of the universe, he wished to show two very important things: first that the Father and Maker of the world was in the truest sense its Lawgiver; second, that he who would observe the laws will accept gladly the duty of following nature and live in accordance with the ordering of the universe, so that his deeds are attuned to harmony with his words and, in turn, his words with his deeds.

Decal. 1: Having related in the preceding treatises the lives of those who according to Moses are men of wisdom, who are set before us in the Holy Books as founders of our nations and were themselves Unwritten Laws (*Decal.* 1–5), I shall now proceed in due course to give full descriptions of the written Laws. . . .

Hypoth. 7.6: Besides these, there is a host of other things that belong to the Unwritten Laws themselves. What a man would hate to suffer he must not do himself to others. What he has not laid down he must not take up either from a garden or a wine press or a threshing floor. He must not take anything great or small from a stack. He must not grudge to give fire to one who needs it, and he must not cut off a stream of water. If poor or crippled people beg him for food, he must give it as an offering of religion to God.[11]

THE *DECALOGUE* OR TEN HEADS

First Commandment

Her. 169: Thus, the first commandment among the duties to God is that which opposes the belief in polytheism and teaches that He is the One and only ruler of the world.

Decal. 155: The first commandment summarizes the laws about the monarchical rule. These laws declare that there is one Cause of the world and one Ruler and King, Who guides the chariot and steers the bark of the universe in safety. . . .

Praem. 24–25a: After this triad comes another triad holier and loved by God, all belonging to one kingship. For it is a father and a son and a grandson upon whom promoted zealously the same goal of life, namely, to be well pleasing to the Maker and Father of the universe. They despised all that the multitude admire: glory and wealth and pleasure. They also laughed at vanity, that web woven of lies and cunningly devised to deceive the beholders. 25a This vanity is the enchanter, who deifies the lifeless things, the great and formidable fort, which entices with the artifices and tricks in every city and captures the souls of the young.[12]

Second Commandment

Her. 169: The second commandment forbids to make gods of things, which are not the causes of existence, employing for that purpose the mischievous arts of the painter and sculptor. Moses drove them out from his own commonwealth and sentenced them to eternal banishment.

Ebr. 109–110: Therefore, he began fashioning gods and filled the inhabited world with idols of stone and wood and numberless other figures wrought in various materials, and decreed great prizes and honors public and private to painters and sculptors, whom the Lawgiver had banished from the boundaries of his commonwealth. He expected to produce piety, but what he accomplished was its opposite, impiety. 110 For polytheism creates atheism in the souls of the foolish, and God's honor is neglected by those who deify the mortal things. For it did not suffice them to fashion images of sun and of moon, or, if they would have it so, of all the earth and all the water, but they even allowed irrational animals and plants to give a share of things imperishable.

Decal. 66: But while all who give worship and service to the sun and the moon and the whole heaven and the world and their chief parts as gods most undoubtedly err by magnifying the subjects above the ruler, their offense is less than that of the others who have given shape to stocks and stones and silver and gold and similar materials, each according to their fancy, and then filled the habitable world with images and wooden figures and the other works of human hands fashioned by the craftsmanship of painting and sculpture, arts that have wrought great mischief in the life of human beings.

Spec. 1.21–22: There are some who put gold and silver in the hands of sculptors as if they were competent to fashion gods. They take the crude material and furthermore use a mortal form for their model to crown the absurdity of shaped gods, as they are supposed to be. After erecting and establishing temples they have built altars, and in their honor they hold sacrifices and processions with other religious rites and ceremonies conducted with the most elaborate care, and the vain shown is treated by priests and priestesses with the utmost possible solemnity. 22 These idolaters are warned by the Father of the universe, saying, "you shall not make gods with me of silver and gold" (Exod. 20:23), teaching openly a direct command, "neither you shall make gods the work of your hands from any other material if you are prevented from using the best," for silver and gold hold first place in the sculptor's materials.

Third Commandment

Decal. 82–83: . . . Let us proceed to investigate carefully the next in order, not to take the name of God in vain (Exod. 20:7). Thus, it is the well-known commandment in the list to the opinion of those who have clear-sighted minds. For the name always is subordinated and stands second to the thing that it represents as the shadow that follows the body. 83 Therefore, after speaking first about the existence and honor of the everlasting Existent next to the sequence of the order, he exhorts about the proper name to be clearly distinguished. For there are manifold and diverse sins of human beings in this part.

Spec. 2.2: The first of these commandments is not to take the name of God in vain. For the word of the good person, it says, must be an oath, firm, steadfast, sincere, and must take a firm stand in truth. If, indeed, an occasion constrains us to swear, the oath should be by a father or mother, their health and goodness of season if they are alive, and their memory if they are dead.[13]

Fourth Commandment

Decal. 96–98: The fourth commandment deals with the holy seventh day, which should be celebrated holily and devotedly. While some cities celebrate once a month, reckoning it from the commencement as shown by the new moon, the Jewish nation never ceases to do so at continuous intervals with six days between each. 97 There is an account recorded in the story of the creation, containing an absolutely and necessary reason for this. It says that the world was created in six days, and that on the seventh day God ceased from

His works and began to contemplate mystically what had been beautifully created. 98 Thus, Moses exhorted those who should live as citizens under this ordered world to follow God in this as in other matters. Thus, he commanded that they should apply themselves to work for six days and rest on the seventh day and turn to the study of wisdom, and that while they thus had leisure for the contemplation of the truths of nature, they should also consider whether any offense against purity had been committed in previous days.

Spec. 2.39: The next Head is concerned with the holy seventh day, which brings in a great number of matters of vital importance, the different kinds of the feasts. . . .

Spec. 2.56: After the continuous and undivided feast, which has neither beginning nor end, the second to be observed is the holy seventh day, happening with six days between. Some have named it "virgin," having before their eyes its surpassing chastity. They also call her the "motherless,[14] begotten by the Father of the whole alone, the ideal form of the male sex with nothing of the female. Seven is the manliest and doughtiest of numbers, well gifted by nature for sovereignty and leadership.[15]

Contempl. 36: The seventh day, since they consider to be all holy and a most complete festival, they deem worthy of special privilege, and on it, after caring for the soul, they also refresh and anoint the body, releasing it, just as they naturally do to their cattle from their continual labors. And they eat nothing sumptuous, only simple bread and salt as a condiment further seasoned by the more luxurious with hyssop, and their drink is spring water.[16]

Fifth Commandment

Leg. 1.99: Let us form an even more precise conception of this. To honor parents is both "eatable" and "nourishing." But the good and wicked honor them differently, the latter because of custom, and these do not "eat food," but they merely eat. When, then, do they eat also "for food"? When, after ruminating on and searching for the reasons, they freely determine that such conduct is noble. The reasons are such as these: they gave us birth, they nurtured us, they educated us, and they have been the causes of all good things. Again, honoring the Existent One is "eatable." But it is also "for food" whenever it is coupled with the explanation of the whole matter and an account of the reasons for it.

Decal. 106–107: After dealing with the seventh day, He gives the fifth commandment, the honor of parents (*QG* 4.202). He placed this commandment on the borderline between the two sets of five commandments; it is the last of the first set in which He has assigned it as the holiest; and it adjoins to the second set that contains the duties toward our fellow human beings. 107 The reason I consider is this: parents by their nature stand on the borderline between the mortal and immortal side of existence. The mortal because of their kinship with human beings and other animals through the perishableness of the body, and the immortal because their act of generation assimilates them to God, the Generator of the universe.

Spec. 2.2b: For these parents are copies and likeness of the divine power, because they have brought into existence those who do not exist.

Spec. 2.224b–225: Now, I proceed to discuss the fifth commandment, which concerns with the honor of parents, which, just as I showed in the discussion devoted to this in particular, stands on the borderline between the human and divine commandments. 225 For parents are midway between divine and human nature, sharing in both: the human, as is so clear, because they have been born and will perish, the divine because they have brought others to birth and have brought forth nonexistent beings into existent beings. For, I think, what God is to the universe, parents are to their children, since just as He has achieved existence for the nonexistent, so they, in imitation of His power, as far as they are capable, immortalize the race.[17]

Sixth Commandment

Decal. 121–123a: Having discussed enough about the honoring of parents, he closes the first set of five commandments. Setting up the second set of five commandments, which contain prohibitions pertaining to duties to fellow human beings, Moses begins with adultery, holding this to be the greatest of crimes. 122 For in the first place it has its source in the love for pleasure, which also effeminates the bodies of those who entertain it, relaxes the sinews of the soul, and wastes away the means of substance, consuming like an unquenchable fire all that it touches and leaving nothing wholesome in the human life. 123a Then, it persuades the adulterer not to do wrong only but also to teach another to share the wrong by setting up a fellowship in a situation where true fellowship is not possible.

Spec. 3.8a: The first commandment in the second tablet is "you shall not commit adultery," because pleasure, I believe, is a mighty force felt throughout the inhabited world, and no part of the world has escaped its domination, neither the denizens of land, nor of sea nor of air.

Hypoth. 7.1: . . . Nothing at all, but everything is clear and simple. If you are a lover of boys, if you have committed adultery with a woman, if you have raped a child, for do not speak of doing so to a boy, but even to a female child (*QG* 4.37–38). Similarly, if you prostitute yourself, or allow any action that your age makes indecent the penalty is death.[18]

Seventh Commandment

Decal. 132–134: The second commandment is not to commit murder. For nature, having begotten man, the most civilized of animals, to be gregarious and sociable, has invited man to a life of unanimity and fellowship by endowing human being with reason, which leads to harmony and reciprocity of feelings. He, who commits murder, should be fully aware that he is subverting the laws and the established principles of nature, excellently inscribed for the well-being of all. 133 Further, he should also realize that he is guilty of sacrilege, the robbery from its Sanctuary of the most sacred of God's possessions. For what votive offering is more sacred or more worthy of reverence than a human being . . . ? 134 But man, the best of living creatures, in virtue of the superior element in his being, the soul, is most nearly akin to heaven, the purest thing in all that exists, and, as most admit, also the Father of the world, possessing in his mind a closer likeness and copy than anything else on earth of the eternal and blessed Archetype.

Spec. 3.83–84: The term murder is used to signify the act of one who has killed a human being, but in truth the act is a sacrilege and the worst of sacrileges; seeing that of all the treasures that the universe has in its store there is nothing more sacred and godlike than man. Man is the glorious cast of a glorious image and is shaped according to the paradigm of the archetypal form of Logos. 84 Therefore, one must suppose that the murderer must be regarded as an offender against piety and holiness, both of which are violated in the highest degree by his action. For his merciless conduct he must be put to death, though indeed, it is a thousand deaths that he deserves instead of the one that he suffers, because his punishment being necessarily single cannot grow into a plurality in which death has no place.

Spec. 3.108–110: If a person is locked together with a pregnant woman and comes to blows with her and strikes her on the belly, and she miscarries, and if the result of the miscarriage is underdeveloped and unshaped, he must be fined for the outrage and for obstructing the artist nature in her creative work of bringing into life the fairest of living creatures, that is man. But, if the offspring has been already shaped and all the limbs have their proper qualities and places in the system, 109 he must die, for that which answers to this description is a human being, which he has destroyed in the laboratory of nature who judges that the hour has not yet come for bringing it out into the light, like the statue lying in a studio requiting nothing more than to be conveyed outside and released from confinement. 110 These ordinances have also prohibited something else more important, the exposure of infants, a sacrilegious practice, which among many other nations, through their innate inhumanity, has come to be regarded with complacence.[19]

Eighth Commandment

Decal. 135: The third commandment of the second set of five is not to steal. He who gapes after what belongs to others greedily is the common enemy of the city; he wishes to rob all people, but he is able only to deprive some, because, while his covetousness extends indefinitely, his feebler capacity cannot keep pace with it but is only restricted to a small space and reaches only to a few.

Spec. 4.2: Anyone who carries off any kind of property belonging to another and to which he has no right must be written down as a public enemy, if he does so openly and with violence, because he combines shameless effrontery with defiance of the law. But if he devises cunningly and tries to avoid observation like a thief, since his shameless impudence in his private capacity, and, as he is liable only for the damage that he has attempted to work, he must repay the stolen goods twofold, and thus, by the damage that he most justly suffers, make full amends for the injustice of his gains.[20]

Ninth Commandment

Decal. 138–140: Speaking fully about stealing, next he proceeds to forbid to bear false witness, knowing that false witnesses are guilty under many important heads, all of them of a grave kind. For in the first place, they violate the sacred truth, which is as sacred as anything that we possess in life, like the sun bestows light upon all things and allows none of them to be overshadowed. 139 Secondly, in addition to bear false witness, they veil the facts as it were in night and profound darkness; they take part with the offenders and against those who are wronged, affirming that they have sure knowledge and thorough apprehension of things that they have neither seen nor heard. 140 And they commit a third transgression even more heinous than the first two. When there is a lack of proofs, either verbal or written, those who have questions in dispute betake themselves to witnesses, whose words are taken by the jurymen as standards in determining the verdicts they are about to give. Since they are obliged to fall back on these alone if there is no other means of testing the truth.

Spec. 4.41–42: "You shall not bear false witness." This is the ninth commandment of the Ten Heads, but the fourth in number of those on the second tablet. Countless are the blessings that it can bring to human life if observed, numberless on the other hand the injuries that it causes if disregarded; 42 for reprehensible as is the false accuser his guilt is less than that of the bearer of false witness. The former acts as his own champion, the latter as the accomplice of another, and if we compare one bad man with another, the iniquity of one who sins for his own sake is less than his who sins for the sake of another.[21]

Tenth Commandment

Decal. 142: The last commandment forbids to desire, which he knew is subversive and the enemy. For all the grievous passions of the soul, which move and shake it out of its proper nature and do not allow it to be sound, are hard to deal with, but desire is the most difficult of all the passions (*QG* 2.37). Therefore, while each of the others seems to be involuntary, an extraneous visitation, and assault from outside, desire alone originates in us, and it is voluntary.

Spec. 4.78b–80: . . . We must proceed to the last of the Ten Words. This, which like each of the rest was delivered in the form of a summary, is "you shall not desire." 79 Each passion is blameworthy, since we are accountable for every immoderate, excessive impulse and for the soul's irrational and unnatural movement. After all, what do both of these definitions describe if not an unleashing of the emotional part of the soul? So, if a man does not set limits to the impulses and does not bridle them, like horses that defy the reins, he is the victim of a virtually fatal passion, and that defiance will cause him to be carried away before he knows it like a driver borne by his team into ravines or impassable abysses, from whence it is hardly possible to escape. 80 But none of the passions is so troublesome as desire of what we have not gotten, things that seem good, though they are not truly good, such desire breeds fierce and endless yearnings. It urges and drives the soul as far as possible into the boundless distance while the object of the chase often flies insolently before it, with its face not its back turned to the pursuer.[22]

NOTES

1. Plutarch, *Alex. fort.* 329A–B (*SVF* 1.262; *HP* 67A).
2. *Congr.* 120; *Prob.* 80.
3. Philo equates the Jewish Law with the Law of Nature and the Unwritten Law. With the Law of Nature: *Ebr.* 47; *Sobr.* 25; *Abr.* 135; *Mos.* 2.7; *Spec.* 1.155, 202; 306; 2.32, 112, 189; 4.204; *Praem.* 42, 108; *Prob.* 30, 37; *Contempl.* 59; *Aet.* 59; *Prov.* 2.23; *QG* 1.27; *QE* 2.3. With the Unwritten Law: *Decal.* 1; *Virt.* 194.
4. Sterling, "Universalizing the Particular: Natural Law in Second Temple Jewish Ethics," 78; Barclay, *Jews in the Mediterranean Diaspora,* 172; Helmut Koester, "ΝΟΜΟΣ ΦΥΣΕΩΣ: The Concept of Natural Law in Greek Thought," in Jacob Neusner, *Religions in Antiquity: Essays in Memory of Erwin Ramsdell Goodenough* (SHR 14; Leiden: Brill, 1968), 521–41; Hindy Najman, "The Law of Nature and the

Authority of Mosaic Law." *SPhA* 11 (1999): 55–73; Martens, "Philo and the 'Higher' Law," 313.

5. See also *Mut.* 150.
6. *Somn.* 2; *Spec.* 3.163; *Abr.* 5.
7. *Leg.* 3.107; *Abr.* 68.
8. *Spec.* 1.314, 324; 4.96; *Flacc.* 121.
9. *Decal.* 2 21; *Praem.* 1–3.
10. Cf. Wis 13:1 15:17; Rom 1:18–32.
11. *Mos.* 2.13–16; natural laws: *Ebr.* 36–37, 46–48; *Migr.* 104–105; *Spec.* 3.11 113; 4.213–215; *Praem.* 108–110; *Prob.* 62–63; ordinances: *Post.* 95; *Migr.* 13 131; *Spec.* 4.143–144, 16 164; *Virt.* 8 87; *Hypoth.* 6.8; *Legat.* 7. There is a comparison made between Philo and Josephus, see Philo, *Hypoth.* 9.1–9 and Josephus, *Against Apion*, 2.190–219.
12. *Spec.* 1.12–20.
13. *Spec.* 3–17, 26–28.
14. *Decal.* 102.
15. *Spec.* 1.168–176; 2.57–64.
16. *Mos.* 2.215–216; *Spec.* 57–59, 65–73, 86–88, 11 115; *Virt.* 98–101; *Hypoth.* 7.15, 17.
17. *Decal.* 108–120; *Spec.* 2.237–251; *Hypoth.* 7.14.
18. *Decal.* 124–131; *Spec.* 3.9–14, 17–59, 72–82.
19. *Spec.* 3.85–177.
20. *Spec.* 4.3–29, 36–40.
21. *Spec.* 4.43–54, 59–77.
22. *Decal.* 143–153; *Spec.* 4.81–99.

BIBLIOGRAPHY

Birnbaum, Ellen. "What in the Name of God Led Philo to Interpret Abraham, Isaac, and Jacob as Learning, Nature, and Practice?" *The Studia Philonica Annual* 28 (2016): 273–96.

Borgen, Peder. "Application of and Commitment to the Law of Moses." *Studia Philonica* 13 (2001): 86–95.

Cohen, Naomi G. "The Greek Virtues and the Mosaic Laws in Philo: An Elucidation of De Specialibus Legibus IV 133–135." *Studia Philonica* 5 (1993): 9–23.

Martens, John W. *One God, One Law: Philo of Alexandria on the Mosaic and Greco-Roman Law*. Ancient Mediterranean and Medieval Texts and Contexts. Vol. 2. Boston: Brill, 2003.

Najman, Hindy. "A Written Copy of the Law of Nature: An Unthinkable Paradox?" *Studia Philonica* 15 (2003): 54–63.

Sterling, Gregory E. "Universalizing the Particular: Natural Law in Second Temple Jewish Ethics." *The Studia Philonica Annual* XV (2003): 64–80.

Svebakken, Hans. *Philo of Alexandria's Exposition of the Tenth Commandment*. Studia Philonica Monographs 6. Atlanta: Society of Biblical Literature, 2012.

Chapter 7

Jewish Worship and Major Observances

Ancient Judaism has been characterized by its many diverse practices and observances in order to live lives pleasing to God. The Jewish way of life was a life of piety. What the Mosaic Law and the *Decalogue* prescribe as a pious way of life according to Philo centered on a set of Jewish worship practices and major observances. This chapter, then, shows a collection of these practices as well as the different prohibitions within the ethical commandments of the *Decalogue* and the particular laws. For Philo, the observance of the High Holy Days is crucial. In *Spec.* 2.41–214 (see also *Spec.* 1.168–242), he describes in greater detail the ten feasts recorded in the law: the feast of Every Day (*Spec.* 2.42–49); the feast of Weeks or Pentecost (*Spec.* 2.179–187); and the Day of Atonement (*Spec.* 2.193–203).

It is important for the reader to look at this chapter in light of, and in relationship to, the topics and themes of Chapter 6; as a matter of fact, this chapter is considered an extension of the Ten Heads, the major ethical points evolving around the particular laws, mostly found in the *Special Laws* 1–4. I chose texts that exhibit what I consider Philo's most essential exposition and/or symbolic interpretations that reflect, once again, the ethical significance of his thought in his biblical interpretation. For example, the reader will encounter both the literal and allegorical interpretations of the practice of prayer, circumcision, Temple, food laws, the priesthood, the Sabbath, the altar, and the Tabernacle; Philo identifies these last two as the symbols of the incorporeal.

Philo offers two reasons why these Jewish observances must be performed: the most important one is *God*, the Creator of the All; another is to thank God for the creation of the universe;[1] and to gain some benefits from God, like forgiveness of sins, and the purification of the body and soul (*Spec.* 2.163). Secondly, these observances foster the ethical conduct of human beings, since their practices lead human beings to have a life *pleasing to God*.[2] For example, the feast of the Day of Atonement is to teach the mind *perfect piety*

(*Spec.* 2.197); and the celebration of the Sabbath is actually the birthday festival of the world (*Spec.* 2.70). They help to gain *perfection of virtue* (*Spec.* 2.68). The feast of the new moon is meant to inculcate lessons of *kindness* and *love of humanity* (*Spec.* 2.141).

The emphasis on the value of the practice of virtues and the avoidance of vices is clearly reflected in Philo's description of the observances and feasts. His philosophical knowledge and the Greek virtue ethics are reflected in the way he is able to connect the cultivation of virtues and the avoidance of vices with the practice of philosophy and the achievement of a genuine and perfect happiness, the goal of human life. It is in this context that Philo speaks of the four Stoic passions; the worst of these is desire, and the virtues of self-control, temperance, love of humanity, and piety, the greatest of virtues. In all, the Jewish Mosaic observances are meant to foster noble character and the practice of virtues. Importantly, the reader would come to get a sense of Philo's own personal ethical character, his attitude toward the Jewish observances and feasts, as well as his devotion and fidelity to his Jewish heritage.

MONOTHEISM

Note

Philo presents his doctrine of monotheism especially in his treatises *On the Decalogue* 52–65 and the *Special Laws* 1.13–65. The end of Philo's treatise *On the Creation*, 170–172 is the climactic moment of his monotheistic view and theological conceptions. He presents a summary of his belief about the Existent One: that the divine exists (against atheism); that God is One (against polytheism); that the world is created; that the world is one, and that God cares for the world (belief in providence). The description of Philo's monotheistic attitude is *theocentric*. Although in some passages Philo recognizes the celestial beings, the sun, the stars, the planets, and heaven itself as "gods,"[3] he gives them the rank of subordinate rulers (*Spec*. 1.19). According to Philo, they have been brought into existence by the Existent One through an act of creation.[4]

God Is One and the World Is One (Credal Formulation)

Opif. 170b–172: Through the exposition of the creation of the world about what we referred, besides many other things Moses taught us especially five that are the fairest and best of all. First, that God is and exists from eternity. This with a view to atheists, some of whom have hesitated and have been of two minds about His eternal existence, while the bolder sort has carried their audacity to the point of declaring that God does not exist at all, but that it is a mere assertion of human beings obscuring the truth with myth and fiction. 171 Second, that God is One. This is with a view to the assertors of polytheism, those who do not blush to transfer from earth to heaven mob-rule, that worst of evil polities. Third, as it has been said already, that the world came into being. This is because of those who think that the world is uncreated and eternal, who thus assign to God no superiority at all. Fourth, that the world too is one as well as its Maker, Who made His work like Himself in accord with its uniqueness, and Who used up for the creation of the universe all the material that exists. For it would not have been the whole had it not been formed and consisted of parts that were wholes. For there are those who suppose that there are more worlds than one, while some think that they are infinite in number. Such men are themselves in very deed infinitely lacking in knowledge of things that it is right and good to know. Fifth, that God also provides for the world. For that the Maker should care for the things made is required continually by the laws and ordinances of nature, and it is in accord with these that parents care for their children. 172 He truly knows these things beforehand not by hearing but understanding. He knows that he has sealed in his soul honorable and highly prized conceptions: that God is and exists from eternity and that He, Who Is, is One, and that He has made the world and it is One, as it says, it is like God in accord with its uniqueness; and that He provides continually for what He has made. He shall lead a life of bliss and blessedness, for he has a character molded by the ordinances of piety and holiness.

Polytheism and Idolatry/Idol Making/Idols

Leg. 3.36–37: For the holy word curses on one setting up in secret a carved or molted image, a work of the hands of the craftsman (Deut. 27:15). For why do you hold bad opinions, that God is like the carved images are, of this or that kind, God the Being is without kind, or that He Who is imperishable is corruptible like the molted images are . . .? For you may think that one is skillful in science, because you have studied methods of persuasion unworthy of an educated man, . . . but your science is discovered unskilled, in that you refuse healing treatment of your soul's grievous malady of ignorance. 37 That the bad man sinks into his own dispersed mind running away from He Who Is; it is testified by Moses, who "smote the Egyptian and hid him in the sand" (Exod. 2:12). This means that he took full account of the man who maintains that the things of the body have the preeminence and holds the things of the soul to have no value at all, and regards pleasures as the end of life.

Mos. 2.205–206: But here by the word "god" he is not alluding to the Primal and Begetter of the universe, but to the gods of the different cities

(*QE* 1.20). They are false gods, being fashioned by the arts of painters and shapers. For the inhabited world is full of idols of wood and stone and such-like images. We must refrain from speaking with disrespect about these, lest any of Moses's disciples get into the habit of treating light the name "god" in general, for it is a title worthy of victory and love. 206 But if any, I will not say blasphemes the Lord of gods and of human beings, but even ventures to utter His name unseasonably, let him suffer the penalty of death.

Decal. 70: If it is proper to say that they indeed sinned, they should have deified the painters and sculptors themselves and have given them honors on a magnificent scale, they leaven them in obscurity and bestow no favor on them, while they regard as gods the figures and pictures made by their workmanship.

Contempl. 7–9: What about the worshipers of statues and images? Their substance is stone and wood, only a little while before utterly destitute of form. Quarrymen and woodcutters cut them out of their congenital structure while their kindred and cognate parts have become urns and foot-basins or some other vessels of a yet ignobler sort, which serve the purposes in darkness rather than in light. 8 As for the gods of the Egyptians, even to mention them is indecent. They have introduced to the divine honors irrational animals, not only of the tame animals but also wild beasts, from every sublunar species; from the land the lion, from the water the native crocodile, from the air the hawk and the Egyptian ibis. 9 Although they see these animals begotten, in need of food, eating voraciously, crammed with excretion, poisonous and devourers of humans, the prey of every sort of disease, and perishing not only by a natural but often by a violent death, still they, civilized men, worship these untamed and ferocious beasts; though rational men, they worship irrational beasts; though they are akin to the Godhead, they worship creatures unworthy of being compared even to the ape-like Thersites; though appointed rulers and masters of creation, they worship creatures that are naturally subjects and slaves.

Legat. 139: What they thought is that they, who are men made into gods, should be regarded so by those who deified dogs, wolves, lions, crocodiles, and many other wild beasts on the land, in the water and the air. Altars, temples, shrines, and sacred precincts have been established throughout the whole of Egypt.[5]

Golden Calf

Post. 158–159: This is the food of the soul, which is suitable for exercise, to consider labor not bitter but very sweet. It is not allowed to all people to participate in this food, but to those only by whom the golden calf, the idol of the Egyptian, the body, is sprinkled over with water having set in fire and broken to pieces. For it is said in the Holy Books that "Moses taking the calf he burnt it down in fire and ground it into powder and threw it into the water and gave the children of Israel to drink it" (Exod. 32:20). 159 For the lover of virtue set on fire by the brilliant appearance of the beautiful, burns up the pleasures of the body, and then chops and grinds them up, using the principle of classification, and then teaches that health, or beauty, or precision of the senses, or complete soundness, including strength and muscular force, are among the bodily "good things," and yet all these are shared with others by men abominable and accursed. Even if they were good things, no bad man would have had part in any of them.

Fug. 90: Therefore, was this the only reason or was it also because the Tribe of Levi, consisting of those who had the care of Tabernacle, rushed up and at one onset slew from the age of puberty upwards, those who fashioned into a god the golden calf, the Egyptian folly? They did this under the impulse of righteous anger accompanied by an inspiration from above and a God-sent possession: "and each man slays brother and neighbor and his nearest" (Exod. 32:27), for the body is the brother of the soul, and the irrational part of us neighbor of the rational, and the word of utterance "next of kin" to mind.[6]

CIRCUMCISION

Note

In terms of the observance of circumcision, Philo emphasizes both the literal and ethical meaning of it. For him, the physical observance of circumcision is an initiation ritual, when a young Jew becomes Jewish. He speaks of the necessity to keep and observe the Mosaic Law, including the literal practice of circumcision.[7] However, the ethical meaning of circumcision is also important for Philo. In *Spec.* 1.8–11, he gives two reasons for circumcision: the first is the removal of excessive pleasure and all passions of the soul, and the second to correct men's delusion of power and pride.[8] His position enhances the control of pleasure and desire and corrects men's erroneous attitude about the power of their sexual organ to procreate (*QE* 2.2 [Exod. 22:21]). For Philo, for example, circumcision is not necessary for becoming a Proselyte or for entering the Jewish way of life. He explains that a Proselyte is not the one who has circumcised his uncircumcision, but the one who has circumcised his desires and sensual pleasures, and the other passions of the soul.[9] True circumcision, therefore, is that of the heart, where the soul is capable to moderate or control the appetites of the passions and vices (*Spec.* 1.305; cf. *Spec.* 1.6).

Worth noting is that Philo does not want to deny the physical observance of circumcision (*Migr.* 92; *QG* 2.52). He is not ready to reject physical circumcision in favor of only the ethical or spiritual character of it because he still sees both as valuable. Philo keeps both meanings not only because of the observance of the Mosaic Law and the caring for the body, but also because the body is the dwelling place of the soul (*Migr.* 93), and because it is important to maintain community identity (*Migr.* 88).[10] Interestingly, when Philo spiritualizes circumcision, it becomes more individualistic. For him, the deeper ethical meaning of circumcision represents the liberation of the individual's mind from the pleasures and bodily passions (*QG* 2.52), for the soul who is not symbolically circumcised, purified, and sanctified of the passions and desires cannot be loyal to God.

Physical and Spiritual Circumcision

Migr. 92–93: It is true that the feast is a symbol of gladness of the soul and of thankfulness to God, but we should not set apart against the festal assemblies of the annual seasons. It is true that receiving circumcision does indeed portray the castration of pleasure and of all the passions and the destruction of impious vainglory, under which the mind has supposed that it was capable of begetting by its own power. On this account, we may not destroy the law laid down for the circumcision (*QG* 2.52; 3.46–48, 52, 61; *QE* 2.2). Since we shall be neglectful of the Temple's holiness and a thousand other things, too, if we pay heed to only those who are being shown by the inner meaning of things. 93 But we should acknowledge these necessary things as resembling the body, and their inner meaning as resembling the soul. Thus, just as we have to take thought for the body, since it is the abode of the soul, we must also provide that one must pay heed to the letter of the law. For observing these, we shall know a clear conception of those things of which these are symbols.

Spec. 1.2–7: The practice that may be a laugh among many people, circumcision of the genital organs, is an action that is highly valued by many other nations, especially by the Egyptians, who are believed to be the most populous and ancient and lovers of philosophy . . . 3 . . . there are four important reasons to be circumcised. 4 First, it secures exemption from serious and incurable disease of the prepuce called carbuncle and, I believe, from the slow fire that it sets up and to which those who retain the foreskin are more susceptible. 5 Secondly, it promotes the cleanliness of the whole body as befits the consecrated order. . . . 6 Third, it assimilates the circumcised member to the heart. For it is prepared for the sake of generation, though it is generated by the Spirit in the heart. . . . 7 And fourth, and the most important reason, is its power to give fertility of offspring. It says that it causes the sperm to have a free course without being scattered into the folds of the foreskin, and therefore the circumcised nations appear to be the most prolific and populous.

Spec. 1.305: These he admonishes with the words, "circumcise the hardness of your heart" (Deut. 10:16), make speed, that is to prune away from the ruling mind the superfluous overgrowths sown and raised by the immoderate appetites of the passions and planted by folly, the evil husbandman of the soul.[11]

FOOD LAWS

Note

Philo deals extensively with the food laws in his treatment of the Tenth Commandment in *Spec.* 4.78–131.[12] The practice of the food laws as part of the whole of the ethical commandments has the moral purpose of improving the character of the individual.[13] Philo follows the Middle Platonic view of dietary regulations, which is the moderation of desire (*epithumia*).[14] Philo offers an ethical explanation of the food laws, which expresses the importance of the literal meaning of this commandment. He takes desire, one of the four Stoic passions, and views it as the worst of all the passions of the soul (*Decal.* 142). Influenced by Middle Platonism, he reinterprets the Tenth Commandment as "you shall not desire" to highlight the ethical character of the commandment. However, the practice of the food laws is not for the extirpation of desire, which is the goal of the Stoics; for Philo, it is to control or moderate desire, which is the goal of Middle Platonists. The process of controlling food and drink is a training that enhances a discipline of self-control.[15] Since certain animals (e.g., pigs) provide an appetizing and delectable repast (*Spec.* 4.103), they can arouse a person's desires and produce gluttony.[16] Philo explains allegorically the process of controlling desire, giving emphasis on how the human soul is to become a "virtue-loving soul," rather than a "lover of pleasure."[17] For him, this is the real meaning of God's command: "You shall eat 'for food'" in Gen. 2.16. Allegorically, "eat" is a symbol for the nourishment of the soul, and the eating "for food" is the way the virtue-loving soul controls desires, passions, and vices by reason (*Leg.* 1.59).

Clean and Unclean Animals: Land, Sea, and Sky

Spec. 4.100–116: Moses did not allow members of the sacred commonwealth simply to eat whatever they wanted without restriction. In fact, he strictly prohibited all of the richest, most succulent types of meat, meat that tickles and teases our treacherous foe pleasure, by prohibiting just the right animal of land, sea, or sky. He knew that these meats could produce the characteristic insatiability of tyrannical desire, once they had ensnared the most slavish of the senses, taste. And insatiability represents a practically incurable problem not only for our souls but also for our bodies. For insatiate desire for food leads to overeating, which in turn leads to indigestion, which is the source and the wellspring of all diseases and infirmities. 101 Now among the different kinds of land animals, we agree, there is none whose meat is so delicious as the pig's, and among the water animals the same may be said of such species as are scaleless . . . having special gifts for inciting to self-control those who have a natural tendency to practice virtue, he trains and drills them by frugality and simple docility and tries to get rid of extravagance. . . . 103 It may be thought just that all of the beasts that feed on human flesh should suffer from human beings what human beings have suffered from them. But Moses, considering what benefits a gentle soul, thinks we should abstain from the enjoyment of these creatures, even though they provide a very appetizing and delectable repast. . . . 104 In fact, Moses makes so extreme an effort to prevent such behavior as to forbid categorically the eating of all carnivorous animals, wishing to restrain preemptively the impulse for revenge against man-eaters. He distinguished between them and the herbivorous, which he grouped with the gentle kind, since, indeed, they are tamed by nature and live on the gentle fruits that the earth produces and do nothing by way of attempting the life of others (*QG* 2.52). . . . 106 He also provides a general test and a scrutiny of these ten animals based on the two signs: the parted hoof and the chewing of the cud. Any kind that lacks both or one of these is unclean. Now, these two are symbols to teacher and learner of the best method suited for acquiring knowledge. . . . 108 . . . Since the way of life is twofold, one leads to vice and the other to virtue, it is necessary to choose what we should choose and avoid the contrary. 109 Therefore all the creatures whose hooves are uniform or multiform are unclean; the one (uniform) because they signify the idea that good and bad have one and the same nature, which is like confusing concave and convex or uphill and downhill in a road; and the other (multiform) because they set before our life many roads, which are rather no roads, to cheat us, for where there is a multitude to choose from it, it is not easy to find the best and most serviceable road. . . . 110 . . . He proceeds to describe such creatures of the water that are clean for eating. These are also distinguished by two signs: fins and scales. Those that lack either or both he dismisses and repudiates. . . . 111 Any that fails to possess either one or both are swept away by the current unable to resist the force of the stream. . . . 112 These two kinds of fish are symbolical, the first of a pleasure-loving soul, the latter of one to which endurance and self-control are dear. For the road that leads to pleasure is downhill and very easy, . . . and the other that leads to self-control is uphill, toilsome no doubt but exceedingly profitable.

... 113 Having the same idea, he declares that all reptiles that have no feet but wriggle along by trailing their belly, or have four legs and many feet are unclean for eating (*QG* 2.57; *QE* 1.19). ... 114 Creeping things that have legs above their feet, so that they can leap from the earth, Moses catalogs these among the clean animals. ... 116 ... He proceeds to examine also the remaining parts of the animal creation, the inhabitants of the air. Of these he rejected a vast number of kinds of winged animals, indeed all that prey on other fowls or on humans, animals that are carnivorous and poisonous and in general use their power to attack others.

Prov. 2.63–65: If swallows live with us, there is nothing to wonder at for we do not attempt to catch them. And the instinct of self-preservation is implanted in both the irrational and rational souls. But birds that we like to eat will have nothing to do with us, for they fear our designs against them except in cases where the law forbids that their kind should be used as food. ... 64 ... I saw a multitude of pigeons at the crossroads and in each house, ... it was not lawful to choose them because they had been from old times forbidden food to the inhabitants. Thus, the creature has been so tamed by its security that it not merely lives under their roof but shares their table regularly and takes delight in the immunity that it enjoys. ... 65 It is a more wonderful sight in Egypt to see; for the human-eating crocodile, the most dangerous of wild animals, which is born and bred in the holiest of rivers, the Nile, understands the benefit of this though it is a deep-water creature.

Temperance

Leg. 2.79: Therefore, how is the healing of their suffering brought about? By the making of another serpent, opposite to that of Eve, namely the principle of temperance. For temperance is the opposite of pleasure, a variable virtue to a variable passion, and a virtue that defends itself against the hostile pleasure (*QE* 2.18). Thus, God exhorts Moses to make the serpent according to temperance, and He says: "make yourself a serpent and set it upon a standard" (Num. 21:8). You see that Moses makes this serpent for no one else, rather for himself, for God commands, "make it for yourself," that you may know that temperance is not a possession of every person but only of the one who loves God.

Leg. 2.98: Thus, let the principle of temperance become a serpent upon the soul whose journey goes through all the circumstances of life and let it seat upon the well-worn track. What does this mean? The path of virtue is unworn, because few walk on it, while the path of vice is well worn.

Agr. 104: The roads of prudence and temperance and of the other virtues, if not untrodden, are at all events unworn. For few is the number of those that walk on them, that have genuinely devoted themselves to the practice of philosophy and set to the only beautiful companionship.

Legat. 5: If the sight of the seniors or instructors or rulers or parents stirs in motion those who want to have a self-respect and a beauty and a zeal for a life of temperance, how firmly based is the virtue and nobility of character, which we may expect to find in souls whose vision has soared above all created things and schooled itself to perceive the uncreated and divine, the First Good and the excellent and the happy, and the blessed. It may be necessarily and genuinely called better than the good, more excellent than the excellent, most blessed than blessedness, more happy than happiness itself, and any perfection there may be greater than these.

Self-Control

Agr. 98–101: Therefore, he, who contemplates the form of endurance, even if he was previously bitten perhaps by the love charm of pleasure, cannot but live. For pleasure menaces the soul with an inevitable death, but self-control holds out to it health and preservation of life; and temperance the averter of evil is an antidote to licentiousness. 99 For every wise man looks upon the beautiful and dear, which is also by all means salvation. So, when Moses prays that it may happen to Dan, either himself, to be a serpent (for the words may be taken either way), he prays for a serpent corresponding to the one made by him, but not like Eve's; for prayer is a request for good things. 100 Therefore, endurance is of a good kind that brings immortality, a perfect good, while pleasure is of an evil kind that brings the greatest suffering, death. Therefore, Moses says: "let Dan become a serpent" not elsewhere than "on the road." 101 For ill-temperance and gluttony and all else that issues from the womb of those immoderate and insatiable pleasures that ever conceive by the abundance of external comforts, never allow the soul to go along the straight course by the highway, but compel it to fall into pits and clefts, until they have utterly destroyed it. But only the practice of endurance and temperance and other virtues secures for the soul a safe journey where there is no slippery block under the feet upon which the soul must stumble and fall. Most fitly, therefore, Moses declares that temperance clings to the right road, since the opposite condition, that of licentiousness, finds no road at all.

Congr. 31–32: Thus, with all the recounting faculties the man of practice mates, with the free and legitimate wives, and also with the slaves and concubines. For it aims at the Leah movement—and the Leah movement creates health in the body and works nobility and justice in the soul. Jacob loves Rachel when wrestling with the passions and when he goes into training to gain self-control and takes his position to oppose all the objects of the senses. . . . 32 . . . Thus, it is Leah through whom it comes to pass that he reaps the higher and dominant blessings, and Rachel, through whom he wins what we may call the spoils of war.

Spec. 4.97: What then is the teaching that he takes as his first step? There are two important things that stand out, food and drink (*QG* 4.77, 186). Moses did not refrain from either of these, but he bridled them with ordinances, the best guide to self-control and to love of humanity and what is the greatest of all, piety.

Spec. 4.124: The fat is prohibited because it is the richest part, and here again he teaches us to practice self-control and foster a zeal for a life of austerity, which relinquishes what is easiest and lies ready at hand, but voluntarily endures anxiety and toils for the acquisition of virtue.

Virt. 189: Since, therefore, nobility is the proper inheritance of a mind that has been purified by perfect purification, one must call only the moderate and just noble, even if their parents were made slaves, home-bred or purchased. But to the evil children of good parents the state of nobility must be closed off.

Prov. 2.70: Therefore, until now, those who have thought for self-control abstain from every one of them and take green vegetables and the fruits of trees as a relish to their bread with the utmost enjoyment. Those who hold that feasting on these animals is natural have had placed over them teachers, censors, and lawgivers, who in the different cities make it their business to restrain the intemperance of their appetites by refusing to allow all people to use them all without restriction.[18]

Desire

Ebr. 102–103: How customary are the very loud outcries of pleasure with which it is accustomed to command what it wills. How continuous is the voice of desire, when it thunders forth its threats against those who do not minister to its wants. How loud and grandiloquent is the voice of each of the other passions? 103 Yet though each of the passions has countless tongues and mouths with which to swell the war-shout, according to the poet's phrase. . . .

Spec. 1.149–150: The opposite of desire is self-control. To practice and to acquire it one must toil, and it be sought zealously with every possible means as the greatest and the most perfect goodness. Self-control is profitable for both the individual and the public. 150 Thus, desire, which is profane, unclean, and unholy, has been driven away beyond the boundaries of virtue, and its banishment is well deserved. But self-control is clean and an undefiled virtue, which depraves all concerns of food and drink and boasts to stand superior to the pleasures of the belly, touch the holy altars and bring with it the attachment of the belly as a reminder that it holds in contempt gluttony and insatiate desire and of all that inflames the tendencies to desires (*QG* 159).[19]

Spec. 4.79–82: [see above] . . . 81 . . . And desire constantly eluded and deprived struggles in vain, bringing the punishment of Tantalus on the wretched soul. Surely, you remember that, as the story goes, that wretch who could never quench his thirst because the water withdraws every time he tried to take a drink. In the same way, whenever he reached for some fruit on the nearby trees, it all disappeared, making barren the fertility of the trees. 82 For just as those unmerciful and relentless mistresses of the body, hunger and thirst, torture it with pains as great as, or greater than, those of the sufferers on the tormentor's wheel. . . . Desire makes the soul empty through oblivion of what is present, and then through memory of what is far away it produces fierce desire and ungovernable madness, and thus creates mistresses harsher than those just mentioned though bearing the same name, hunger and thirst, . . . not for enjoyment of the belly but for money, glory, authority, beauty, and other many innumerable things that are considered enviable and worthy of great effort to human life.[20]

Tyranny of Passions/Irrational Passion

Leg. 2.99–102: "Biting the horse's heel." . . . the passions are likened to a horse. For the passion, like a horse, is full, impulsive, self-willed, and naturally unruly. But the principle of temperance loves to bite and wound and destroy the passion. When the passion with its heel bitten has stumbled "the horseman shall fall backwards." We must understand by "the horseman" the mind that sets foot on the passions, which falls off the passions when they are brought to a reckoning and overthrown. 100 Well, it is not that the soul falls forward. Let him not get in advance of the passions, but be behind them, and he shall learn self-control. And there is a principle in what is said. For if the mind, after starting out to do wrong, drops behind and fails backwards, it will not do the wrong thing. And if, after experiencing an impulse to an irrational passion, it does not follow it up but stays behind, it will bear fruit, the most beautiful reward, even freedom from passion (*QG* 4.222). 101 That is why the prophet, understanding the falling backwards to be freed from evil things, adds the words: "waiting for the salvation of the Lord." For he is saved by the Lord who falls away from the passions and comes short of realizing them in act. May my soul have such a fall and never mount the unruly passion, wild like a bounding capering horse, that, having waited for God's salvation, it may be truly happy. 102 This is why Moses in the song praises God, that "he cast a horse and a rider into the sea" (Exod. 15:1). He means that God casts to utter ruin and the bottomless abyss the four passions and the wretched mind mounted on them.

Leg. 3.248–250: "Thorns and whirring sounds shall it bring forth to you" (Gen. 3:18). But what else can produce, and grow, and shoot up in the soul of a foolish man but the passions that goad and wound it? (*QG* 4.235). To these, using figures, he has given the name of thorny plants, which the irrational impulse, like a fire, meets first, and ranging herself with them burns up and consumes all the soul's possessions. . . . 249 You see that the fire, the irrational impulse, does not set on fire the thorny plants, but it succeeds. For being a seeker after the passions it finds what it desired to get. And when it has found it, it burns up these three things: perfect virtue, progress, and natural goodness. Thus, he brings alongside virtue to the threshing-floor, for as the fruit has been gathered together herein, so in the soul of the wise have been gathered noble things. To the standing corn he brings alongside progress, since it is either incomplete or earnestly set on its completeness. He likens goodness of natural disposition to the field because it is receptive of the seeds of virtue. 250 And each of the passions he calls thistles, because they are threefold, the passion itself, that which produces it, and the finished result of these. For instance, pleasure, the pleasant, enjoying pleasure; desire, the desirable, desiring; grief, the sorrowful, grieving; fear, the fearful, fearing.

SEXUAL IMMORALITY

Gluttony/Belly

Ebr. 220–222: Certainly, all these three were shown to be eunuchs and barren of wisdom. It was the butler with whom the mind, whose kingdom is the belly, made his compact of peace. For the love of wine is exceedingly strong in the human race, and it is unique in this that it does not produce satiety. For whereas everyone is satisfied with sleep, food, sexual intercourse, and the like, this is rarely so with strong unmixed drink and particularly with practiced topers. 221 They drink yet they are not thirsty, and while they begin with smaller cups, as they advance they call for the wine to be poured in larger goblets. . . . 222 But even then, the insatiable craving within them rages just as if it were still starving. "For their vine is of the vine of Sodom," as Moses says, "and their vine-branch of Gomorrah. Their grapes are grapes of gall, a cluster of bitterness to them. Their wine is the wrath of dragons and the incurable wrath of asps" (Deut. 32:32–33). Sodom is indeed interpreted as "barrenness and blindness," and Moses here likens to a vine and its produce those who are under the thrall of greediness for wine and gluttony and of the other most disgraceful pleasures (*QG* 4.234).

Migr. 66: Some men, exceeding all bounds, not only indulge in all that comes under the description of desire, but also acquire that passion, which is akin to passion, that is anger, wishing to rekindle all the irrational part of the soul to destroy the mind. For that which has been said, "upon your breast and belly you shall go" (Gen. 3:14). In the literal sense it applies to the serpent but in reality it is a truly divine oracle that applies to every irrational man, who is a passion-loving man. For the breast is the abode of anger and desire dwells in the belly.

Somn. 2.155–158a: . . . As for gluttony it has two forms, drink and food, and the spices and the flavorings needed are by no means simple in the former, but innumerable in the latter. These are, indeed, entrusted to two caretakers: the liquor treated with nicety to a chief butler, the more elaborate edibles to a chief baker. 156 There is a carefully considered meaning in describing the dreams as appearing to these two men in a single night. For both strive eagerly to serve the same need, not simple food, but they prepare it with pleasure and delight. Although the hard work of each of them is about half the food, they are both concerned with the whole. 157 Also, each half attracts the other, for after eating the men immediately desire to drink, and after drinking, they immediately wish to eat, and this is one of the chief reasons for assigning the same time to the dreams of both. 158a Therefore, the chief butler is drunkenness and the chief baker gluttony. . . .

Somn. 2.182: . . . I am appointed to be a cupbearer, not to one invested with temperance and piety and the other virtues, but to the very greedy and immoderate and unjust man, one who was very proud in impiety, and once who dared to say, "I know not the Lord" (Exod. 5:2).

Spec. 3.9–10: The natural pleasure is frequently greatly to blame when the craving for it is immoderate and insatiable; for instance, when it takes the form of voracious gluttony, even though nothing of the food is of the forbidden kind, and the passionate desire for women shown by men who in their craze for sexual intercourse behave unchastely, not with the wives of others, but with their own. 10 But the blame in most of these cases is of the body more than of the soul. The body seems to contain a great amount of fire and moisture; the fire as it consumes the material set before it quickly demands a second supply; moisture is transitory, leading through the genital organs; it creates irritations, itching, and titillations without end.[21]

Virt. 163–164: Therefore, Moses in all his excellent revelations exhorts them to refrain from all sins, but particularly from arrogance (*QG* 4.237). Then, he gives them a reminder of things that are apt to inflame this passion, that is excessive satiety of the belly and an extravagant surplus of houses, land, and cattle. For they immediately lose control over themselves, being elated and puffed up, for whom the only hope of their cure is to never utterly forget God. 164 For as when the sun has risen, the darkness disappears, and all things are filled with light, so in the same way, when God, the intelligible Sun, appears and shines upon the soul, the darkness of passions and vices is dispelled, and that purest and most venerable form, the form of exceedingly brilliant virtue, reveals itself.

Sexual Pleasure

Ebr. 223b: . . . when God passed well-deserved sentence upon the impious, and the heavens rained instead of water the unquenchable flames of thunderbolt. In such a soul all that grows is passionate desire, which is barren of excellence and blinded to all that is worthy divine, and this he compares to a wine; not that which is the mother of fruits, but a vine that proves to be the bearer of bitterness and wickedness and villainy and both anger and fury, and savage moods and tempters; and the wine that stings the soul like vipers and venomous asps, and their bites none can cure.

Det. 113: His plight is that to which a human being would come, if he were always eating or drinking, and never being filled, or indulging perpetually in sexual pleasures with his cravings after sexual intercourse continually in full force (*QG* 2.46). For wickedness is brought about by emptiness, and strength by fullness; and insatiability is the hunger that is experienced when an abundant supply of food is combined with dire intemperance, and the wretched ones are fully burdened, while their appetites are empty desires and still thirsting.

Somn. 2.13: The same way the pleasures of the body fall down upon us in gathered force like a cataract deluding and obliterating one after another all the things of the mind. Then, after a short time, wisdom with strong and vehement Spirit slackens the stream of pleasures and softens in general all the appetites and ambitions that the bodily senses kindle in us.

Agr. 37–38: Gluttony is naturally followed by her attendant, sexual pleasure, bringing on extraordinary madness, fierce desire, and most grievous frenzy. For when men have been loaded up with overeating and strong drink and heavy intoxication, they are no longer able to control themselves, but they haste to indulge their sexual pleasures; they burst in and beset doors until they have drained off the great vehemence of their passion and find it possible to rest. 38 This is apparently the reason why nature placed the organs of sexual lust where nature did, assuming that they do not like hunger but are roused to their special activities when fullness of food leads the way.

Congr. 59–60a: Therefore, the wicked person begets vice by his legitimate wife and passion by his concubine. For the soul as a whole is the legitimate companion of reasoning, and if it be a soul of guilt it begets vices. The bodily nature is the concubine, and it is seen that through it passion is generated. For the body is the place of pleasures and desires (*QG* 4.40–42). 60a This concubine is called Timna, whose name translated is "tossing faintness." For the soul faints and loses power in passion.[22]

JERUSALEM

Pilgrimage

Spec. 1.69–70: Countless multitudes from countless cities come to the Temple at every feast, some over land, and others over sea, from east and west and north and south. They take the Temple for their port as a general refuge and safe asylum from the bustle and great turmoil of life. There, they seek to find calm weather and, released from the cares whose yoke has been heavy upon them from their earliest years, to enjoy a brief breathing space in cheerful tranquility. 70 Filled with propitious hopes they devote the leisure, as is their important duty to holiness and the honoring of God. Friendships are formed between those who did not know each other, and the sacrifices and libations are the occasion of reciprocity of feeling and constitute the surest pledge that all are of one unanimous faith.

Prov. 2.64: There is a city on the sea of Syria, named Ascalon. While I was there at a time when I was on my way to our ancestral Temple to offer both prayers and sacrifices. . . .

Jerusalem and Mother City

Conf. 78: Therefore, when they have stayed a while in their bodies and have understood through them all that sense and mortality are to be shown, they return again to the place from which they set out at first, a native country, a heavenly country in which it is their citizenship and hold in honor the earthly place in which they dwell for a while. For to those who found a colony instead of a metropolis receive the land, I suppose, as their native country. But those who are travelers abroad from their land that sent them forth remain together with those who are away from the home, to which also they yearn to return.

Fug. 94–95: These are the causes for the murderers of unintentional homicide taking refuge only in the cities of the temple-keepers. We must say next why there are six in number. It would seem, then, that the oldest and strongest and best Mother City (*QG* 4.178), something more than just a city, is the divine Word, and that to take refuge first in it is supremely advantageous. 95 The other five cities, being as it were colonies, are powers of Him who speaks that Word, their leader being the creative power, according to which the Creator fashioned the world with a Word. And the second is the royal power, according to which He Who has created governs what has come into being. The third is the gracious power, through which the Artificer has compassion and has mercy on his own work. The fourth is the legislative power, by which He prohibits those things that should not be done.

Flacc. 46: The Jews are so numerous that there is not one country than can contain all the Jews. For this reason, they settle in most of the wealthiest countries of Europe and Asia, both their islands and mainland. However, they regard the Holy City as their main city. It is where the Holy Temple of the Most High God stands. But the regions they obtained as inheritance from their fathers, grandfathers, great-grandfathers, and even the most remote ancestors, to live in, they regard as their fatherland where they were born and brought up. There are also some regions where they came as immigrants at the time of their foundation, much to the satisfaction of the founders.

Legat. 281–282a: About our Holy City, I must say what benefits me to say. She, as I said, is my native city, and also my Mother City not only of the one country of Judea, but also of many others, because of the colonies sent out from time to time into the neighboring countries Egypt, Phoenicia, the part of Syria called the Hollow, and also the rest of the regions lying far apart of Pamphylia, Cilicia, most of Asia up to Bithynia and the corners of Pontus. ... 282a But not only are the continents full of Jewish colonies, but also the most highly esteemed of the islands, such as Euboea, Cyprus, and Crete.[23]

TEMPLE/SANCTUARY

Note

In Philo's writings, the Temple stands at the heart of Judaism.[24] Unlike other Hellenistic Jews, Philo emphasizes two dimensions of the practice of the various observances regarding the Temples: the earthly and the spiritual Temples. Both Temples and their practices have ethical value.[25] Concerning the earthly Temple, for example, the various Jewish practices for and at the Jerusalem Temple are expressions of pious deeds that inculcate the virtue of piety. Philo links closely the Temple observances with monotheism. The practices of prayers, hymns,[26] daily or perpetual holy rites,[27] sacrifices,[28] first fruits,[29] offerings or votive offerings,[30] donations, and sacred services[31] promote true piety toward God.[32] Within his monotheistic view, Philo exhorts pilgrimage to the Jerusalem Temple. It is to this Temple that the Diaspora Alexandrian Jews are urged to come in pilgrimage for the religious observances and feasts.[33] The physical Temple is the incentive for a desire for piety and all the other virtues.

Metaphorically, the spiritual Temple is the highest and, in the truest sense, the holy Temple of God, the whole universe (*Spec.* 1.66). In this sense, the altar is replaced by the most sacred of all existence, the holy vestments by the stars, and the priest by the angels, all of these belonging to the intelligible realm. According to Philo, the Existent One cannot dwell literally in any earthly building (*Cher.* 99), because the Supreme and Eternal God could only dwell in a worthy mind (*Cher.* 99–101). Philo believes that people, whose minds are pious, are in a holy place with their minds even if they are not present physically (*Leg.* 1.62). The true Temple is within the human soul. He internalizes and spiritualizes the Jerusalem Temple in a way that the physical reality of the Temple remains very important.[34] Although the temple language becomes in some instances spiritualized, the religious observances in and for the Jerusalem Temple are maintained to preserve Jewish piety, ethical values, as well as community unity.

Temple of Jerusalem

Somn. 1.149a: It is clear that many groups of the wicked colonists are being removed, so that the One, the Good One, may enter the house (*QE* 2.115). Therefore, take up seriously! O soul, to become the house of God, His Holy Temple, the most beautiful dwelling place.

Somn. 1.215: I believe there are two Temples of God: one of them is the universe, in which the high priest is His first-born, the divine Logos, and the other is the rational soul, whose priest is the man of truth, the outward and visible image of whom is he who offers the prayers and sacrifices handed down from our fathers, who has been commissioned to wear the aforesaid tunic, which is a replica of the whole heaven, so that the universe may join in the holy rites with human and human with the universe.

Mos. 2.72: Thus, if they had already taken the land into which they were removing, they would necessarily have set firmly a very famous Temple on the purest place with very expensive stones for its material and build great walls around it and with houses for the temple-keepers, and call by name the place the Holy City.

Spec. 1.152, 156: Above all, none of the donors should reproach the recipients; first, it exhorts to bring the first fruits into the Temple, then, from this place they should be taken by the priests. (*QE* 1.10) It was the proper course that the first fruits should be brought in thanksgiving to God by those whose life in all its aspects is blessed by His beneficence and then by Him, since He needs nothing, freely bestowed with all reverence and honor on those who serve and minister as temple servants. . . . 156 After bestowing these great sources of revenue on the priests, He did not ignore those who are in the second order. They are the temple servants (*QG* 4.151). Some of these are stationed at the doors as gatekeepers at the very entrances, some within in front of the Temple to prevent any unlawful person from setting foot therein, either intentionally or unintentionally. Some inspect around it turn by turn at night and day assigned by lot, night-watchmen and day-watchmen. Others sweep out the porticoes and the open court, remove the rubbish, and take care of the purity.

Legat. 156–157a: He knew also that they have houses of prayer and met together in them, especially on the sacred sevenths (or sabbaths), when they are instructed together in their ancestral philosophy. He also knew that they collect money for sacred purposes from their first fruits and send them to Jerusalem by those who take up sacrifices (*QG* 1.62). 157a Though, nevertheless, he neither expelled them from Rome nor deprived them of their Roman citizenship, because they were careful to preserve their Jewish citizenship, nor took any violent measures against the houses of prayer, nor prevented them from gathering together to receive instructions in their laws, nor opposed their offerings of the first fruits.

Legat. 188: He managed with difficulty while sobbing and breathing spasmodically to say, "Our temple is lost, Gaius has ordered a colossal statue to be set up within the inner Temple dedicated to himself under the name of Zeus."

Legat. 198: They replied, "you know the supreme and first cause, which is also known by all men. Gaius wishes to be thought a god and has assumed that the Jews will be the only dissentients, on whom he could inflict no greater injury than the ruin of the sacredness of their Temple. He has been instructed that the Temple in Jerusalem is the most beautiful in comparison to all the temples everywhere, from endless ages embellished by unceasing and unsparing expenditure.

Legat. 203a: After reading the letter, Gaius ordered a colossal statue coated with gold, something more richly furnished and much more magnificent than the rich altar of bricks built in Jamnia, should be set up in the Temple of the Mother City.

Legat. 212: And above all, a more peculiar and remarkable aspect is their zeal for the Temple. Indeed, zeal is their greatest sign, for death without mercy has been established against those of other races who enter into its inner precincts. For the outer parts of the Temple are open to all wherever they come from.

Legat. 265: Your honorable and good citizens of every race, only those men who do not acknowledge Gaius to be a god, appear now to be desiring to plot even my death in their obstinate disobedience. When I ordered to set up a statue of Zeus in the Temple as object of worship, they raised the whole of their people and issued forth from the city and country nominally to make a petition. The truth is that they opposed to the orders that I had imposed upon them.

Legat. 278–279a: As you know me, Jerusalem is my native city, in which is situated the Holy Temple of the Most High God (*QE* 1.12). I received kings from grandfathers and ancestors. Most of them had the title of high priest (*QE* 2.105, 107) and considered their kingship to be inferior to the priesthood and held that the office of high priest was as superior in excellence to that of a king, as God is superior to men. 279a As my lot is cast in such a nation, fatherland, and Temple, I bind beyond everything. For the nation, that it may not bear the opposite intention of the truth, when from the very first, it has been the most pious and holiest nation well disposed from the beginning to all your house.

Legat. 346: . . . and the Temple in the Holy City, which its sanctity was left untouched, being judged to have all rights of a Sanctuary, he was proceeding to convert and change the form into a temple of his own to bear the name of Gaius, the new Zeus made manifest.[35]

Priesthood/Priest/High Priest

Somn. 2.185: But the high priest is unblemished, perfect, the husband of a virgin (Lev. 21:12–13), who, with wrong belief, has never been made a woman, but who rather has forsaken the things that are feminine through the company of her husband (Gen. 18:11). And not only is this man a husband able to sow the seed of undefiled and virgin thoughts, but he is also a father of holy words.

Mos. 2.66–68: . . . Third, one must give further an account of the priesthood. The greatest and most necessary characteristic of a high priest is piety, which Moses practiced in a very high degree and at the same time made use of his natural good gift. . . . 67 Therefore, he came to love God and be loved by Him as have been few others, being inspired by heavenly love, and honoring the Ruler of everything, and being in return honored by Him in a particular way. And it was an honor well adapted to the wise man to serve the One, Who truly Is, and the service of God is a practice of the priesthood. This is privilege, a blessing that nothing in the world can surpass, was given to him as his due, and oracles instructed him in all that pertains to rites of worship and the sacred tasks of his ministry. 68 But first, it is necessary to be pure in soul as in body, nothing attributing to passion, but purifying himself from everything that belongs to the mortal nature, food and drink, and intercourse with women.

Mos. 2.133–135: Therefore, the high priest, being equipped in this way, is properly prepared for the holy duties, so that when he enters to offer the ancestral prayers and sacrifices, there may enter along with him the whole universe through which he brings examples: the long robe an example of the air, the pomegranate of the water (*QE* 2.119), the flower trimming of the earth, the scarlet of fire, and the mantel over his shoulders of heaven itself. . . . 134 For he who has been consecrated to the Father of the world needs to conceive a desire for an intercessor, the most perfect son of virtue, so that sins may be remembered no more and good gifts showered in abundance.

135 Perhaps, indeed, he is also teaching beforehand the servant of God to learn the lesson, even if he is unable to make himself worthy of the Creator of the world, he should try to be continuously worthy of the world itself. As he wears a vesture that represents the world. His first duty is to carry the pattern enshrined in his heart, and so be in a sense transformed from a human being into the nature of the world, and if one may dare to say so, and in speaking of truth one may well dare to speak the truth, become a microcosm himself.

Mos. 2.174: Since the consecrated persons consisted of more than one order, those who are made priests and have been entrusted to offer prayers and sacrifices and the other holy rites and to penetrate to the innermost Sanctuary, and those who are none but sometimes called temple attendants who had none of these duties, but had the duty of taking care of and guarding the Temple and the things in it both day and night. The faction has become the cause of innumerable evils to many persons in many places and gained ground here also. The temple attendants attacked the priests attempting to deprive their privileges, which belonged to them, and they thought to accomplish this easily, since they were many times more numerous that the others.

Mos. 2.275–276: . . . when I was speaking of the prophet as a high priest, he himself was under possession and was fulfilled at not long period afterwards, but at the very moment when he was prophesizing. 276 There are two groups of servants of the Temple: the higher consisting of priests and the lower consisting of temple attendants. And at this time there were three priests (Aaron, Eleazar, and Ithamar), but many thousand temple attendants.

Spec. 1.80–84: With regard to the priests there are laws. It has been ordained that the priest should be complete and perfect, without any mutilation in the body (Lev. 21:17–21; 22:4). That is, no parts of the body must be lacking or have been mutilated, nor on the other hand redundant, whether the excrescence be congenital or an aftergrowth due to disease. Nor must the skin change into leprosy or into malignant tetters or warts or any other eruptive growth. 81 For if the body of the priest, which is mortal by nature, must be scrutinized to see that it is not harmed by any misfortune, much more is the immortal soul, which we say was impressed after the Image of the Existent (Gen. 1:27). And the Logos is the Image of God through whom the whole world was fashioned. 82 After providing for his pure family from a noble stock and his perfection in both body and soul, the legislation deals with his clothing, which the priest must accept when he is about to carry out the holy services to God. 83 The dress is a tunic of linen and girdle, which covers the private parts. It is a custom not to reveal the genitals at the altar precincts. The tunic makes the priests nimble in their ministry. For in this undress, with nothing more than the short tunics, they are attired to move with unhampered rapidity when training the soul. That is when they bring forward the victims and the votive offerings and the libations and all the other useful sacrifices

(*QE* 2.101). 84 With regard to the high priest, it is said that he is bidden to put on a similar dress when he enters the inner Sanctuary to offer incense, because its fine linen is not like wool produced by mortal creatures who are subject to death, and also to wear another robe,the formation of which is very complicated. So, in this it would seem to be a likeness and copy of the universe.

Spec. 1.96–97: It is expressed that the high priest should first have an image of the All reflecting upon him, so that from the continuous contemplation of the All he may naturally render his own life worthy of the whole. Secondly, by being a fellow minister in the holy works, he should have the whole universe as his fellow-ministrant. Most suitable and very right it is that the one who is a priest consecrated to the Father of the world should take with him also the Father's son, the universe, for the service of the One Who fashioned and made the All. 97 . . . Among the other nations the priests are accustomed to performing religious duties of prayers and sacrifices for their kinsmen and friends and fellow-countrymen only, but the high priest of the Jews makes prayers and give thanks not only on behalf of the whole humanity but also on behalf of the parts of nature, earth, water, air, fire. He performs prayers and thanksgivings, for he holds the world to be his fatherland, the very truth it is; on its behalf, he is accustomed to propitiate the Ruler with supplication and litanies, imploring Him to make His creature a partaker of His own kindly and merciful nature.

Spec. 1.101–102: Since a priest is a man before he is a priest and must be bound to have sexual intercourse, an impulse from necessity, Moses seeks for him a marriage with a pure virgin, whose parents and grandparents and ancestors are equally pure, highly distinguished for their nobility of character, and hence their excellence based on birth. 102 . . . For the rights and duties of the priest are of special kind and the office duties demand an even tenor of blamelessness from birth to death.

Spec. 4.98: He exhorts them to offer a sacrifice as first fruits some of their grain, wine, oil, sheep, and other goods, and distribute them for sacrifices and for gifts to the officiating priests: the former out of thanksgiving to God for the bounty and abundance of everything, and the latter out of gratitude for the sacred-Temple service, in order that the priests might receive a reward for their services of the holy duties.

Legat. 306–307: Therefore, at that time they were round shields on which no image has been painted. And now it is a colossal statue. Then, also the erection was in the house of the governors; but they say, that which is now contemplated is to be in the inmost part of the Temple, in the inaccessible Sanctuary itself, into which the great priest enters once a year only on the fast as it is called, to offer prayers and incense according to the ancestral practice for a full supply of blessings and prosperity and peace for all humanity. 307 And if any priest, not to say about the other Jews, and not merely one of the lowest priests, but of those who are ranked directly below the first, goes in either by himself or with the high priest, and further even if the high priest enters on two days in the year or three or four times on the same day, death without appeal is his doom.[36]

JEWISH FESTIVALS

Sacrifices

Mos. 2.159–160: Many sacrifices were necessarily brought every day and especially in assemblies and festivals on behalf of both each individual and all in general, and for a multitude of different reasons. This piety shown by a populous nation made it necessary to have also a multitude of temple-attendants for the sacred services. 160 The election of these officers was made in a novel and not in the ordinary manner. He appointed one of the twelve tribes according to birth, giving them the office as the prize and reward of a deed pleasing to God.

Spec. 1.161b–166: . . . Next, Moses proceeds to give instructions concerning the animals suitable for sacrifice (*QE* 2.98–99). 162 Of the animals used for this purpose some are confined to the dry land, and others fly in the air. Of the winged animals he took in preference creatures that are divided into numberless tribes, all of which he ignored except only two classes: dove and turtle-dove, the dove because it is the gentlest of those whose nature is tame and gregarious, and the turtle-dove because it is the tamest of those that are naturally solitary. 163 Animals of the dry land are unspeakably great flocks, and the number of their varieties is innumerably rich. All of these he passed over and selected three animals based on the superiority of birth, oxen and sheep, and goats. These are the gentlest and tamest animals. . . . 166 All the animals selected must be perfect, with no affliction troubling any parts of their body, unharmed throughout, and without a share of defilement. At any rate, so great is the forethought, not only by those who bring up the sacrifices but also by those who offer the sacrifices, that the most highly approved of the priests, selected according to birth for the inspection of their physical blemishes, examine them from the head to the extremities of the feet, both the visible parts and those that are concealed under the belly and thighs, for fear that some small blemish has passed unobserved.

Spec. 1.194: Having so much discoursed about these subjects, Moses begins to divide the kinds of sacrifices into three classes. He calls them respectively the whole-burnt offering, the preservation offering, and the sin offering. To each of these he adds the adornment of suitable ritual, in which he succeeds admirably in combining decorum with reverence.

Spec. 1.277a: The symbolical meaning is nothing else than this: what is honorable before God is not the number of victims offered to God, but the true purity of the rational spirit in the one who makes a sacrifice.[37]

Spec. 1.271–272: To such high-minded people, I would say that God does not rejoice in burnt offerings, even if someone offers an offering of a hundred oxen.[38] For all things are His possessions; yet though He possesses, He is in need of nothing. But He rejoices with those who in their minds love God and with people who practice holiness, and from these He accepts plain meal or barley, ritual cakes, and the cheapest things, as if they were costly things, rather than those of expensive cost. 272 Indeed, although the worshipers may bring nothing else, they bring themselves and offer the best sacrifice, the full and perfect oblation of nobleness, as they honor with hymns and thanksgiving to God, the Benefactor and Savior, sometimes with the organs of speech and other times without the tongue and mouth, when in the soul alone their minds recite the detailed narrative and utter the cry of praise. For the ears of human beings cannot reach to the perception of such.

Sin-Offering

Spec. 1.190: Thus, the general sacrifices in the form of burnt offerings performed on behalf of the nation or, to speak more correctly, on behalf of all human beings, have now been described to the best of my ability. But these burnt offerings are accompanied on each day of a feast by the sacrifice called the sin offering, which is offered for the remission of sins. Its flesh is placed aside to be eaten by the priests.

Spec. 1.226–229: So much for these. Now we must consider the third kind of sacrifice next. It is called sin offering. This has been divided into several parts, those concerned with the kinds of persons and those concerned with the kinds of sacrificial victims. As to the persons, the high priest is distinguished from the whole nation and the ruler as a class from the men of the uncultivated people. As to the victims, they may be a male calf, a he-goat, a she-goat or ewe-lamb. 227 Another distinction made is one that is most essential between voluntary and unvoluntary sins. For those who have acknowledged their sin are changing their way for the better, while they who reproach themselves for their errors are seeking a blameless life as their refuge. 228 The sins, then, of the high priest and those of the whole nation are purified with an animal equal in value. . . . 229 For it is necessary that in matters of sacrifice the ruler should be superior to the uncultivated person and the nation superior to the ruler, since it is proper that the whole should always be superior to the part. . . . But the equality of honor that the high priest enjoys is evidently not so much on his own account, because he is the servant of the nation, giving thanks in common for all through the holiest of prayers and the purest sacrifices.[39]

Prayer

Ebr. 125–126: Pray then to God that you never become a leader in the wine song, never, that is, to say voluntarily take the first step on the path that leads to ignorance and folly. For, I say, involuntarily evils are but half evils and lighter matters as deliberate sins. . . . 126 But if your prayers are fulfilled you cannot longer remain a layman but will obtain the office that is the greatest of the authorities, the priesthood. For it is the work of priests and servants of God alone to sacrifice sobriety, and in steadfastness of mind to resist the wine-cup and everything that causes folly.

Ebr. 224: We may offer prayer that these may be averted, and implore the all-merciful God, so that this wild wine may also be destroyed and may declare to the eunuchs and all those who are barren of virtue everlasting vanishment, and that, instead of them, He may plant in the garden of our souls trees of right instruction, and He may grant us fruits of genuine worth and true virility and powers of reason, capable of begetting good actions and also of bringing the virtues to their faithfulness, gifted with the strength to bind together and keep safe for ever all that is akin to real happiness.

Mut. 188: But some of those who are more courageous might come forward and say that the utterance does not even indicate any disbelief, but a prayer, that if joy, the best of good emotions, is to be born, its birth should be confined to the numbers ninety and one hundred, that so the perfect good may enter on its existence under perfect numbers.

Mut. 204: Therefore, then it is "this Ishmael" for whose health alone the man of virtue prays, because it is those others who do not hear sincerely the holy teachings whom Moses openly forbade to resort to the assembly of the Ruler of the universe.[40]

Mos. 1.184–185: When they were engaged in such lamentations, Moses supplicated to God again that, knowing the weakness of animals, and especially of human beings, and the necessities of the body, which depends on food and is tied to the harsh mistresses, meat and drink, He should pardon the disheartened and also satisfy the deficiency of all; not at some distant time but with a prompt and immediate gift, considering the natural negligence of mortality, which desires quick advantage for the support. 185 He sent out beforehand the power of His grace, and opening the vigilant eye of the suppliant's soul, he showed him a tree, which He commanded him to lift up and cast into the springs (*QG* 2.63), possibly formed by nature to exercise a virtue that had hitherto remained unknown, or possibly created in that moment for the first time for the service into which it was destined to serve.

The Feast of the Tabernacle

Ebr. 134–135: We may conceive the Tabernacle and the altar as ideas, the former the symbol of incorporeal virtue and the latter the symbol of the sensible image. Now, the altar and what is on it can be easily seen, for it is constructed out of doors and with unquenchable fire. . . . It is never consumed, and thus by night and by day it is in bright light. 135 But the Tabernacle and all its contents are invisible, because they are placed not only in the innermost place and in the inner Sanctuary, but also because anyone who touched them, or with a very curious eye looked upon them, was punished with death according to the Law. . . . The only exception made is for one who should be free from all defects, not wasting himself with any passion great or small, but endowed with a nature sound and complete and perfect in every respect.

Spec. 1.189: On the fifteenth day of this month at the full moon it is held the feast of the Tabernacles, as it is called, and on this feast the supply of sacrificial offerings is on a greater scale. For during seven days seventy calves are being sacrificed, and fourteen rams and ninety-eight lambs; all these animals are entirely burnt. It is also commanded that the holy eighth day be held as a custom and be observed as holy. This last must be treated in detail when the subject about the feast comes up for discussion. On this day as many offerings are brought as on the feast that begins the sacred month.

Spec. 2.204: The last of the annual feasts, called Tabernacles, takes place at the autumn equinox. From this feast have been offered two morals. First, it is necessary to honor equality and hate inequality, for the former is justice, and the latter is the source and fountain of injustice. The former is akin to open sunlight, and the latter to darkness. Second, it is that after all the fruits are made perfect, it is our duty to give thanks to God, Who brought them to perfection and is the source of all good things only.[41]

The Feast of the Trumpets

Spec. 1.186–187: When the third season has come in the seventh month at the autumnal equinox, there is held at its outset the sacred-month-day called trumpet day, about which I have spoken before (see *Spec.* 1.180). On the tenth day is the fast, which is not only carefully observed by those who practice piety and holiness, but also by those who never do their religious duties in the rest of their life. For all stand in awe, overcome by the holiness of the day; and at that time the worse compete with the better in self-control and virtue. 187 The high dignity of this day has two aspects, one as a festival, and the other as a purification and escape from sins, for which forgiveness has been given by the bounties of the graciousness of God, Who holds him in honor in the same way He does to the one who does not sin.

Spec. 2.188–192: Next is the holy time of the month when it was customary to sound a trumpet at the same time with those who bring up sacrifices to the Temple. Its name of trumpet feast is derived from this. There are two reasons for it: one is particular to the nation, and the other is common to all human beings. . . . 189 For, then, the sound of the trumpet sounded forth from heaven, which seems likely to suppose that it reached the ends of the universe, so that the event might strike terror even into those who were far from the spot almost reaching the extremities of the earth, who would come to the natural conclusion that such mighty signs portended mighty consequences. . . . 190 This is a significance peculiar to the nation. And what follows is common to all human beings. The trumpet is the instrument used in war, both to sound the advance against the enemy when the moment comes for engaging battle, and also for recalling the troops when they have to separate and return to their respective camps. . . . 192 Therefore, the law declared this feast named trumpet of the instrument of war to establish peace as thank-offering to God the peace-maker and peace-keeper. He destroys faction in cities and in the various parts of the universe and creates plenty and fertility and abundance of other good things and leaves no fuel of fruits of destruction to be rekindled.

The Feast of the Fast

Spec. 2.193–197: . . . And after the feast of the trumpets comes the fast. Perhaps some of those who are not in accordance with the established doctrine and are not ashamed to censure the beautiful things will ask, what kind of feast is it, in which there are no gatherings, and common meal, and hosts, and banquet guests, and many unmixed drinks and very costly tables, nor generous displays and equipment of all the accompaniments of a public banquet . . . ? 194 It is in these and through these that men, in ignorance of what true merriment is, consider that the merriment of a feast is to be found. This the clear-seeing eyes of the all-wise Moses discerned, and therefore, he called the fast a feast, the greatest of the feasts, in his native tongue a Sabbath of sabbaths, and as the Greeks would say a seven of sevens, and a holier than the holy. He gave it this name for many reasons. 195 First, because of self-control, which is always and everywhere exhorting them to show this in all the affairs of life, in controlling the tongue and the belly and the organs below the belly. . . . 196 Second, because the holy day is entirely devoted to prayers and supplications, and human beings move their leisure from morning to evening in nothing else but offering suppliant prayers, in which they zealously seek to propitiate God and ask for remission of their sins, voluntarily and involuntarily. . . . 197 Third, because of the time in which the celebration of the fast occurs, that is when all the annual fruits of the earth have been gathered together. To eat and drink of these without delay would, he held, show gluttony, but to fast and refrain from taking them as food is an expression of piety. Piety teaches the mind not to put trust in what stands readily prepared before us as though it were the source of health and life. For often its presence proves injurious and its absence beneficial.

The Sabbath

Cher. 86–87: The precept is this. Only God keeps a feast really and truly. For He alone rejoices, and He alone delights in, and He alone cheers, and He has come together with unmixed war to bring peace. He is free from grief and fear and has no share of evil things, unquestionably correct, free from pain, untiring, and full of perfect happiness. His nature is the most perfect; He is himself the summit, end, and limit, and the limit of happiness is God, having a share with nothing other than to improvement. . . . 87 And therefore Moses often calls in his laws the Sabbath, which means rest, God's Sabbath (Exod. 20:10; *QE* 1.9), not of human beings. He lays His finger on an essential fact in the nature of things. For in all truth there is but one thing in the universe that rests, that is God.

The Feast of Passover

Spec. 1.181: In the first season, which he names springtime and its equinox the first season, he ordained that what is called the feast of the unleavened bread should be observed for seven days. He declared that this is a feast that should be carried equally in honor in the holy ritual assigned to them. For he ordered ten sacrifices to be offered each day, as they are for the new moons, making the total number of whole-burnt offerings seventy apart from those dealing with the sin-offerings.

Spec. 2.145: After the new moon is the fourth feast of the crossing over. This feast was called by the Hebrews Pascha in their ancestral tongue (*QE* 1.4). In this festival many thousands of victims were sacrificed from noon until evening by the whole people. Old and young alike honored that day and the priesthood with high dignity. At other times, the priests according to the ordinance of the law perform religious rites, such as the public sacrifices and those offered by private individuals. But on this occasion the whole nation performs the sacred rites and acts as priest with pure hands and complete immunity.[42]

The Feast of the New Moon

Spec. 1.177–178a: Having given these orders with regard to the seventh days, he deals with the new moons. He says that it is necessary to sacrifice whole-burnt offerings, ten all together: two calves, one ram, seven lambs. Since the cycle of the month in which the moon brings to completion is a perfect whole, he considered it worthy that in order to perform priestly functions the number of animals to be sacrificed should be perfect. 178a Ten is a perfect number, and he exceedingly distributed it well into the things above mentioned.

Spec. 2.140–142a: Following the order stated above, we record a third type of feast, which we will make known. It is the new moon, or beginning of the lunar month, the time from the conjunction to a conjunction, which is distinguished in the mathematical schools. The new moon holds its place among the feasts for many reasons. First, because it is the beginning of the month, and the beginning in honor of number and of time. Second, because when it arrives nothing is left without a light in heaven. . . . 141 Third, because it is the stronger or more powerful element at that time and it supplies the help that is needed to the smaller and weaker body. For it is just then that the sun begins to illumine the moon with the light, which we perceive, and the moon reveals its own beauty to the eye. . . . 142a Fourth, because it is the moon that traverses the zodiac in a shorter fixed period than any other heavenly body (*QE* 2.112).

The Feast of the Great Vow

Spec. 1.247–248: After arranging these ordinances about each particular kind of sacrifice, whole-burnt sacrifice, preservation-offering, and sin-offering, he ordained rules for another feast, which partakes of the three, so that they may show friendships and kingship between them. 248 . . . When some people offered first-fruits from every part of their possession, for instance, in wheat, barley, oil, wine, and their finest orchard-fruits and also in the first-born males of their livestock, consecrated in the case of the clean animals and valued at an adequate compensation in the case of unclean animals, having no longer material resources with which they will delight in piety, they actually dedicate and consecrate themselves, showing an amazing sanctification and a surpassing devotion to God. And thus, it is appropriately called the great vow, for every man is his own greatest possession, and this even he now gives up and abandons.

The Feast of the Sheaf

Spec. 2.162–163: Within the feast there is another feast following directly after the first day. This is called the feast of the sheaf, a name given to it from the ceremony that consists in bringing to the altar a sheaf as a first fruit, both of the land that has been given to the nation to dwell in and of the whole human race in general. 163 The reason is that the priest has the same relation to a city that the nation of the Jews has to the whole inhabited world. For the holy office in very truth belongs to the nation because it carries out all the rites of purification and in both body and soul obeys the injunctions of the divine laws, which restrict the pleasures of the belly and the parts below the stomach (*QG* 4.168) . . . setting reason to guide the irrational senses and also to check and to rein in the wild and extravagant impulses of the soul.[43]

NOTES

1. *Spec.* 1.193–197; 209–210, 242; 2.204, 209, 156.
2. *Spec.* 1.201, 215.
3. *Opif.* 27; *Decal.* 53–57; *Spec.* 1.19; *Aet.* 10, 20; *Mos.* 1.158. In Wis. 13:1–9, the author recognizes the celestial beings as gods, yet in less elaborated form than Philo (see also Paul, 1 Cor. 8:5).
4. *Leg.* 1.41; 3.82 (Deut. 4:39). Harry Austryn Wolfson, *Philo: Foundations of Religious Philosophy in Judaism, Christianity, and Islam* (2 vols.; Cambridge: Harvard University Press, 1948), 1:173, 1:201.
5. *Leg.* 1.48–52; *Ebr.* 95–96; *Mos.* 1.298–299; 2.161–166; *Spec.* 1.56–59, 79; *Virt.* 102–104, 221–222.
6. *Mos.* 2.268–270; *Spec.* 3.125–126.
7. *Migr.* 86–93 (Gen. 12:2). Although bodily circumcision was not required for entering the Jewish community (*QE* 2.2), it was one of the commandments that all Jews had to obey.
8. Philo explains that excessive pleasure befuddles and confuses the human mind, especially during intercourse, which according to Philo, is the greatest pleasure. So, the excision of a piece of the male organ, which ministers the intercourse, appeases the excessive and superfluous pleasure.
9. Neil J. McEleney, "Conversion, Circumcision, and the Law." *NTS* 20 (1974): 328–29; J. Nolland, "Uncircumcised Proselytes?" *JSJ* 12 (1981): 173–94.
10. In Philo, we could also find a strong Jewish "philosophical" apology against Greek perception of circumcision as an obscene act.
11. *Migr.* 224.
12. Cf. *Decal.* 174, 51.
13. *Spec.* 4.100–118. Like in *Let. Arist.* 128–171, for the author, such dietary regulations demonstrate Jewish superiority (cf. 4 Maccabees).

14. For a discussion, see Svebakken, *Philo of Alexandria's Exposition of the Tenth Commandment*, 20–31.

15. *Somn.* 1.93–94; *QG* 4.167.

16. *Somn.* 2.155, 215; *Spec.* 1.50.

17. *Leg.* 1.90–106.

18. *Leg.* 2.79, 97–98; *Det.* 72; *Agr.* 102–106; *Mut.* 1.236–237; 2.181–184; *Hypoth.* 7.11; *Legat.* 4–6.

19. *Spec.* 4.92–94.

20. *Migr.* 61–66; *Her.* 192–194, 268–273; *Decal.* 149; *Spec.* 4.78–91, 113–115.

21. *Leg.* 3.140–144; *Post.* 180; *Congr.* 80; *Abr.* 133–136, 147–150; *Mos.* 1.160–162; *Spec.* 2.49–50; 4.100–101, 127–128; *Virt.* 136–137; *Contempl.* 55–56; *Prov.* 2.18–20.

22. *Post.* 155–157; *Deus* 111–112; *Agr.* 21–22, 36–38; *Congr.* 58–59; *Det.* 109–111; *Ebr.* 220–223; *Conf.* 90–94; *Migr.* 26–29; *Fug.* 143–146; *Somn.* 2.276–278; *Ios.* 49–51; *Mos.* 1.305; 2.185–186; *Spec.* 2.50; 4.129–131; *Praem.* 124; *Contempl.* 55–56.

23. *Mos.* 2.72; *Legat.* 156, 203, 225–226, 281–293, 330–333.

24. Philo mentions the Temple in his lists of important Jewish practical values (*Migr.* 92). For a good treatment on the Temple in Philo, see Borgen, "Application of and Commitment to the Law of Moses." *SPhA* 13 (2001): 86–95; Aryeh Kasher, "Jerusalem as 'Metropolis' in Philo's National Consciousness." *Cathedra* 11 (1979): 45–56; Hans-Josef Klauck, "Die heilige Stadt: Jerusalem bei Philo und Lukas." *Kairos* 28/3–4 (1986): 129–51.

25. What Philo writes in *Somn.* 1.215 is different from *Spec.* 1.66–67.

26. *Spec.* 2.209; *Contempl.* 88; *Legat.* 280.

27. *Ebr.* 18; *Sobr.* 40; *Congr.* 98.

28. *Somn.* 1.194; *Abr.* 171; *Mos.* 2.270; *Spec.* 193; *QE* 2.99.

29. *Mos.* 1.254; *Spec.* 1.78, 248; *Legat.* 316.

30. *Abr.* 177; *Legat.* 319.

31. *Mos.* 1.317; *Flacc.* 48.

32. Cf. *Mos.* 1.303; *Spec.* 1.317.

33. *Spec.* 1.316; 2.216.

34. *Spec.* 1.74, 76; *Legat.* 157, 198, 203; 232, 290, 310, 346; *Prov.* 2.64.

35. *Migr.* 92; *Prob.* 148; *Legat.* 208, 220–221, 306–308, 314–315.

36. *Mos.* 2.109–119, 141–152, 275–276; *Spec.* 1.105–116; *Praem.* 74–78.

37. *Spec.* 1.168–182, 297–298.

38. Cf. Hosea 6:6.

39. *Spec.* 1.230–234; 2.215–222; burnt offering: *Spec.* 1.194–209, 212–215; preservation offering: *Spec.* 1.224–225.

40. *Sobr.* 53–54; *Mut.* 209–213; *Contempl.* 24–26.

41. *Fug.* 93–94; *Spec.* 2.205–211.

42. *Spec.* 2.150–162.

43. *Spec.* 2.167–178.

BIBLIOGRAPHY

Barclay, John M. G. "Paul and Philo on Circumcision: Romans 2:25–29 in Social and Cultural Context." *New Testament Studies* 44 (1998): 536–56.

Birnbaum, Ellen. *The Place of Judaism in Philo's Thought: Israel, Jews, and Proselytes*. Brown Judaic Studies 290. Studia Philonica Annual Monograph Series 2. Atlanta, GA: Scholars Press, 1996.

James, T. "Philo on Circumcision." *South African Medical Journal* 50 (1976): 1409–12.

LaPorte, Jean. "The High Priest in Philo of Alexandria." *The Studia Philonica Annual* 3 (1991): 71–82.

Mendelson, Alan. *Philo's Jewish Identity*. Brown Judaic Studies 161. Atlanta, GA: Scholars Press, 1988.

Pearce, Sarah. "Jerusalem as 'Mother-City' in the Writings of Philo of Alexandria." Pages 19–36 in *Negotiating Diaspora: Jewish Strategies in the Roman Empire*. Edited by John M. G. Barclay. London: T & T Clark, 2004.

Smitt, P. "Ritual Competition and Ritual Failure in Philo's *De vita contemplative*." Pages 19–39 in *Felix Culpa*. Leiden, The Netherlands: Brill, 2021.

Index

Abel, 125–26, 127, 128
Abraham, 16, 64, 84, 93, 107, 114, 139n7; instruction of, 128–29; Isaac and, 131–32; in three elements to acquire virtue, 99–101
Adam, 62, 117, 124
adultery, 149
Alexander, Tiberius Julio, viii–ix
Alexandria, viii
Alexandrian Jews, viii
allegorical interpretation of "the fall," 117–20
allegorical interpretations, x, 84–89
angels (daimones), 17–20, 41, 46n16, 128
anti-anthropomorphism, 11–12, 24n17
Archangel, 17, 19
archetypal seal, 83
Aristobulus, 24n17
Aristotle, 112
astrology, 63
athletic language in practice of virtues, 98–102

beasts, 158
Bezaleel, 32–33
biblical characters, 123
biblical characters, Jewish names, 123, 139n7; Abraham as, 129; Adam as, 124; Cain and Abel as, 124–26, 127, 139n2; Enoch as, 127; Essenes as, 124, 138; Hagar as, 134–35; Hannah as, 135–36; Isaac as, 131–32; Jacob as, 130–31; Leah as, 135; Methuselah as, 137–38; Moses as, 137; Noah as, 127–28; Phineas as, 137; Rebekah as, 135; Sarah as, 133–34; Seth as, 127; Tamar as, 136; *Therapeutae* as, 124, 138
blood, 36, 51, 67
breath, 12, 52, 54, 55, 56, 57, 67
burnt-offerings, 131, 177–78

Cain, 82, 105, 115, 125–26, 128
Cain and Abel, 124–26, 127
cause of creation, 29–32, 36, 46n5, 46n6
circumcision, 184n7; Philo on, 159–60, 184n8, 184n10
citizenship, viii
Colson, F. H., xiii
concubine, 67
conferences, vii
The Contemplative Life and the Giants (Philo), vii
cosmology: cause of creation, 29–32, 46n6; creation, 27–28, 46n5; creation of "two worlds," 34–39, 46n9, 46n13; divine Logos, 26–27, 32–34,

46n9; potencies of God/powers of God/"Others," 37–39, 46n13
courage, 86–87, 88–89
craftsmanship, 146–47
creation, 27–29
Credal Formulation, 156–57

daimones. *See* angels
Dan, 118, 164
daughters, 72
death, 70–71, 125, 149, 150, 177; of souls, 137–38
Decalogue (Ten Heads, Ten Words): first commandment in, 146; second commandment in, 146–47; third commandment in, 147; fourth commandment in, 147–48; fifth commandment in, 142, 148–49; sixth commandment in, 149; seventh commandment in, 150; eighth commandment in, 151; ninth commandment in, 151–52; tenth commandment in, 152; creation in, 144; God in, 144; history in, 144, 145; vices in, 142; virtues in, 141–43
De Migratione Abrahami (*Migr.*), 4
De Posteritate Caini, 3–4
desire, 115–16, 119, 152; food laws and, 161, 165–66
Deuteronomy, 123
divine Logos, 26–27, 43; Bezaleel in, 32–33; harmony as, 33–34, 46n9; *Logos of God* in, 32; Lord as shepherd in, 33
divine Word, 170
doctrine of creation, 25–32, 46nn5–6
drink, 167–68

economics, 92
Eden, 87–89
education, ix, 16–17, 24n15, 73, 108, 134–35
education and prophecy: laws in, 75–76; teachers on, 74–75
eighth commandment, 151

Enoch, 127
Ephraim, 64, 65
epithumia (moderation of desire), 161
Esau, 98, 126, 130
Essenes, ix, 124, 138
eunuch, 58–59
Eve, 118
Existent One, 1–5, 23n1, 30, 124
Exodus (*QE*), xii

faith, 89, 90, 95–96, 114
false witnesses, 151–52
fathers, 42, 75–76, 111
fear, 115–16
feast of fast, 181–82
feast of great vow, 183
feast of new moon, 183
feast of sheaf, 184
female, 69–71. *See also* male *versus* female; women
feminine form, 65
fifth commandment, 142, 148–49
first commandment, 146
fishes, 49–50
food laws: character related to, 161, 184n13; clean and unclean animals in, 161–63; desire and, 161, 165–66; passions/irrational passion and, 166–67; self-control and, 164–66; temperance and, 163–64
four cardinal virtues, 84–89
four elements, 41–42, 46n16
four passions, 115–17, 156
four rivers of Eden, 87–89
fourth commandment, 147–48

Gaius Caligula (emperor), viii
Garden of Eden, 58, 79n14, 85, 94, 109
gender, 65
generic virtues: courage as, 86–87, 88–89; justice as, 86–87, 88–89; prudence and, 85, 86–87, 88–89; temperance as, 86–87, 88–89
God, 61–62, 155; name of, 1–2, 6–7, 23n12, 147

God and Logos: Cherubim in, 15; memory in, 15; "place" in, 15–16
God and mind: boundaries in, 8; flight of, 10–11; Good in, 9; graciousness of, 10; Moses and, 8, 9; patriarchs in, 9–10, 24n15; Pharaoh and, 8–9; virtue in, 9–10
God and Spirit (*Pneuma*): Joseph and, 21; knowledge of, 20–21; life goals and, 22–23; Moses with, 20, 21–22; raining of food from, 23
God has no human form, 11–12
Godhead, Monad, Dyad, 12–14
God-like, 103, 104–6
gods, 157–58
God's providence: as craftsman, 43; damage and, 45; divine Logos as, 43; elements in, 45; future as, 43; harmonies of, 44–45; human beings in, 43–44; Israel as, 45; Law of Nature in, 45; nourishment as, 44; refuge of, 43; revelation as, 45; reverence toward, 44; time related to, 43; universe as, 43; voluntary and involuntary sins and, 44
gold, 85, 87–88
golden calf, 158–59
grace, 136
great vow, feast of, 183
grief, 115, 116

Hagar, 19; knowledge from, 134; middle education of, 134–35; Moses on, 134; senses from, 134–35
Hannah, 135–36
happiness, 81, 103–4; as human life goal, 102–4
harmony, 33–34, 46n9
head, 52, 63. *See also* Ten Heads
healing, 138
heaven, 34, 35
Hellenistic Jewish authors, x
herds, 118
High Holy Days, 155
high priest, 173–77, 178–79

holiness, 92–94
Holy City, 172
horse analogy, 166
hostility, 88
human beings: breath of, 52; divine Spirit of, 49; fishes compared to, 49–50; fishes related to, 49–50; four elements of, 49; head of, 52; in human nature, 49–54; as image of God, 48–49, 50–52; minds of, 49, 50–51, 52, 53, 79n5; mortality of, 53; reasoning of, 50, 52, 53; right actions of, 53; sequence for, 50–51; soul and, 49–50, 79n16; superiority of, 52–53; test of, 54; virtues of, 52; water related to, 51; woman as, 51; World of Ideas and, 49
human life goal, 22–23, 102–8; God-like as, 103; happiness as, 102–4
human nature: creatures compared to, 50; earth and, 51–52; first human and, 55; Garden of Eden and, 58; God's mind in, 48; human beings in, 49–54; Image of God and, 48, 52, 53, 55, 57; immunity of, 53; life-creating and divine spirit in, 54–58; minds of, 50–51, 52, 53, 56–57, 58, 79n5, 79n14; mortal and immortal related to, 53; reasoning of, 50, 54–55, 57; right actions of, 53; senses and, 48, 52–53, 79n5; sequence of, 50; virtues of, 52; of women, 51
human sexuality, 73–74

idolaters, 146–47
idols, 146, 157–59
ignorance, 94, 111–12
Image of God: human beings as, 48–49, 50–51; human nature and, 48, 52, 53, 55, 57; as Logos as first-born, 17; in Philo's anthropology, 47
images, 146–47
imitation of God, 106–7
immortality, 94

impiety, 109–10, 146; divine natures and, 110; godlessness related to, 110; offenders of, 110
infants, exposure of, 150
intellect, 60
intelligible world, creation of, 34–35
Isaac, 100, 101, 103, 104; Abraham and, 131–32; burnt-offerings related to, 131; Esau and, 126; as "self-learned," 129, 139n7; wisdom of, 132
Ishmael, 179
Israel: as God's providence, 45; name of, 130. *See also* Jacob
Issachar, 135

Jacob, 58, 76, 99, 100, 101–2; Esau and, 126, 130; Logos and Angels and, 17–18; as "practice," 129, 130, 139n7; Rachel and, 164–65
Jerusalem, 170–71
Jethro, 75
Jewish festivals: feast of fast in, 181–82; feast of great vow in, 183; feast of new moon in, 183; feast of Passover in, 182; feast of sheaf in, 184; feast of Tabernacle in, 180; feast of trumpets in, 180–81; prayer in, 179; Sabbath in, 155–56, 182; sacrifices in, 177–78; sin offering in, 177–79
Jewish Law and *Decalogue*, xiii–xiv, 153n11, 184n3; circumcision in, 159–61, 184n7, 184n10; *Decalogue* in, 142–45; *Decalogue* or ten heads, 141–42, 145–52; food laws in, 161–67, 184n13; Jerusalem in, 170–71; Jewish festivals in, 177–84; monotheism in, 156–59; Mosaic Law in, 141, 145; nature of Mosaic Law, 145; sexual immorality in, 167–69, 184n8; *Special Laws* in, 141; Temple/Sanctuary in, 171–77, 185n24; Unwritten Law as, 141, 142, 145, 152n3
Jewish War (Josephus), viii

Jewish worship and major observances: circumcision in, 159–61, 184nn7–8, 184n10; food laws in, 161–67, 184n13; God related to, 155; High Holy Days in, 155; monotheism in, 156–59
Joseph, 21, 64–65, 132–33
Josephus, viii, 153n11
Jubal, 112–13
Judah, 135, 136
justice, 86–87, 88–89, 90, 133

knowledge, 94–95

Laban, 111
Lamech, 137–38
laws, 69, 75–76, 156, 164–66; Unwritten, 141, 142, 145, 152n3. *See also* Jewish Law; Jewish Law and *Decalogue*; Mosaic Law
LCL. *See* Loeb Classical Library
Leah, 71, 76, 107, 135, 164–65
Levi, 61–62, 131, 159
Lewy, Hans, vii
life-creating and divine spirit: breath in, 54, 55, 56, 57; senses in, 54–55, 57–58; soul in, 54–55; virtues in, 55–56; water related to, 51, 56
Loeb Classical Library (LCL), xii, xiii
Logos, 1, 87, 172
Logos and Angels: destruction in, 18–19; Hagar in, 19; health from, 18; Jacob and, 17–18; King's road for, 18; Ruler and, 19; sovereign Ruler in, 19–20; Word of God as, 17–18
Logos as first-born: Archangel in, 17; Image of God as, 17; shepherd in, 17; understanding as, 17
Logos as rock: divine wisdom as, 16; education in, 16–17; "manna" as, 16–17; soul nourishments as, 16
Logos's role in creation, 32–34, 46n9
LXX. *See* Pentateuch
Lysimachus, Alexander, viii

makeup of human: body and flesh in, 65–66; memory in, 63–65, 79nn17–18; sense-perception in, 66; soul in, 66–67; tripartite of human soul in, 63, 79n16

males: division related to, 68; feminine compared to, 68; in hiding, 67–68; laws for, 69; souls and, 68–69

male *versus* female, 71–73

man: Adam as, 117; mind of, 117–18; soul of, 118

man and woman: female in, 69–73; male in, 67–69, 71–73

Manasseh, 64, 65

marriage, 74, 138

masculine form, 65

means: Moses on, 112–13, 114; virtues as, 112

memory, 15, 79n17; animal chewing cud and, 64; eternality of, 63–64; forgotten in, 65; Joseph related to, 64–65; repetition in, 79n18

menstruation, 36, 51

meteorology, 92

Methuselah, 137–38

middle path, 112–14

Middle Platonism, x, 161

mind: Adam related to, 124; human and, 59–60; of human nature, 50–51, 52, 53, 56–57, 58, 79n5, 79n14; of Moses, 137; nature of, 58–59; sense-perceptions and, 60–63; shepherd compared to, 111. *See also* nature of mind

mind and human: as discoverer, 60; indivisibility of, 59–60; passion in, 60; two natures in, 59–60

mind and sense-perception: Adam in, 62; astrology in, 63; good mind in, 62; senseless mind in, 62; Uncreated in, 62–63; watching in, 62

mind *versus* sense-perception: God in, 61–62; intellect in, 60; Levi on, 61–62; passions in, 61; perception in, 61; soul in, 60

Miriam, 137

miscarriage, 150

moderation of desire (*epithumia*), 161

Monad: essence as, 13; hearing related to, 12–13; Maker as, 12; Moses and, 13; unmixed as, 12

Monad and Dyad: birth in, 13; distinctions of, 13–14; diviners in, 14; female and male as, 13; light in, 14; matter in, 13–14

monotheism: Credal Formulation of, 156–57; golden calf and, 158–59; polytheism and idolatry compared to, 157–58; theocentrism of, 156, 184n3

Mosaic Law, 141, 145; of circumcision, 159, 184n7

Moses, 2, 102, 105–7, 118, 157; Adam related to, 124; on Cain, 125; cause of creation and, 29; in creation of sensible world, 36; on divine Logos, 32; on education and prophecy, 74–75; in God and Logos, 16; God and mind and, 8, 9; God and Spirit with, 20, 21–22; golden calf and, 159; on Hagar, 134; on means, 112–13, 114; mind of, 137; Monad and, 13; in nature of world, 40; on passion, 166; in potencies of God/powers of God/"Others," 37, 38–39; on prayer, 179; prophecy/prophet and, 77–78; on self-control, 164; as Spokesperson, 143; on transcendence of God, 7; wisdom of, 109

mother, 70

Mother City, 170–71

motherless, 148

mothers and fathers, 75–76

murder, prohibition of, 150

music, 93–94, 95, 137

name: of Abraham, 129; of God, 1–2, 6–7, 23n12, 147; of Israel, 130; of Noah, 127

native country, 170–71

nature: of soul, 112; truths of, 148

nature of God: characteristics of, 2–3; *On the Creation* related to, 3; Existent One, 2, 3–5; God and mind, 8–11, 24n15; Greek philosophical language in, 3; Judaism's superiority in, 3–4; piety in, 3; *pronoia* in, 3; Transcendence of God as, 5–8; uniqueness in, 3

nature of mind: earth-born and, 59; eunuch related to, 58–59; God-born and, 59; heaven-born and, 59; myth about giants and, 59

nature of world (world of becoming): "beginning" in, 40; Moses in, 40; newborn nourishment in, 40

newborn nourishment, 40

new moon, feast of, 183

ninth commandment, 151–52

Noah, 77, 99, 106; name of, 127; virtues of, 128

On Abraham (Philo), 128–29, 139n7

one kingship, 146

On the Contemplative Life (Philo), ix

On the Creation (Philo), 3, 156

oracles, 134

order, 87

parents, 90–91, 157; divinity of, 148–49; impiety related to, 109–10

passions, 60, 61, 156, 166–67; fear and grief as, 115–16; pleasure and desire as, 115; pleasure related to, 114; reason and, 114–15; rebirth and, 116–17; senses and, 116; soul related to, 116; stoic four passions and, 114–17; virtue and vice related to, 115

Passover, feast of, 182

patriarchs, 141; God and mind and, 9–10. *See also specific patriarchs*

Pentateuch (LXX), xiii

perfect human, 96–97

Philo, the person: biography on, viii; character of, ix–x; citizenship of, viii; education of, ix; family of, viii–ix

Philonic Corpus: abbreviations of, xiv–xv; allegorism in, xi; anti-Semitism related to, xi; division of, xi; extent of, x; interpretations of, xi–xiii, xiii; popularity of, xi; preservation of, x–xi; relevance of, xii; summaries in, xiii–xiv; Ten Commandments in, xi; translations of, xii–xiii

Philo of Alexandria (Winston), vii–viii

Philo's anthropology: contrasts in, 48; ethics in, 47–48; genders in, 48; human nature in, 48–58; human sexuality in, 73–74; humans in, 47; Image of God in, 47; makeup of human in, 63–67; man and woman, 67–73; Middle Platonic categories of, 47; mind in, 58–63; Plato on, 47; *Timaeus* on, 47

Philo's doctrine of creation: cause of creation in, 25; God's transcendence in, 25; providence from, 26; Stoic Logos in, 25; "two worlds" in, 25. *See also* cosmology

Philo's doctrine of ethics: allegorical interpretation of "the fall" in, 117–20; athletic language in practice of virtues in, 98–102; faith in, 95–96; to follow God in, 107–8; four cardinal virtues in, 84–89; four rivers of Eden in, 87–89; generic virtues in, 85–87; God-like in, 103, 104–6; Greek influence in, 81; happiness in, 81, 103–4; health in, 92; Hellenistic Jewish tradition in, 81–82; holiness in, 92–94; human life goal in, 102–8; ignorance in, 111–12; imitation of God in, 106–7; impiety in, 109–10; Logos and virtue in, 87; the mean in, 112–14; middle path between two extremes in, 112–14; passions and stoic four passions in, 114–17; piety in, 81, 89–93; practice of vices in, 108–12; practice of virtues in, 96–97;

Index

prize in, 98–99; three elements to acquire virtue in, 99–102; virtue-ethics in, 82–84; virtue *par excellence* and key virtues in, 89–96; virtues in, 81–82, 95–102; wisdom and knowledge in, 94–95

philosophical doctrines, ix

philosophy, 95

Philo's theology: anti-anthropomorphism in, 11–12, 24n17; corrupted text related to, 23n11, 24n13; Dyad in, 2; Existent One in, 1–2, 3–5, 23n1; God and mind, 8–11, 24n15; God and Spirit, 20–23; God has no human form, 11–12; Godhead, Monad, Dyad, 12–14; God's name in, 1–2, 6, 23n12; God's Providence, 43–45; Logos in, 1; mind in, 1; Monad in, 2; Moses in, 2; nature of God, 2–11, 23nn11–12, 24n13; nature of world in, 24n15, 40; potencies of God/powers of God/"Others," 24n13, 37–39; relationship between God and Logos, 14–20; Spirit in, 1; transcendence in, 1, 2; Transcendence of God, 5–8, 23nn11–12, 24n13; view of creation, 40–41; world/cosmos/universe, 40–45

Phineas, 137

phronēsis. *See* prudence

physical and spiritual circumcision, 160–61

piety, 81, 89–91, 146; of priesthood/priest/high priest, 174

pilgrimage, 170

Plato, 2, 139n7

Plato's *Timaeus*, 2

pleasure, 9, 115, 116, 118–20, 169; adultery related to, 149; death related to, 149; passions related to, 114

Pneuma. *See* Spirit

polytheism, 146, 157–58

"possession," 124–25

potencies of God/powers of God/"Others": chastisement in, 37–38; corporeal objects in, 39; Creator and Maker in, 38; Lord and God in, 37, 46n13; Moses in, 37, 38–39; Noah in, 37; sense-perception in, 39; Sovereign in, 38; subjects in, 38; world in, 39

powers, 106–7

practice of vices: appetite for, 109; council against, 109; education and, 108; inconvenience of, 108; soul and, 108–9; trees analogy in, 108

practice of virtues, 96–97

prayer, 179

priesthood/priest/high priest: bodies of, 175; clothing of, 175–76; of death, 177; gratitude for, 176; high priests of, 173–74, 176, 178–79; piety of, 174; priests of, 175; privilege of, 174–75; sexual intercourse of, 176; temple attendants and, 175; universe of, 174–75, 176

privileged position, viii–ix

prize, 98–99

property theft, 151

prophecy/prophet: fasting for, 78; instruments of, 78; mind and, 76–77; Moses and, 77–78; sense-perception and, 76–77; soul and, 76; Spirit in, 77–78; widow and, 76

Protagoras, 127

providence (*pronoia*), 3

prudence (*phronēsis*), 90, 113, 139n7; generic virtues and, 85, 86–87, 88–89

QE. *See* Exodus

Questions and Answers of Genesis (*QG*), xii

Rachel, 164–65

reason, 119; attention related to, 111; in life-creating and divine spirit, 54–55; passions and, 114–15

reasoning: of human beings, 50, 52, 53; of human nature, 50, 54–55
Rebekah, 64, 100, 126, 135
relationship between God and Logos: God and Logos, 15–16; Logos and Angels, 17–20; Logos as First-born, 17; Logos as rock, 16–17; sensible world in, 14; Stoic Logos in, 14
royal road, 113
Ruben, 131
Runia, David T., xi

sacrifices, 125–26, 131, 177–78
sacrificial rites, 93
Samuel, 135–36
Sarah, 82, 84, 99, 129, 131, 133–34
scholarship, vii
Scholer, David M., xii–xiii
science, 157
sculptors, 146–47
second commandment, 146–47
self-control, 72–73, 95, 161; food laws and, 164–66
self-lovers, 126
Seneca, 139n7
sense-perceptions, 66, 70, 118, 119; in creation of sensible world, 36–37; in male *versus* female, 72; minds and, 60–63
senses, 54–55, 57–58; from Hagar, 134–35; human nature and, 48, 52–53, 79n5
sensible world, 14; creation of, 36–37
Seth, 127
seventh commandment, 150
seventh day, 147–48
sex, 119; clothing and, 74; competition and, 73; education related to, 73; immortality and, 74; marriage and, 74; souls and, 73–74, 120; virtues and, 73
sexual immorality, 184n8; gluttony/belly in, 167–69; sexual pleasure in, 169
sexual intercourse, 176
sexual pleasure, 169

sheaf, feast of, 184
shepherd: Abel as, 125; mind compared to, 111
sight, 130, 137, 138
sin offerings, 177–79
sixth commandment, 149
snake, 118–20
Society of Biblical Literature, vii
Society of New Testament Studies, vii
Sodom, 167
souls, 8, 16, 60, 63, 97, 123, 157; blood related to, 67; breath related to, 67; concubine related to, 67; death of, 137–38; eating related to, 161; emotion of, 152, 166–67; healing of, 138; human beings and, 49–50, 79n16; knowledge of, 94–95; in life-creating and divine spirit, 54–55; Logos and, 172; in makeup of human, 66–67; male and, 68–69; in male *versus* female, 72; of man, 118; power of persuasion, 108–9; practice of vices and, 108–9; sex and, 73–74, 120; "virtue-loving soul," 143; virtues of, 66, 157; whole and dominant part of, 66–67
sourcebook, xii–xiv
Special Laws (Philo), 156
Spirit (*Pneuma*), 1, 49, 54–58; in cosmology, 26–27; in creation of intelligible world, 34; in prophecy/prophet, 77–78. *See also* God and Spirit
Spirit of God, 20–23
spiritual circumcision, 160–61
stealing, 151
Stoics, 161

Tabernacle, 159
Tabernacle, feast of, 180
Tamar, 136
temperance, 90; food laws and, 163–64; as generic virtues, 86–87, 88–89
Temple, 90, 93

Temple of Jerusalem: first fruits in, 172, 173; high priest in, 173–77, 178–79; Holy City as, 172; statue in, 173, 174; universe as, 172; watchmen at, 172–73
Temple/Sanctuary, 185n25; earthly and spiritual, 171; heart in, 171, 185n24; minds as, 171–72; priesthood/priest/high priest in, 174–77; soul as, 172; Temple of Jerusalem in, 172–74
Ten Commandments, xi, 93–94
Ten Heads, 155. *See also* Decalogue
tenth commandment, 152, 161
theocentrism, 156, 184n3
Therapeutae, 124, 138
third commandment, 147
3 Jewish Philosophers (Lewy), vii
three elements to acquire virtue, 99–102
three patriarchs, 128–29, 139n7
Timaeus (Philo), 26
traditions of interpretations, ix–x
transcendence of God, 24n13; judges and, 7; Logos of, 6; Monad as, 7–8; Moses on, 7; names of, 6–7; nourishment of, 6; as One, 7; potency of, 6; presence of, 6; resting-place in, 5–6; space and place of, 6
tripartite of human soul, 63, 79n16
trumpets, feast of, 180–81
truths, 147; of cause of creation, 30; false witnesses against, 151–52; of nature, 148
"Two Worlds," creation of, 34–39, 46n9, 46n13
tyranny of passions/irrational passion, 166–67

Unwritten Law, 141, 142, 145, 152n3

vanity, 146
vices, 108–12
view of creation: Cause in, 41; equal rights in, 40; false testimony in, 41; goodness in, 41; sellers and buyers in, 40–41; stranger or sojourner in, 40
virginity, 148, 174; of Rebekah, 126
virtue-ethics, 82–84
"virtue-loving soul," 143
virtue *par excellence* and key virtues, 92–96; courage in, 89, 91; courtesy in, 90–91; faith in, 89, 90; holiness in, 89; justice in, 89, 90; piety in, 89–91; prudence in, 89, 90; Sophists in, 90; temperance in, 89, 90; Temple in, 90
virtues, 52, 71, 85–89, 100; of Abraham, 128–29; archetypal seal of, 83; corruption and, 83–84; fugitive compared to, 124; in God and mind, 9–10; happiness as, 82; of Joseph, 132; in life-creating and divine spirit, 55–56; means as, 112; modesty as, 82; of Noah, 128; nuts related to, 84; in pairs, 128; perfection of, 156; in Philo's doctrine of ethics, 81–82, 95–102; prayers for, 179; of rational beings, 82–83; of Rebekah, 126; of Sarah, 84; sex and, 73; of souls, 66, 157; Tabernacle and, 83; of Tamar, 136; in triads, 128–29
virtues and vices, 123–24
vision of God, 97
voluntary and involuntary sins, 44, 112

watering. *See* Seth
Wendland, 24n13
Whitaker, G. H., xiii
wine, 167, 179
Winston, David, vii–viii, ix
wisdom, 16, 65, 97; of Hannah, 135–36; of Isaac, 132; of Moses, 109; of Rebekah, 135
wisdom and knowledge, 94–95
witnesses, false, 151–52
Wolfson, Harry, xi
women, 36, 51, 69–73; in allegorical interpretation of "the fall," 118; three patriarchs without, 128

Word of God, 113
The Works of Philo Complete and Unabridged (Yonge and Scholer), xii–xiii
world/cosmos/universe, 43–45; four elements in, 41–42, 46n16; nature of the world in, 40; view of creation in, 40–41
world of becoming, 40
World of Ideas (Plato), 26

Yonge, C. D., xii–xiii

About the Author

Nélida Naveros Córdova, CDP, has a doctorate in New Testament and Early Christianity and is an assistant professor of biblical studies and director of graduate programs in theology and ministry at Spring Hill College in Mobile, Alabama. Nélida is the author of *Philo of Alexandria's Ethical Discourse: Living in the Power of Piety*; *To Live in the Spirit: Paul and the Spirit of God*; *God's Presence in Creation*; and numerous scholarly articles. She has presented papers at international and national conventions. She enjoys cooking, dancing, gardening, knitting, sewing, listening to music, and playing volleyball.

www.ingramcontent.com/pod-product-compliance
Lightning Source LLC
Chambersburg PA
CBHW061445300426
44114CB00014B/1846